WOMEN, WITCHCRAFT,
AND THE INQUISITION IN SPAIN
AND THE NEW WORLD

NEW HISPANISMS
Cultural and Literary Studies

ANNE J. CRUZ, SERIES EDITOR

WOMEN
WITCHCRAFT
AND THE
INQUISITION
IN SPAIN AND THE
NEW WORLD

EDITED BY

María Jesús Zamora Calvo

LOUISIANA STATE UNIVERSITY PRESS   BATON ROUGE

Published by Louisiana State University Press
lsupress.org

DESIGNER: Michelle A. Neustrom
TYPEFACE: Minion Pro

LIBRARY OF CONGRESS CATALOGING-IN-PUBLICATION DATA

Names: Zamora Calvo, María Jesús, editor.
Title: Women, witchcraft, and the Inquisition in Spain and the New World /
    edited by María Jesús Zamora Calvo.
Description: Baton Rouge : Louisiana State University Press, [2021] | Series:
    New Hispanisms : cultural and literary studies | Includes bibliographical
    references and index.
Identifiers: LCCN 2021006865 (print) | LCCN 2021006866 (ebook) |
    ISBN 978-0-8071-7561-3 (cloth) | ISBN 978-0-8071-7644-3 (pdf) |
    ISBN 978-0-8071-7645-0 (epub)
Subjects: LCSH: Inquisition—Spain. | Inquisition—Latin America. | Spain—
    Church history. | Spain—Colonies. | Witch hunting—History. | Women—
    Violence against—History.
Classification: LCC BX1735 .W593 2021 (print) | LCC BX1735 (ebook) |
    DDC 272/.20946—dc23
LC record available at https://lccn.loc.gov/2021006865
LC ebook record available at https://lccn.loc.gov/2021006866

✤ CONTENTS ✤

✦ ACKNOWLEDGMENTS ✦

My greatest debt is to my family: my son, my husband, my mother, my brothers, to whom this book is dedicated with my dearest love. To thank every colleague who contributed an insight, criticism, or reference would be impossible; I am grateful to all. Special thanks go to my students at the Universidad Autónoma de Madrid (UAM), Spain, for their care and curiosity, and for their enthusiasm and vitality. To Anne J. Cruz, soul and heart of this book: thank you so much.

I thank all those persons and institutions that have contributed to publishing this book: R&D Excellence Project for the Ministry of Economy and Competitiveness of Spain (FEM2016-78192-P), financed by the State Agency for Research (Agencia Estatal de Investigación—AEI) and the European Regional Development Fund (ERDF, EU); as well as the research group "Magical Mentalities and Anti-Superstition Discourse (Sixteenth, Seventeenth, and Eighteenth Centuries)," Universidad Autónoma de Madrid.

To my contributors, my thanks for your trust in this project and for helping us bring back from oblivion these unique women who, with their own voices, fought against the restrictions imposed on them by the Inquisition of their time. May their names and identities be remembered so that society today will not forget where we come from and perceive a clearer path to follow.

Read and reflect—skillful reader—; we dedicate this book to you.

WOMEN, WITCHCRAFT,
AND THE INQUISITION IN SPAIN
AND THE NEW WORLD

✝

Introduction

MARÍA JESÚS ZAMORA CALVO

A mong Inquisition files, there are numerous cases of women who break their silence to relate the reasons why they were prosecuted by an Inquisition that did its utmost to erase their names and identities from history. Women represented a minority of cases brought before the Spanish and American tribunals. Mostly poor and uneducated, they were often accused of such minor offenses as witchcraft and sorcery. Yet, while these offenses rarely led to forceful physical punishment, the persecution, public discipline, and imprisonment suffered by the accused were nonetheless traumatic and unjust. In a system as closed and secretive as the Inquisition was, its rule hierarchical and misogynistic, women came under laws, punishments, and judgments that were frequently arbitrary and capricious. The essays in this volume bring to light inquisitorial cases in which women were subjected to anonymous accusations, secret detentions, persistent interrogations, and sentences that almost always led to conviction, and whose prosecutions frequently cast a shadow of hatred, rejection, and marginalization.

During the last few decades, scholars have examined the roles of women during the inquisitional period and in so doing have contributed to the reclamation of women's history in the early modern period. Historical monographs have uncovered the lives and voices of women buried in inquisitional records and testimonies and underscored the perils women faced against the authoritarian structures of church and state in early modern Spain and the Americas.[1] The essays in this collection continue and complement the work begun by these pioneers in their own studies of women under trial by the Inquisition and who were branded in many cases as heretics and witches. *Women, Witchcraft, and the Inqui-*

sition in Spain and the New World thus intends to contribute not only to cultural studies of the Inquisition, but especially to the research carried out on women and gender in Spain as well as in the New World during the sixteenth, seventeenth, and eighteenth centuries.

The Spanish Inquisition has been amply studied and its history is well known: established in 1478 to regulate all deviation from Catholic orthodoxy, it was as fundamental to the Spanish monarchical project—both in the Iberian peninsula and in its territories abroad—as to Counter-Reformation policies. Under its first Inquisitor, Tomás de Torquemada (1420–98), the Holy Office focused primarily on the prosecution of converted Jews (*conversos*) who heretically reverted to Judaism. Soon, however, it expanded to pursue other forms of heresy and offenses against the faith, such as bigamy, blasphemy, sorcery, and witchcraft. Between the fifteenth and sixteenth centuries, the gradual establishment of tribunals throughout Iberian peninsular territories evidenced the increasing reach of the Holy Office's institutional power and the expansion of its bureaucratic apparatus.

In the New World, inquisitorial tribunals were initially established in Mexico and Lima in 1571. Forty years later, the need for a third American tribunal became evident, as the first two proved incapable of effectively surveilling Spain's Caribbean territories, whose economic relevance had expanded greatly. Thus, in 1610, a third inquisitorial outpost was established in Cartagena de Indias in modern-day Colombia, a key Caribbean commercial enclave. In theory, Spanish American tribunals had the same responsibilities as their counterparts in the metropolis. Yet, the geographic, demographic, economic, and sociopolitical particularities of the Spanish Monarchy's viceroyalties created a chasm between the letter and the practice of inquisitorial prosecution overseas.

Geographical distance between the Holy Office in Madrid and the other tribunals, on both sides of the Atlantic, led to procedural, theoretical, and structural differences. Often these variations were the result of material conditions. At a bureaucratic level, American tribunals faced budgetary restrictions reflected in the reduction of the number of functionaries and the adjustment of strategies of control. Inquisitorial ruling also diverged in terms of the subjects and practices targeted and sentenced. To mention a few key distinctions, whereas in Spain the prosecution of *conversos* had been the institution's central concern mostly from the fifteenth to the seventeenth centuries, it became a major preoccupation of American tribunals in the mid-seventeenth century only when fears of Jewish conspiracies surged in vice-regal territories. In Spain, the Inquisition could prosecute any of the Catholic subjects of the Crown it deemed suspect, while in the Americas its jurisdiction excluded indigenous peoples. In Spain, blasphemy and witchcraft were charges dealt universally, but in the Americas, these quickly became racialized and targeted predominantly at African and Afro-descendant peoples, both free and enslaved. In sum, over the course of three hundred and fifty years (1478–1834), the Holy Office produced a broad range of cases that changed from place to place, revealing an institution that requires nuanced approaches to understand its complexities and fissures.

This is the context framing the present book, which offers ten multidisciplinary essays on women who, under accusations as diverse as witchcraft, bigamy, false beatitude, and heresy, came before the Inquisition in Spain and the New World to account for their lives. The authors propose to study their social status, analyze their motivations, determine the characteristics of their trials, and understand the justifications for their trials. The collection's overarching hypothesis is that, in all cases of women subject to imprisonment, interrogation, and judgment, there exists the specter of contempt, humiliation, silencing, and denial of their very self. In their varied scholarly approaches and sources, the essays contribute to the intellectual and cultural history of women under the Inquisition.[2]

The first part of the volume, "Women and the Spanish Inquisition," begins by addressing cases of women that were registered in the peninsular Inquisition. In the first essay, Beatriz Moncó Rebollo focuses on the presence of women in matters such as witchcraft, sorcery, possession, and diabolical pacts from an anthropological perspective. She delves into the study of inquisitorial trials that helped to construct the binomial figure of the woman/devil and caused social fear. The author notes that the female realm in the early modern period is the domestic space, and she demonstrates that it is in the field of spirituality that women had a leading role, ironically attained through the devil, as instanced by the possessed nuns of the convent of San Plácido in Madrid.

The desire to control its imagery and perhaps even to veil the sufferings of women under inquisitorial power is what is at stake in the Inquisition's commission of the painting analyzed by Sonia Pérez-Villanueva, *Profanación de un crucifijo o Familia de herejes azotando un crucifijo*, by the Spanish artist Francisco Rizi. Pérez-Villanueva's historical analysis reveals how the painting of a Portuguese crypto-Jewish family and the women's beauty, during a perilous time of increased migration of Portuguese to Spain, depicts a moment that abets the Inquisition, yet symbolically denounces its anti-Semitic and anti-Portuguese patriarchal legacy.

In my essay, I delineate the cultural perceptions of those elderly, widowed, and sickly women who found in witchcraft a way of life in sixteenth-century Castile. These elderly women echoed the stereotypes that popular culture had passed on from ancient times of females who attributed to themselves magical powers in order to survive. This is the case of Catalina Mateo, a woman accused of sorcery and prosecuted by the court of Toledo. Through her Inquisition file, I analyze the various factors that led to the marginalization of elderly women in a society that excluded and discarded them. I delve into the fear that old age caused at that time and the mechanisms activated to rid society of these women who, like Catalina Mateo, became the scapegoat for crimes they never committed.

Moving from the Spanish peninsula to the New World, the second part of the volume deals with studies of women prosecuted by the Inquisition tribunals of New Spain and Cartagena de Indias. It begins with Alberto Ortiz's comprehensive history of the Inquisition's concerns with binding spells, or ligatures, exemplified by cases cited from treatises such as the *Malleus Maleficarum* (Speyer: Peter Drach, 1487) and Francesco Guazzo's *Compendium Maleficarum* (Milan: Collegio Ambrosiano, 1624), as well as the case against the Portuguese Gypsy, María de la Concepción, which took place in New Spain in the seventeenth century. As eroticism was an important element in the cultural production of the early modern world, it is not uncommon that there would be a great variety of erotic manifestations in the history of witchcraft.[3] The practice of "ligature" or "binding," for example, was a real concern for the inquisitorial authorities because of its diabolical affiliation and its challenge to free will. Each public case where this magical affectation appeared generated great fear in men and in society in general. The presumed obstruction of reproductive powers and control of the sexual organs through witchcraft stood also as a sign of eroticism, an activity of witches, an inquisitional problem, and a factor of fear.

Cecilia López-Ridaura further develops the theme of enchantments in New Spain that were dedicated to the control of male sexual potency. To this topic, Henrich Kramer and Jacob Sprenger devoted four sections of the well-known manual of witches *Malleus Maleficarum,* which has attracted the attention of numerous scholars who have analyzed the passages from different perspectives. In her essay, López-Ridaura examines how the approaches described in the medieval treatise, in particular the application of the hex of ligature, are reflected in the eighteenth-century testimonies collected by the Inquisition in New Spain. In a wealth of examples taken from the Mexican archives, López-Ridaura traces the cultural heritage of medieval beliefs from the *Malleus Maleficarum* as recorded in the cases of eighteenth-century enchantresses.

Robin Ann Rice's essay, "Midwives, Folk Medicine, and Magic in Early Modern Mexico," focuses on midwives and the complaints against them for exercising, whether correctly or incorrectly, their profession. In this study, the author intends to examine the extent to which the medical conventions of New Spain encouraged not only women in general but particularly *mulatas* and African descendants to become involved in a type of medicine that involves medieval Christian superstition along with pre-Columbian and African folk medicine. Rice presents several cases to illustrate the possible misunderstanding or misinterpretation of the Mexican midwife in the early modern period.

Women's poetry in New Spain rarely appeared as evidence of guilt in the inquisitorial trials against women in cases of blasphemy or heresy, much less when they had written the verses themselves. Yadira Munguía has devoted her research to searching for allusions to female poets in New Spain that appear in cases of the Holy Office, such as the cases of Catalina de Eslava and Sor Juana Inés de la Cruz. An unusual example is that of Felipa Olaeta, whose poetry Munguía investigates in her essay, "Self-Denunciation before the Inquisition: The Case of Felipa Olaeta in Eighteenth-Century New Spain." Olaeta, an eighteenth-century layperson and author of several poems, reported herself for outside-the-norm and even heretical pronouncements she believed she had incurred in comments and songs.

Another intriguing example of the interactions of popular discourses with Inquisition cases is the essay by Claudia Carranza Vera and Jair Antonio Acevedo López, "The Personification of Erysipelas in Two Eighteenth-Century Spells from New Spain." Here, Carranza and her colleague focus their attention on the spell protecting against erysipelas and its different versions from the sixteenth century to today. Noting that there are few studies that deal with the popular spell combating the disease that has long circulated in Mexico, their essay analyzes histories collected in the records of the Holy Office in New Spain, where references to the plant and the disease are found, and the link between the two. These cases hold great interest because, for various reasons, they are given credit for actions and even feelings, which humanize them, and which, in several cases, are perceived as female entities or as possessing traits typical of the female sex.

Inquisitorial discourse itself helped construct the figure of the witch, which relies on misogynist belief in women's evil nature. Graciela Rodríguez Castañón's essay delves thoroughly into the cultural imaginary and its influence on inquisitorial cases in New Spain to revise the concept of sorcery's significance in the sixteenth and seventeenth centuries, a concept that emerges marked by its ideas of and prejudices against women. For Rodríguez Castañón, at the center of this problem lies the differentiating thought of gender, which considers women as transmitters of evil. The inquisitorial notions applied in a majority of trials against women accused of witchcraft were based on a complex network of traditional beliefs and interpretations held by theologians, as in the example of Juana la Catañona.

No women from any ethnic group escaped the Inquisition's scrutiny, as the last essay in the collection confirms. Ana María Díaz Burgos's essay, "Marital Pains, Heterodox Cures: Alternative Economies of Sorcery and Witchcraft during the Cartagena de Indias Inquisition," takes us to another inquisitorial court closely linked to Spain and Mexico, that of Cartagena de Indias in Nueva Granada (modern Colombia). In 1613, Lorenzana de Acereto, a twenty-seven-year-old Creole (*criolla*) woman, wife of the port city's royal scribe, was prosecuted for witchcraft and superstition.[4] Twenty years later, in 1633, the Inquisition tried Elena de la Cruz, a Spanish woman of forty years of age, resident of Tolú and wife of a prominent captain, for the same offenses. The author argues that by focusing on the language deployed, we may trace both women's participation in alternative economies of healing in which people exchange words, objects, and rituals from Iberian, African, and indigenous traditions. Furthermore, these two cases evince the changes in the authorities' zeal to condemn women during the first three decades of the Inquisition in Cartagena de Indias and its vicinity.

In all the essays, the intent has been to give a varied and fair vision of the women who, for one reason or another, were forced to face the Inquisition tribunals of Spain and the New World. As experts in the field of Inquisition studies, the authors present essays that promote the collaboration of specialists in different disciplines such as literature, history, law, iconography, and anthropology. They offer different and enriching points of view of women and of the Inquisition. A significant supplementary aim of these essays has been to retrieve the documentation of trials, confessions, letters, diaries, and other documents deserving of location, preservation, and digitization. The volume thus performs a documentary rescue that brings to light an important part of the early modern cultural heritage that for centuries has remained unheard and unread. It offers new avenues of study that expand the previous illuminating historical perspectives of women and the Inquisition and encourages scholars to consider these new directions.

NOTES

1. Among the numerous studies on women and the Inquisition are María Helena Sánchez Ortega, *La mujer y la sexualidad en el Antiguo Régimen: La perspectiva inquisitorial* (Madrid: Akal, 1992); Richard L. Kagan, *Lucrecia's Dreams: Politics and Prophecy in*

Sixteenth-Century Spain (Berkeley: University of California Press, 1995); Mary E. Giles, *Women in the Inquisition: Spain and the New World* (Baltimore: Johns Hopkins University Press, 1999); Georgina Dopico-Black, *Perfect Wives, Other Women: Adultery and Inquisition in Early Modern Spain* (Durham, NC, and London: Duke University Press, 2001); Martha Few, *Women Who Live Evil Lives: Gender, Religion and the Politics of Power in Colonial Guatemala* (Austin: University of Texas Press, 2002); Adelina Sarrión, *Beatas y endemoniadas: Mujeres heterodoxas ante la Inquisición, Siglos XVI a XIX* (Madrid: Alianza Editorial, 2003); Nora E. Jaffary, *False Mystics: Deviant Orthodoxy in Colonial Mexico* (Lincoln and London: University of Nebraska Press, 2004); Lisa Vollendorf, *The Lives of Women: A New History of Inquisitional Spain* (Nashville: Vanderbilt University Press, 2005); Joan Bristol, *Christians, Blasphemers, and Witches: Afro-Mexican Ritual Practice in the Seventeenth Century* (Albuquerque: University of New Mexico Press, 2007); Stacey Schlau, *Gendered Crime and Punishment: Women and/in the Hispanic Inquisitions* (Leiden: Brill, 2013); Nicole von Germeten, *Violent Delights, Violent Ends: Sex, Race, and Honor in Colonial Cartagena de Indias* (Albuquerque: University of New Mexico Press, 2013); and Pablo F. Gómez, *The Experiential Caribbean: Creating Knowledge and Healing in the Early Modern Atlantic* (Chapel Hill: University of North Carolina Press, 2017).

2. The essays extend the research presented in the following academic conferences: *Mulieres Inquisitionis: La mujer frente a la Inquisición en España* (2017); *Mujeres quebradas: La Inquisición y su violencia hacia la heterodoxia en Nueva España* (2018); and the special issue of *Edad de Oro: Revista de Filología Hispánica* (38; 2019): https://revistas.uam.es/edadoro/issue/view/edadoro2019.38, product of the project "La mujer frente a la Inquisición española y novohispana" (FEM2016–78192-P), R&D of Excellence for the Ministry of Economy and Competitiveness of Spain, and the research group "Magical Mentalities and Anti-Superstition Discourse (Sixteenth, Seventeenth, and Eighteenth Centuries)" of the Universidad Autónoma de Madrid.

3. Following norms of sexual conduct imposed by the Counter-Reformation, cultural representations of early modern sensuality were translated into an erotic narrative that dealt with sensuality in terms of chastity or marriage. Ironically, the Inquisition, which was otherwise dedicated to persecute religious heterodoxy, did not bother to censor the kind of literary eroticism that revealed human fallibility and thereby allowed copious production of texts and erotic images as long as they did not stimulate "lust or incontinence of mind" (Adelina Sarrión, *Beatas y endemoniadas* [Madrid: Alianza Editorial, 2003]).

4. Creole, or *criollo,* refers to a child of Spaniards who was born in the New World.

I

WOMEN
AND THE
SPANISH
INQUISITION

✠

Defeated Demons, Battered Women

The Bodies of Diabolical Possession

BEATRIZ MONCÓ REBOLLO

The Value of the Senses

The Baroque period in Spain was a paradoxical time when what was considered orthodox and what was considered heterodox coexisted daily. At a time when doctrinal teaching was carried out from the pulpits and most of the population was illiterate, it was of vital importance to tackle any personal interpretations of the doctrine. Power, in all its dimensions, formulated identities and consciences, constructed certainties and values, and, in the end, built the channels through which individuals interpreted and thought about the world, others, and themselves. Orthodox boundaries of doctrine and spirit were drawn with male strokes. Men were the owners of the truth; they implemented and propagated doctrine. It was also men who held the religious, political, social, economic, and symbolic power. The few women in history who had gained a certain prominence were often perceived as alterations to a perfect canvas; they were defects that had to be refined, controlled, or removed.

Nevertheless, particularly during the sixteenth and seventeenth centuries, in the world of religiosity and spirituality women took on a leading role that the dominant gender order (and specifically religious power as its instrument) considered utterly inappropriate and even transgressive. Religious movements such as *beatas, alumbradas,* and Molinists (as collective examples), and even spiritual teachers who were cloistered or considered special individuals, represented a path by which women who became archetypes of female holiness and those who faced inquisitorial power for their reputation as believers in heterodoxy coexisted.

Indeed, it was easier to distinguish between conceptual categories than to conduct a doctrinal and behavioral analysis of facts and beliefs in each particular circumstance. This was the case not only because of the different levels of reality and experience, but also because mystical visionaries and deceived simpletons were placed in the same ideological frame of reference, and both used similar terms and images to talk about angels, spirits, and demonic apparitions. For this reason, we should keep in mind that, as contemporaries, the former and the latter both moved within a common belief framework dictated by the religious orthodoxy supported and funded by men of the church—who, as previously noted, were in charge of that orthodoxy and of the church. Therefore, it will be essential to analyze the context of the events, their discourse and inter-pretation, as well as the individuals who produced them. It comes as no surprise that women make up a majority of those accused of witchcraft, sorcery, possession, and diabolical pacts, nor that in many inquisitorial trials we find a wide panorama of events that can clearly be traced back to the construction of the binomial woman/devil.

Since the Middle Ages, the devil has had a large presence in both or-thodox and heterodox practices and has played a prominent role in their development. Ultimately, in a dualistic world, the belief in a divine being forced the existence of a figure that could represent and explain the mul-tiple facets of evil. Thus, throughout the history of western civilization Satan has played an important role, and perceptions of and about him have reflected historical movements. Satan was not, therefore, new for the Spaniards of the Baroque period, but his particular characteristics and representations were. The early modern period's social, cultural, political, and religious upheavals produced a more day-to-day, quarrelsome devil, one who needed to be fought in close combat with a warlike force that entailed both his defeat and that of his human hosts.

Accordingly, Satan was a cultural figure of the first order and a core part of the belief systems of early modern Europe and the New World. It is not surprising, then, that there are hundreds of texts on demonology, sorcery, witchcraft, incubi, succubi, manuals for experts, hexes, spells, and superstitions. All these texts construe a devilish figure: the antonym of divinity, contrary to all human value. These works led first theologians and then preachers to outline cultural models to be taught through and legitimized by sermons in church and in the streets. We are confronted, then, with a devil born in homily, constructed from the pulpit just as were the figures of his human minions (witches, for example) or the possessed. It is therefore not surprising to find that, in one way or another, the devil is mentioned frequently in inquisitorial trials—not only those addressing witchcraft, but also those addressing sorcery, magic, and different spiritualities like those of visionaries and the *alumbradas*.

Bodies and the Inquisition

Early modern Catholicism leaned toward asceticism, the perception that spirit and body are opposed, antagonistic realities. In this view, the body represents materiality, the world, the earthly, the flesh, temptation, and sin. It is an obstacle along the path to glory, an anchor which prevents us from elevating our spirits and omitting our physical needs. At times, the body's needs are expanded to transform into capital sins, as with gluttony or lust. This body, which binds us to the world and gives an account of our weaknesses, must be tempered, and even punished. We must diminish its prominence, render it void, and leave it behind so that the spirit, after this oblivion, may attain the importance it deserves. Fasting, discipline, and sexual abstinence are the first steps toward reaching a state of grace and perfection.

Paradoxically, it could be said that the doctrine of the Church takes the body into account precisely to write it off, making it the perfect place to pay for one's faults, make sacrifices, and experience temptations. We are the body; we live and die and feel and experience with it; we hate, we yearn, and we dream with it. To the inquisitors, the body is the stage where the dramatization of good and evil, of truth and deception, and of orthodoxy and heterodoxy is carried out. The body is the legitimate object that may be harmed, tortured, and killed in the name of—and for the sake of—the divinity.

In the inquisitorial trial of a member of the mystical *alumbrado* cult, María de Cazalla, we read that "after a few turns of the rope on her legs," she confessed her guilt. However, if one includes every detail and tells the truth, they tensed the rope binding her hands and arms. Her head was held with another rope, and a cloth was put over her face and nose until the jug—"which holds about half an *açumbre,* little more or less"— was empty.[1] The strings continued to tighten and a second jug was emptied over her face, causing her to suffocate and choke. We will not delve here into the distinctive constructions of the female and male bodies, but we do wish to state for the record that the nakedness these women endured prior to being tormented and manipulated bodily by their tormentors had added symbolic value because of their gender. It is truly poignant to recall here that on that day, October 10, 1534, María de Cazalla lamented the protocol imposed on her: "And they will strip the women," she said, adding later that "much greater is the fear of the insult than the shame." Indeed, what is at stake is not only bodily pain but personal humiliation.[2]

By contrast, inquisitorial violence managed to legitimize itself. The same idea of surveillance that characterized faith—the continued persecution of evil that influenced the core of the doctrine—excused both the means and the costs. A culture such as Spain's, supported by a religion such as Catholicism in which blood and pain were normalized and even considered artistic and sanctified, did not reject suffering outright as a suitable instrument of the law, especially when the suffering bodies belonged to "altered" women—to those "others" transformed into Moors, Jewish converts, *alumbradas,* or heretics. Certainly, what we call "necropolitics" (Mbembe 2006) today can be tracked throughout the history of power. In this essay, through the inquisitorial trials, we explore the female body in pain, and its torment and torture, as a means of reaching the truth. At its peak, as we have noted elsewhere (Moncó 2017), pain cannot be expressed with language; it can be expressed only with screams that have no communicative meaning. Words, in short, aestheticize reality.

From another perspective, the body also plays a notable leading role in other types of unorthodox behavior, especially when accompanied by the figure of the devil. Consider, for instance, that the witches' bodies are marked by signature characteristics and certain special signifiers. The demonic marks on the eyes and skin signify property and servitude, but at the same time, they also speak to the truth or falsehood of the claim that the woman is a vassal of the devil. In this mystical world, one can speak of visible and noticeable bodily signs that the inquisitors must seek, find, and interpret.

Moreover, the hermeneutics of the body can be expanded to include sexualized bodies in the coven (which we will not address in the limited space of this essay) and particularly unusual, abnormal, strange, altered bodies, such as the bodies of the possessed. As mentioned earlier, in the sixteenth and seventeenth centuries, there is an extensive elaboration of the devil, who is normalized as a part of everyday life and on human bodies. No longer can an extraordinary pact be made with him; as in the case of witches, the devil merges himself with the bodies of those he possesses and is present and real in their day-to-day lives. Evil is no longer doctrine and abstraction, faith, and belief, but becomes palpable, as a visible and sensorial experience. The devil allows himself to be seen and heard. He can be felt through the body of the possessed. He becomes word and gesture.

Women and Demonic Possession

Women's common scope of action in the early modern period was limited to the domestic space or the spaces which, out of necessity, pertained to their trade. Of the women whose names stood out within the orthodox world of the Church, some, such as Teresa of Ávila or Catherine of Siena, were suspected of heterodoxy. Nevertheless, during this period, the sphere of spirituality is a space where women begin to let themselves be heard, largely in the company of the devil.

In his work *Espejo místico en que el hombre interior se mira prácticamente ilustrado para los conocimientos de Dios y el ejercicio de las virtudes* (Mystical Mirror wherein the Inner Man Sees Himself Virtually Enlightened for God's Knowledge and the Practice of Virtues), the Franciscan Capuchin José de Naxara clearly states a belief that several authorities have posed since the Middle Ages: the devil has the right to enter human bodies to possess and torment them. And furthermore, he does so because God allows it. As Fray Luis de la Concepción explains: "[God] wanting this, so as to purify the soul, and for other high ends, wishing our wellness, or that faults and sins cease, or that we may fulfill the sentence those already committed deserve, or finally, that our own praise may increase, so that this praise, in turn, belongs to glory, chosen as aspiration and reward" (1983, 2).[3]

Possession lies, hence, within the realm of the diabolical and the divine. It represents a paradoxical picture reinforced by the presence of the conjurer and the divine weapons he employs. God and Satan uphold a dispute in which the former—the supreme power—allows temptation and pain in order to demonstrate this supremacy by resolving the possession and returning the possessed to their usual state. In the end, that is what exorcism is: a ritual that refers to normality and to order and balance, common desires at the core of many spells and mystical agents.[4]

In the demonic drama, there are two opposing powerful figures. Just as it is important to know the signs of true possession, it is essential that the exorcist holds certain virtues and characteristics that allow him to fight evil. This is another aspect that expert demonologists assert over and over; it is not a coincidence that many diabolical possessions used to arise precisely from the desires and behaviors of the exorcist himself. As late as the eighteenth century, Benito Jerónimo Feijoo (1961), for example, criticized in no uncertain terms the strictness with which some exorcists sought out the signs of possession: "[The exorcists use] certain incense, which they say has the effectiveness to strangely disturb the demons [. . .] For this incense they make use of rue, St. John's wort, goat's horn, human feces [. . .] what we experience is that any man or woman, if the smell of disgusting and foul-smelling things is brought close to the nose, the individual is upset, disturbed, anguished and does everything possible to step away" (1961, 31).[5]

It is therefore essential that incantations to exorcise demons be carried out by persons with appropriate characteristics and qualities. They must be clerics ordained by the bishop, says Pedro Ciruelo (1952), and any layperson who claims to have the ability to cast out demons must be reproved and suspected; in this context, according to Gaspar Navarro (1631), we must keep in mind that only priests receive the power to conjure from the hands of Christ himself, and they must be of proven quality and virtue.

An exorcism, moreover, is both a difficult task and an extraordinary moment, since it is the only time when it is permissible to establish a relationship with the devil. Following a suggestion made by Thomas Aquinas, Kramer and Sprenger's *Malleus Maleficarum* (1492) had stipulated the characteristics of an exorcism: First, no words that had an invocation to the demon should be used, and it was not advisable to use any unknown names, false statements, formulas, or gestures devoid of content. Second, it was inadvisable to hope that any writing, reading, or other nonverbal methods would work. Furthermore, it was forbidden to speak divine words, which belonged to the Holy Scriptures.[6]

Familiarity with many cases of demonic possession and the way they were analyzed confirms that these requirements were no more than wishful thinking, as they were usually unfulfilled. In fact, the very same authoritative texts amply acknowledge the existence of this issue; for instance, Castañega (1529) warns of it in chapter 20, which he devotes to conjurers and the spells of the possessed, and Ciruelo (1952) emphasizes the danger of turning the exorcism into a show by allowing uneducated people to witness the exorcisms, questioning the demon, arguing with him, or becoming entangled in the trap of demanding answers or signs of his presence. Noydens, a true master of leading and guiding the process of an exorcism, warns in his *Práctica de exorcistas y ministros de la Iglesia* (Practice of Exorcists and Ministers of the Church) (1660) that the exorcist must keep his soul clean at all costs and avoid any vanity and praise for performing his task, always bearing in mind that no power over the devil can ever be assumed.

We acknowledge, once again, that demonic possession is paradoxical and swings between truth and error, between the suffering possessed and the lying one, and between the skillful and suitable conjurer and the creator of a fiction. Visions of demons can be found in both the stories of the mystics (the case of Teresa of Ávila is well known) and the cases of devout women who assessed their grace by the number of devils they had had. This allows us to compare among a wide spectrum of cases that each have singular qualities in their staging, resolution, judgment, and analytical dimensions.

As described above, diabolical possession is built doctrinally, represented socially and culturally, and recreated and staged bodily. All these forces allow for a hermeneutics of diabolical signs to become visible, and they are transmitted through the body of the possessed, and through the speech of demons and conjurers and that of possessed females. Conduct and words are thus two significant platforms through which diabolical signs are revealed to the senses.

It was also common for demonic possession to be made visible collectively, like a contagion, multiplying amongst those affected to the point that some authorities spoke of devils coming out of one body only to enter others. In this sense, it is paradigmatic that certain groups of women—especially those focused on spirituality and religiosity—made excellent breeding grounds for the numbers of possessions to rise; one might even say that the more impenetrable the group was, the more likely demons were to appear. For this reason, perhaps, alongside women of untarnished religiosity, we find a good number of religious women who make deception their mystical sign of identity (see Imirizaldu [1977] and also Lisón Tolosana's *Demonios y exorcismos* [1990]) or meet with the devil precisely within the walls of their convent. However, if in some ways we can speak of a cultural pattern of possession, it is also true that each case presents specific singularities, because ultimately diabolical possession gives voice to religious belief, sense, rationality, spirituality, and mysticism, but also to madness, boredom, sadness, pain, loneliness, anguish, and fear, among other things.

By Their Signs Ye Shall Know Them: A Cartography of the Possessed Body

In the last two decades of the sixteenth century, and in the early seventeenth century, the figure of the devil is gradually constructed as habitual and becomes omnipresent in most proceedings against unorthodox practices. In addition, in both common folk tales and the works of the authorities, the devil is adapted to fit the most common situations, even within the doctrine. It is symptomatic of this change that María Martínez, during her trial before an inquisitorial court, declares that all human beings have a guardian demon, but also that the Jesuit Francisco Suárez, a learned philosopher and theologian, would raise the same idea in his work *De Angelis* in 1620. Little by little, this incarnation of evil is adapted, to some extent, to serve as an explanation for all human misery. Satan does not hide; he no longer has the need for expressed diabolical pacts (which is not to say they no longer exist). He becomes a habitual occurrence, expressed daily through disease, misfortune, fear, and disorder. And the more he does, the more popular and familiar he becomes; the more his semantic and hermeneutic field widens; the more he expresses himself through the senses and feelings. In this way, revelations, trances, ecstasies, and possessed bodies become palpable evidence of diabolical power.

The devil leaves a trace when he communicates with human beings. It is not only the darkness of spirit and soul produced by sin, not only the restlessness that leads to temptation and the struggle between good and evil: there are specific signals, visible, distinguishable, and known, that become a guide for diagnosing his presence. In diabolic possession, one or several demons enter the body of a person and take hold of her will, forming a perfect pair in which the human body serves the will of the other(s). To put it another way: the devil has no body and the possessed has no will. Under this understanding, the alterations or suffering of the former are key to understanding or speculating about what occurs with the latter. One might say that diabolical possession has to be dramatized to be seen and must be seen in order to be confirmed and believed. Consequently, the possessed body is the stage where the keys to demonic possession are noticeably, physically, represented. What, then, are these keys?

In a general sense, they are all those physical manifestations on and with the body of the possessed that appear without intercession of her will (since she has none). Therefore, in the context of devils and extraordinary events, these acts manifest themselves through gestural hyperbole, through the irrational and unusual, and through the extraordinary and the nonhuman. Considering the data on the different cases of demonic possession, one could make a catalog of behaviors that would reinforce exactly what the manuals of exorcists and inquisitors advise. The possessed are not sick, despite the fact that some of their symptoms (vomiting, tremors, hot flashes, etc.) could make them seem so; therefore, according to the *Roman Ritual*, "the drugs of medicine confer no benefit."

People can do extraordinary things when possessed, both on the physical plane—for example, they can levitate or go under a trance until their pulse stops—or on the intellectual plane, where they may speak multiple languages or have the gift of clairvoyance. The presence of the devil in their bodies torments them greatly—they endure the suffering of their hearts being crushed, stomach pains and headaches, their jaws dislocated, bruising and terrible cramps all over—and they perform strange, unusual, or excessive movements, such as jumping, tossing restlessly from one side to the other, or lying on the ground, unable to walk. The devil may also force them to make obscene gestures that are neither usual nor appropriate to their sex or age nor to their social and legal status. In short, they are called maniacs for good reason.

During diabolical possessions, Satan is very talkative and speaks with a woman's voice. There are no silent possessions. The bedeviled speak nonstop; they teach the neighbors their doctrines and tell them about dreams and visions; they have and transmit opinions, reveal the devil's doctrine, and construct narratives with their words that subsequently become first-hand sources for the inquisitors.

It is interesting to see how there is a genuinely overwhelming struggle for space in the possession. The entry of a devil into a person's body could be a private and internal act; ultimately, one is inserted into the other. But as previously noted, the possession can only be interpreted and signified if it is manifest—if it comes to the surface; if there is conclusive external evidence of possession.[7] The process entails the transformation of a subject into an object—of a body into an instrument—which establishes an interesting reciprocity between the devil and his possessed: body and will are exchanged for alienation and, in a certain sense, innocence. It is this substitution of body and will that sets the abducted free: she may scream all she wants; she may vociferate obscenities, move compulsively, kick, roar, cry, insult, curse . . . but it is not she who does it. Rather, it is her possessed body; her will and her humanity have been alienated, usurped. There is therefore no just way to punish the possessed, since she no longer exists as a person. If she is possessed, her essence as an individual has been diluted; it is the devil who is addressed, cursed, threatened, intimidated, battered, bashed, and wounded. This is the exorcist practice, its rationale, its significance. Obviously, the problem arises from the fact that in this confrontation between good and evil, as mentioned at the beginning of this essay, the battle is played out on the body of a woman, and it is her body (it is *her,* in fact) that suffers these blows, slaps, and mistreatment.

The exorcist appropriates a clear prominence by assuming the role of the champion of good, the protagonist of divine hosts whose weapons will be the words of the gospel, holy water, the cross, relics, the ornamentation and attires of his office, and even his own person. He becomes the arm of God from the moment he puts the powers that special ordination has conferred on him on the line. His symbolic space is that of Good; his physical space is the Church.

Thus, it is important to bear in mind that the cultural construction of a possessed person requires that words be combined with gestures. Let us remember that the majority of people who witnessed an exorcism did not know how to read and write, misunderstood the Latin of ecclesiastical ritual, and knew the doctrine only by what they heard and saw. In this alliance between the audible and the visible, there is a common pattern, as we have seen, but there is also space for creative variations that—even though they may represent the same basic pattern—broaden the spectrum of possession to encompass each individual case's singular characteristics. These variations undoubtedly reinforce the basic model, but they each add brushstrokes to an evolving doxastic picture that open channels toward new aspects of possession.

In this sense, the body of the possessed becomes a map where each of the diabolical onslaughts takes shape, creating a specific, visible, distinguishable, and identifiable body language—a language that constructs a narrative which serves to codify a given event, legitimize it, and even bestow signs of credibility upon it. Referring to the Loudun possessions, Michel de Certeau (1980) writes:[8] "As the story gets fragmented in (proper) nouns and functions, it erases referencing the beings to substitute them for a series of different and combined stories: the pulse, the digestion, the mouth, the tongue, or the legs" (69).[9]

Indeed, fragments of meaningful and even distinctive bodily stories are formed. The nuns of San Plácido in Madrid are fettered by diabolical manifestations both day and night (see Moncó 1989). They are in distress and continuous vigil; "suddenly enthralled," they "fell to the ground as struck dead from terror," and walked about "distraught and mournful, drained, soul scorched with countless agonies." In this narrative, there are various visible signs that give an account of an aimless and incapable body taken, manipulated, abused, and tormented by a superior will: "Here was the speed of the spins, the agility in the jumps, the fierceness of the voices in the screams, [. . .] the serious illnesses, the distorting swellings, continuous tremors, deadly assaults [. . .] impetuously left their cells [. . .] threw themselves in the water and on the snow [. . .] went up attics with tremulous motions[. . .] immersed themselves in the troughs of cold water [. . .] with eyes ablaze."[10] In addition, the nuns of San Plácido boasted a possession which was truly paradigmatic in its physical manifestations: their faces twisted from stillness to fierceness in an instant; they leapt to massive heights and fled from sacred attributes; their tongues grew thick; their veins became green; their teeth creaked and they foamed at the mouth; their nostrils flared colossally, and their hair stood abristle, and pallor covered their faces while the lips began to bruise.

Despite the fact that the due protocol was followed and the doctor was called (of course, per the *Ritual,* he was not able to do anything to help the women), it seems clear that devils preyed on the women in San Plácido. Here is the case of the first possessed, on September 8, 1625: "the day of the Nativity of Our Lady, we saw a nun make such grimaces, deal such blows, and throwing the relics and images that we deemed her mad." Subsequently, if further confirmation is necessary, there is the doctor's account: "With incredible cries and feelings [the devil] said that it was not only him who was in that house, that others were in most of the sisters."[11]

We find a similar case in Tramacastilla. That diabolical epidemic lasted from 1637 to 1642, spreading throughout the town, as well as through Sandiniés, Villanua, Saqués, Sallent, Jaca, Pueyo de Jaca, and Piedrafita de Jaca (Gari Lacruz 1991). Besides the corresponding inquisitorial minutes, a text by the exorcist Francisco Blasco Lanuza, *Patrocinio de ángeles y combate de demonios* (Patronage of Angels and Combat of Demons), published in 1652, chronicles the possessions in a particular case in this Alto Aragón area. The number of people affected by possession exceeds the seventy-two identified in Tramacastilla and Sandiniés, although it was not as high as the numbers sometimes mentioned in other texts.[12]

In this case, diabolical signals were found not only on the bodies of the possessed, but even in the accidents and discomfort that the animals in the area suffered. The rector of Tramacastilla's dog was abruptly crippled and could be healed only by incantations, while the mule carrying Blasco Lanuza himself toward the scene "became lame so that it could not lean on its front leg and this without wounds or injuries of any kind" (Blasco Lanuza 1652, 847). As in the previous case, the animal was healed only through the use of spells.

Besides giving us more extensive analytical keys, these cases demonstrate that the relationship between the rural world and the devil and his minions has singular aspects that are not found in cities. It is significant not only that these animals are domestic, and therefore very close to human beings, but also that the possession manifests through the unusual, the sudden, the befallen, and the uncontrollable, thus creating a social and symbolic disorder that only an exorcism can undo.

The possessed women from Aragon were very young, ranging from eight to twenty-five years of age, both married and unmarried. Their bodies, however, repeatedly deliver the same message with similar signals. Blasco Lanuza (1652) writes:

> Often marked as obsessed, with a deep sleep, when they come to hear the divine offices, something prevents them from uttering vocal prayers, from looking at the consecrated host when the priest at mass offers it, and reveal themselves in black form, hinder the confession, deprived of their senses before receiving absolution, very reluctant to receive the Blessed Sacrament, knocked to the ground, and refuse to speak entirely as if their throats were locked. Other times they feel fatal grief, as when left to their good judgment they don their rosaries, and bear them in such a manner they seem to suffer unbearable pains, and shed tears with sweats, cry to the heavens, begging for mercy. They also often abstain from food and drink for three, four and five days, causing wonder at their vigor. They feel as if ants crawled between the skin and the flesh, up and down with great speed. They are often crippled, in the arms or hands, or legs, those

parts of the body left numb, and with spells, holy relics, and the invocations of saints, the cause recedes and frees them to use such members. On
some occasions they discover secret things, take pieces of silver and other
jewels, and hide them in very distant places, where they are later found,
forcing the demons with spells to manifest those objects. At all times they
experience great inequalities, because in some, the possessed suffer un-
ending hiccups, deep sighs, multiple and unmanageable curls, stirring
sobs, heavy melancholy, such vomit as tear at their hearts and insides,
hot flashes, headaches, forceful burning pains at their sides, head, stomach and belly, terrible accidents. They throw themselves from high posts
remaining unscathed. Demons speak through them in different figures,
persuading to vices and heresies. (836)[13]

The cases of possession are varied and cumulative. The bodies of the
possessed display characteristics and certainties that reflect a cultural
pattern. However, it is true that by analyzing each case separately—by
delving into each one of them—one can identify distinct issues generated
by other social or personal variables. The possessed women of Aragon
caused actual economic problems in their respective towns by altering the
economic-agricultural rhythms: the poor people, who saw maniacs flour-
ishing everywhere, lived in continuous penance and devoted their time to
processions, masses, and rituals rather than to their fields and livestock.
None of this happened in Loudun or Madrid. Life in a convent in a city
of importance, which was subject to certain religious hierarchies, shaped
other patterns in the possessions there. Interestingly, in both Loudun and
Madrid there were certain political components that were absent from
the cases in Aragon. However, the experts in conjuring were prevalent in
all of them: the exorcists.

Pedagogy of Cruelty: The Bodies of Demons

As stated above, it was well known that demons inhabited a body when
the aforementioned behaviors were observed, and that these behaviors
were not the result of diseases that doctors could cure. Often (as in the
paradigmatic case of San Plácido), the doctor himself suggested the ex-

orcism, or the devil even demanded it vociferously from the body of the possessed (San Plácido, again). Sometimes the devils entered the abducted by means of a spell cast by a sorcerer (in Loudun and Urbain, Grandier; and in Tramacastilla, Pedro de Arruebo and Miguel Guillén), though it was a debatable question whether this occurred because the demons commanded it or because the demoniacs vomited spells, as in the case of Aragon.[14]

In one way or another, at the moment the damage materialized, so did the remedy, which was none other than exorcism by the hand of the conjurer. As previously noted, the exorcists were meant to be men of special disposition, strong in will and faith, because their joust was with Satan himself—nothing more and nothing less. The ritual took the form of a struggle, recalling the first battle, in which Light defeated Darkness, and for this reason, it is usual to find linguistic terms that remind us of this conflictive nature. Words such as battle, war, feud, and the like punctuate texts about exorcisms: Noydens warns that all weapons against the infernal enemy must be readied against the "fiendish invasion of the armies of hell," writes Blasco Lanuza (1652, 855). These armies, he tells us, are as organized as the angelic ones, presided over by seven generals (25–223 and 487–90). With faith as armor, the forces of Light must defeat and conquer them—and not only them, but all those who follow them, be they possessed, witches, or merely heretics. And for this purpose, nothing is better than an exorcist endowed with spiritual ammunition (holy water, crosses, Bibles, prayers) and his own strength and conviction; it is no coincidence that, in many cases, it is he who configures and feeds the demonic possession.

There is also another controversial aspect that, in our opinion, lends a unique character to each case of exorcism: the use of force against the devil. Just as dialectical dispute with the demons had advocates and opponents, a face-to-face confrontation with Satan was permitted and recommended, especially for the educational function it could serve when it was performed so everyone could observe it—at church, for example, as experts recommended. Thus, it is possible to make a typology of exorcisms according to the space in which they were conducted, pointing to each space's relationship with the use of physical force against the devil.

In the case of Tramacastilla, the conjurer himself tells us he secured a possessed woman by the neck with his stole because she slithered like a serpent. At that time, this violent act seemed appropriate to weaken the devil, and ordinary, because it was also used in one of the exorcisms performed on Magdalena de la Cruz to have her manifest and confess her family devil, Serafinito (Imirizaldu 1977, 47–48). These cruel and humiliating actions were justified in the context of personal combat with hell, but it was fully understood, of course, that the beatings and slaps to the demon were received by the body of the possessed. In the infamous case of Loudun, all exorcisms were performed before spectators, some of whom even came from other communities to watch. Barré, one of the exorcists, was in charge of the show.[15] During the third exorcism, the prioress Jeanne des Anges fell to the ground; she howled, writhed, and ground her teeth with such fury that two of them cracked, and with tremendous screams she warned that there were seven demons in her body. On October 8, 1632, Barré ordered that an immense enema be given to Jeanne des Anges, and with that, he accomplished his first victory. Asmodeus, the demon who dwelled in the prioress's underbelly, came out of her with multiple cries before the admiring audience. Days later, on October 13, 1632, Barré struck again. He confronted a demon (and a woman), who grunted and roared like a lion, startling everyone present. Nine days later, after her legs and arms had been secured, he cursed at her over and over, amidst screams and threats, slapping her. The devil resisted, and violence continued until Jeanne des Anges, a woman of small size with bone tuberculosis and vertebrae that had been bent since childhood, exclaimed among disconsolate cries: "Oh Jesus, you kill me. Dear god, my heart hurts. Leave me, I implore you. I cannot handle this anymore! I am so torn apart, I think I have a broken rib"[16] (Certeau 1980, 70).[17]

Demons do not suffer physical pain; only the possessed suffer. And the demons of these women are unique, singular, and nontransferable. Pain attains existence through the person experiencing it, since it lacks ontological existence beyond the comprehension of the afflicted individual. Pain blurs the person, and it does so even more dramatically in this case, where a cultural construction has absorbed all their humanity.

Fortunately, not all exorcisms nor all inquisitorial courts made torment and pain their guide to the truth.[18] Fray Francisco García Calderón, principal conjurer to the nuns of San Plácido, never used physical force against them.[19] The abuse was of a different ilk, not only due to Calderón's own personal characteristics, but also because the demons of San Plácido were internal, cloistered in intimate and closed spaces, a special *communitas* of demoniacs. These were devils centered on the doctrine and policy, demons made into words (Moncó 1989).

The exorcists, the exorcisms, and possession itself are a *vademecum* of symptoms: the signs of possession are uttered from the pulpits; they are seen, confirmed, learned, and replicated again and again, sometimes adorned with a diverse range of personal brushstrokes (personal desires, fears, hopes, disappointments, etc.). For men and women of the seventeenth century, possession was something known, transmitted, and taught by means of multiple sources, some of which are still preserved today, even outside the covers of specialized books. How can we forget the aesthetic power of Giotto, who portrayed these terrified multiform demons taking flight over towers and roofs?[20] How could we fail to appreciate the many diabolical manifestations captured in sculptures in the churches and cathedrals that punctuate the Spanish landscape? Burgos, Ávila, Jaca, Palencia, Zaragoza are all perfect stops on an itinerary throughout Catholic Europe to help us appreciate how Satan has permeated the daily lives of several groups of people. Once again, these sources ratify the experience of the demonic and open the figure of the devil to multiple representations: flesh, temptation, the Final Judgment, possession, and hellish punishment. It is true that not all are equally explicit, and also that our perceptions and feelings before certain representations are not the same as they might be before a painting, sculpted stone, a stage performance, or a work of literature, or film.[21] These manifestations may serve different purposes (doctrinal, artistic, or merely ludic), but they form a chorus that speaks to us with many different voices about profound human problems. As Lisón Tolosana wrote, "Satan has an impossible semantics-referential range, inconsistent: it is everything and nothing, reality and fantasy, abstraction and substitution, empiricism, moral reflection, metaphysics and anthropology" (1990, 101). In conclusion, we face a representation of evil that personifies paradox, ambivalence, and ambiguity.

NOTES

1. Half an *açumbre* is a little more than a liter of water.

2. Physical suffering as a means to the truth took precedence in these punishments. This is demonstrated by the variety of instruments of torture.

3. "Queriéndolo (Dios), para purificar más al alma, y por otros altísimos fines, deseando nuestro bien, o porque cesen culpas y pecados, o porque satisfagamos por la pena que los ya cometidos merecen, o finalmente, por aumentarse más los méritos, para que a la gloria, a que como fin y premio fue elegida, correspondan iguales merecimientos."

4. See, for example, the series of poems, prayers, and expressions referenced by Lisón Tolosana on wise women and witches (1979, especially 136 et seq. and 170 et seq.).

5. "(Los exorcistas utilizan) ciertos sahumerios, los cuales dicen tienen la eficacia de molestar extrañamente a los demonios [. . .] Usan para estos sahumerios de la ruda, del hipericón, del cuerno de cabra, del estiércol humano [. . .] lo que experimentamos es que cualquier hombre o mujer, si le dan humo a las narices con cosas asquerosas y fétidas, se conmueve, se inquieta, se congoja y hace todo lo posible por apartarse." This incense was also common in many places in Spain as protection from and banishment of witches. The analogy is that evil (from the devil and/or witch) is fought with incense's evil (smell).

6. The devil had multiple names, as Morgado García explains (1999, 33–34). It is interesting, however, that in some cases, possessed women rejected the most common names, such as Satan, Beelzebub, Behemoth, Lucifer, Belial, Leviathan, Asmodeus, Astaroth, Belphegor, etc. We find these names in literature and some other, more comical ones, such as *El Diablo Cojuelo* (*The Lame Devil*) by Luis Vélez de Guevara, and even ridiculous descriptions such as Diego Torres Villarroel's in *Los desahuciados del mundo y de la gloria* (The Destitute of This World and of Glory).

7. Some manuals warned that many sinful people had demons in their body but fled the exorcist by not revealing themselves. In some cases of collective possession (San Plácido, for example, which we discuss later) the possessed themselves warned that some of their peers were under the devil's influence despite the fact that their demons failed to manifest themselves. The use of the term is quite symptomatic.

8. Loudon is a French city belonging to the department of Vienne in the Poitou-Charentes region, northwest of Poitiers. The Ursuline nuns of a convent school there, headed by Superior Jeanne des Anges, were possessed and took part in conjurations.

9. "Comme le récit se fragmente en noms (propres) et en rôles, il efface la référence à des êtres pour leur sustituer une série d'histoires différentes et combinées: celle du pouls, celle de la digestion, celle de la bouche, de la langue ou des jambes."

10. "Aquí hubo la velocidad de las vueltas, la agilidad en los saltos, la fiereza de las voces en los aullidos, [. . .] las enfermedades graves, las hinchazones disformes, los temblores continuos, los acometimientos a la muerte [. . .] impetuosamente se salían de las celdas [. . .] se arrojaban sobre el agua y la nieve [. . .] se subían a los desvanes con

movimientos de azogadas [. . .] se metían en las artesas de agua fría [. . .] con los ojos encendidos." I have added the statements by the prioress, Teresa Valle de la Cerda, and the defense of Fray Antonio Pérez.

11. Teresa Valle de la Cerda. Memorial files 40 and 41. Folch and Cardona files 154 and 154.

12. Pellicer, in his *Avisos,* states that the number of the affected was over 1,600. Luisa de Padilla, Countess of Aranda, in her text *Elogios de la verdad e invectiva contra la mentira,* published in 1640, indicates that the women possessed were more than 250 (Gari Lacruz 1991, 164).

13. "Suelen señalarse obsesas, con un profundo sueño, cuando entran a oír los Divinos oficios impídenlas el decir oración vocal, no las dejan mirar a la hostia consagrada, cuando alza el sacerdote en la misa, y se la traslucen en forma negra, ponen estorbo en la confesión, privándolas de sentidos antes de dar la absolución, resisten mucho al tiempo de recibir el Santísimo Sacramento derribándolas en tierra, y se ponen como candados en la garganta. Otras veces sienten mortales congojas, porque dejándolas en buen juicio se ponen los corazones, y los cargan de tal modo que padecen ansias de muerte, y derramando lágrimas con sudores, dan gritos al cielo, pidiendo misericordia. También impiden muchas veces el comer, y beber, por tres, cuatro y cinco días, dejando admiración porque no quedan desfallecidas. Sienten ellas que andan como hormigas entre la piel y la carne, subiendo y bajando con mucha velocidad. Quedan tullidas muchas veces, en los brazos, o manos, o piernas, estando por algún tiempo como insensibles aquellas partes del cuerpo, y con los conjuros, con santas reliquias, e invocaciones de santos, se aparta la causa, quedando libres para usar de tales miembros. En algunas ocasiones descubren cosas secretas, toman piezas de plata y otras alhajas, y las ocultan en puestos muy distantes, donde se hallan después, haciéndolos manifestar a los mismos demonios con los conjuros. En todos tiempos se experimentan grandes desigualdades, porque en algunas espiritada causan hipos continuos, suspiros grandes, y multiplicados risos, sin poderlos atajar, llantos que enternecen, melancolías pesadísimas, vómitos, que parecen han de trocar el corazón y entrañas por la boca, calenturas ardientes, dolores de ijada vehementísimos, y de cabeza, de estómago y de vientre, terribles accidentes. Arrójanse de altos puestos sin recibir daño. Háblanlas los demonios en diversas figuras, persuadiendo a vicios y herejías."

14. Pedro de Arruebo was well known in the area. According to Jeanne des Anges, Grandier had been possessed by a bouquet of roses she had hidden in her corset. The prioress and Grandier never met.

15. This is similar to Aragon. Father Luis de la Concepción, eyewitness, describes several of these scenes. See also Gari Lacruz 1991, 170.

16. "Ha, Jesus, vous tuez me. Mon Dieu, le coeur fait me mal. Laissez moi, je vous prie. Puis Je n'en plus [. . .] que j'endure! Je suis toute Belle, je crois avoir une côte rompue."

17. Corresponding to the original of the BNP, files Fr. 7619, f. 11.

18. However, the differences among the different tribunals and the inquisitorial rationale of some inquisitors and those of the supreme tribunal are remarkable.

19. One of the women's counselors informed the Inquisition in a letter that her demon so tightened her jaws that when they tried to open her mouth, they cracked her cheek (Moncó 1989). The physical force against her did not come from the exorcist.

20. The fresco *The Expulsion of the Demons from Arezzo* is in the Basilica of St. Francis in Assisi.

21. The case of Loudun was made into film (Jerzy Kawalerowicz, *Matka Joanna od Aniołów* [1961], and Ken Russell, *The Devils* [1971]); the case of San Plácido became a play (Domingo Miras, *Las alumbradas de la Encarnación Benita* [1989]).

WORKS CITED

Blasco Lanuza, Francisco de. 1652. *Patrocinio de ángeles y combate de demonios*. San Juan de la Peña: Juan Nogués.

Castañega, Martín de. 1529. *Tratado muy sotil y bien fundado de las supersticiones y hechicerías y vanos conjuros y alusiones y otras cosas tocantes y de la posibilidad e remedio de ellas*. Logroño: Miguel de Eguía.

Certeau, Michel de. 1980. *La possession de Loudun*. Paris: Gallimard.

Ciruelo, Pedro. 1952. *Reprobación de las supersticiones y hechicerías*. Madrid: Joyas Bibliográficas.

Concepción, Luis de la. 1983. *Práctica de conjurar*. Barcelona: Editorial Humanitas.

Feijoo, Benito Jerónimo. 1961. *Teatro crítico universal*. Madrid: BAE.

Gari Lacruz, Ángel. 1991. *Brujería e Inquisición en el Alto Aragón en la primera mitad del siglo XVII*. Zaragoza: Diputación General de Aragón.

Imirizaldu, Jesús. 1977. *Monjas y beatas embaucadoras*. Madrid: Editorial Nacional.

Kramer, Heinrich, and Jacob Sprenger. 1492. *Malleus Maleficarum*. Spira: Peter Drach.

Lisón Tolosana, Carmelo. 1979. *Brujería, estructura social y simbolismo en Galicia*. Madrid: Akal.

———. 1990. *Demonios y exorcismos en los siglos de oro (La España mental I)*. Madrid: Akal.

Mbembe, Achille. 2006. "Nécropolitique." In *Traversées, diasporas, modernités: Raisons Politiques*, ed. Eleni Varikas, 29–60. Paris: Prensses de Sciences Po/Paris VIII.

Moncó, Beatriz. 1989. *Mujer y demonio: Una pareja barroca*. Madrid: Instituto de Sociología Aplicada.

———. 2017. "El cuerpo enfermo y sus cuidados: Identidades y representaciones de género." In *Cuidar el cuerpo vulnerable, perfeccionar lo humano*, ed. V. Roqué Sánchez and J. Guerrero Muñoz, 103–33. Madrid: Dykinson.

Morgado García, Arturo. 1999. *Demonios, magos y brujas en la España Moderna*. Cádiz: Universidad de Cádiz.

Navarro, Gaspar. 1631. *Tribunal de superstición ladina*. Huesca: Pedro Blusón.

Naxara, Fray Joseph de. 1672. *Espejo mýstico en que el hombre interior se mira . . . para los conocimientos de Dios y el exercicio de las virtudes*. Madrid: Lucas Antonio de Bedmar.

Noydens, Benito Remigio. 1660. *Práctica de exorcistas y ministros de la Iglesia*. Valencia: Imprenta del Molino de la Revella.

Suárez, Francisco. 1620. *De Angelis*. Lyon: Horacio Cardon.

✞

The "Fallen Women" of Francisco Rizi's *Profanación de un crucifijo o Familia de herejes azotando un crucifijo*

SONIA PÉREZ-VILLANUEVA

O n July 4, 1632, Madrid celebrated a public trial of the Inquisition, an auto de fe, where forty-two prisoners heard their sentences and another four were tried *in absentia*.[1] The auto de fe
was a premeditated spectacle promoting the success of the Inquisitional
court. The primary objective of the trial was to offer a public exhibition
of the punishment of three families of Portuguese origin who were accused of practicing Judaism and desecrating an image of Christ in one
of their houses on Las Infantas Street near the center of Madrid. Seven
members of these Portuguese families were sentenced to death.[2] Two days
later, the Inquisition ordered the demolition of the house where the image of Christ had supposedly been desecrated and, in its place, the construction of a monastery in memory of the assaults committed against
Christ. In 1639, memories of the house were rendered invisible by the
powerful presence of the new convent of the Capuchins de la Paciencia
de Cristo, which was inaugurated under the invocation of the Patience of
Christ, Our Lord. The Inquisition commissioned five paintings to deco-
rate the walls of the convent and secure in Spanish history a version of
the story about the profanation of Christ and consequent punishment of
the family.

The artists who performed the task of creating a visual memory of the
event were Francisco Camilo (*Ultrajes al Crucifijo o Cristo de las Injurias*,
1651), Francisco Fernández (*Herejes maltratando un crucifijo*, 1651), Andrés
de Vargas (*Martirio del Brasero*, 1651), and Francisco Rizi (*Profanación*

de un crucifijo o Familia de herejes azotando un crucifijo and *El expolio de Cristo o Cristo de la Paciencia,* 1651). The convent was subsequently demolished in 1837 and the artworks were sent to the museum known as the Museo de la Trinidad in Madrid. In his recent study of the paintings, Pereda affirms that "the paintings reconstructed the scene of the crime with well-documented care, they describe the details of the acts, identify each of their protagonists, and most importantly, transform the spectators into witnesses of the occurrence" (2017, 213). The images' narratives thus became truth in the eyes of history.

The paintings continued their journey when the museum was dissolved in 1872 and most of its works were sent to the Prado Museum in Madrid. In 1986, the museum hosted the exhibition "Carreño, Herrera, and Rizi" as part of the reopening of the Villahermosa Palace, which now houses the Thyssen-Bornemisza Museum. Francisco Rizi's *Profanación de un crucifijo o Familia de herejes azotando un crucifijo,* known under both titles, was restored for the exhibition, highlighting the ancient story of the Portuguese family and their desecration of Christ. The painting would subsequently form part of the itinerant exhibition "Art in the Court of Philip IV" that traveled throughout Spain. It is now in storage with a digital presence on the museum website, where the viewer will find the following description:

> The narrated events took place in Madrid around 1630. In the houses of Licenciado Parquero [sic], located on the street of Las Infantas, lived a family of Judaizers, of Portuguese origin, composed of the married couple, *two very beautiful daughters* and a six-year-old boy. They had already encountered some problems with the court of the Inquisition. In their house they had, under the canopy of the hall, a crucifix, half a meter high (41 cm), to make apparent ostentation of their Christian faith. On Wednesday and Friday, during the night, there was a group of fifteen Judaizers who, in different ways, tortured the image by dragging it with ropes and hawthorn sticks. When the image complained on one occasion of the martyrdom that it suffered, even spouting blood that splashed on its executioners, they decided to burn it and finish destroying it with hacking it to pieces. The son's indiscretion in alerting the Holy Office led

it to discover what had happened and to apply the typical punishment of burning at the stake. (museodelprado.es. My italics)

The Prado Museum website replicates the words of Jesús Urrea, curator of the exhibition "Art in the Court of Philip IV," to describe Rizi's painting in 1994. Five centuries after its commission, the visual memory of the Inquisition remains. The Prado description of Rizi's painting excludes the identities of the members of the family, narrates the events as if they were the truth, avoids any reference to the violence that the family suffered, and what is more disturbing, emphasizes the beauty of the young women in the painting. The narrative proves the enduring propagandistic power of images commissioned by the Inquisition throughout time. In Pereda's words, "the canvases constitute sole proof of what occurred; they are the point of contact between testimony and fiction, the site where testimony becomes deception (*engaño*), and fiction, disillusion (*desengaño*)" (2017, 256).[3]

It must be noted that images of the Spanish Inquisition commissioned by the Holy Office itself are scarce, with perhaps fewer than two hundred images that reflect scenes, symbols, or protagonists of the Spanish Inquisition. In those images, there are hardly any representations of violence against women. It is as if women had not been the victims of the punishments of the Inquisition. What is more likely is that the Inquisition commissioned the iconography to erase or hide female suffering, as is the case in Rizi's painting. Indeed, the Holy Office maintained a minimum number of images that represented the procedures of its inquisitorial work and at no time allowed representations of its trials, except for select autos de fe. The Holy Office mastered how its brand was portrayed in Spain, and its iconography was chosen in such a strategic way that it had an ideological effect on the society of the time and even beyond. The promotion of Rizi's painting, therefore, was no accident (Pérez-Villanueva 2017, 148–49).

This essay serves as an homage to Leonor Rodríguez, María Rodríguez, Guiomar Rodríguez, Isabel Núñez Álvarez, Beatriz Núñez, Beatriz Enríquez, Violante Méndez, Victoria Méndez, and their families. It aims to show how Rizi's painting deploys symbolic elements to portray a version of the story favorable to the Inquisition, but also appealing as a cultural truth to Christians throughout time. It will explore the role of women in the crypto-Judaic tradition and the importance of the beauty reflected in the young women and its symbolic relationship to the "fallen woman." This essay recovers an important story of three families and the suffering they unjustly endured, and in so doing it denounces the patriarchal, anti-Semitic, and anti-Portuguese visual legacy of the Spanish Inquisition.

Political and Historical Background: With a Grain of Salt

The early seventeenth-century context for the auto de fe of July 4, 1632, is characterized by the forces of the Inquisition reacting to an increased migration of Portuguese at a time of economic, political, and military peril. These forces were catalyzed on April 16, 1581, when Philip II was crowned king of Portugal, resulting in the political unification of the Iberian peninsula that would last until the 1640s. Unification opened new professional and commercial opportunities, and many Portuguese families migrated to Spain. Portuguese migration increased some forty years later when, during a time of political, economic, and military crisis, Philip IV's favorite, the Count-Duke of Olivares, created new policies to sustain the economy and generate the tax revenue needed to support war efforts in Europe and New Spain. One policy advanced by Olivares was to welcome Portuguese merchants and financiers to Castile, many of whom became the Crown's bankers and tax collectors. The relationship between Olivares and Philip IV grew stronger, but the arrival of greater numbers of Portuguese was not well received in Spain, where they were increasingly subjected to accusations of heresy and Judaism.[4]

Olivares's policies were highly criticized by the Old Christian population, who believed the king's favorite was an ally of the crypto-Jewish community. The Old Christians viewed the Portuguese migration as an intrusion of Judaism on their Christian lands. Olivares was feeling pressure from the Old Christian community and was increasingly desperate and alone. In a letter sent to the Marquis of Aytona in March of 1632, Olivares complained, "With so much work and so little help. I can't keep going . . . I am incapable of making bread from stones" (Elliott 1986, 438). In desperation, Olivares turned to the Crown's monopoly on the supply of salt. He saw in the salt monopoly the miracle he was looking for and increased the tax on salt to generate 9 million ducats for the Crown (Elliott 1986, 438). However, Olivares's tax on salt would exacerbate an already tense relationship between Spanish citizens and Portuguese migrants. Most of the collectors of the salt tax were Portuguese bankers, and the tax would become associated with the Portuguese migrant population. Violent reactions against Portuguese families were reported. In Elliott's words, "on the outskirts of Bilbao a rich Portuguese, who had lived there for twenty-five years, had his house burnt to the ground; in the province of Guipuzcoa, bordering on Vizcaya, native Portuguese were forbidden on pain of life and forfeiture of property to involve themselves in revenue-collecting" (Elliott 1986, 450).

The fear of being persecuted provoked quarrels among the Portuguese living in Spain, some of whom turned against each other to prove their "true" conversion to Christianity so that they could protect themselves from the Old Christians and ultimately from the Inquisition. That was the case with Juana de Silva, a Portuguese woman who lived in Madrid near Las Infantas Street. De Silva accused Beatriz Núñez and Miguel Rodríguez—and their families—of practicing non-Christian activities in their house (Pulido Serrano 2002, 123–25).[5] Between July 12, 1630, and September 3, 1630, all members of the three families were detained and accused of practicing Judaism and of desecrating an image of Christ.[6]

It is uncanny that the house on this street where the accused Portuguese families lived was located in front of a salt store, as Elena Núñez, daughter of Beatriz Núñez, reveals in her testimony: "Then they moved to *Las Infantas* Street opposite the house *where salt is sold;* the house in which these people lived, together with her brother and the children of her brother-in-law Enrique Méndez, who also moved in with these women; the house which was sometimes visited by this woman and her mother Beatriz Núñez and her sister Seraphina" (*Trial of Faith for Violante Méndez,* n.p., my italics).[7] Officials working for the Holy Office measured every move with strategic care. It is highly likely that these families were selected for persecution at least in part for their proximity to the salt store.

By the time the three families of Las Infantas Street heard their sentences on July 4, 1632, they had already spent two years in prison. In the extravagant auto de fe in the Plaza Mayor of Madrid, they were presented in front of the royal family and their escort, important political figures, an overwhelming presence of many important members of the Inquisition, and thousands of spectators. The Count-Duke of Olivares was seated near the king. Olivares had no allegiance to the Portuguese he had encouraged to come to Spain and serve the Crown. With his revenue problem solved with the salt tax, he had then seen an opportunity to consolidate his political power and relationship with the Spanish people by aligning with the spectacle of the auto de fe. With the Crown, Olivares, and the mass of people watching, Ana Rodríguez, a twelve-year-old girl, was sentenced to one year in prison; Elena Núñez (an adult) was sentenced to one hundred lashes and life imprisonment; Violante Núñez Méndez, twenty-two, and Beatriz Enríquez, sixteen, were sentenced to life imprisonment; Adults Beatriz Núñez, Hernán Báez, Isabel Núñez Álvárez, Leonor Rodríguez, and Miguel Rodríguez were sentenced to death at the stake. Beatriz Rodríguez, daughter of Hernán Báez and Leonor Rodríguez, was sentenced to death *in absentia* (Gómez Mora, 12r and 14v–14r).

The case of the three families on Las Infantas Street reflects an anti-Semitic reality of suspicion, persecution, and cruelty. The auto de fe was perhaps also a way for Olivares to recast his position with the Spanish people. Miguel Rodríguez and Isabel Núñez, Hernán Báez and Leonor Rodríguez, and the widow Beatriz Núñez were clearly scapegoats. They had worked as humble textile merchants whose commercial interests had nothing to do with the salt store nearby. The destruction of their house was a symbolic erasure of the synagogue, and the construction of a convent of Capuchins in its place became the triumph of the Church. As will be shown below, Francisco Rizi's painting *Profanación de un crucifijo o Familia de herejes azotando un crucifijo* gathers important propagandistic messages that were meant to communicate the victory of Catholicism over Judaism. The convent was a central image, a terrifying and constant threat of the Inquisition, and with its proximity to the salt store, a permanent reminder of the Portuguese threat that further justified the existence of the Inquisition. Rizi's painting put forth a testimony of falsehoods, a permanent political statement aligned with the interests of Olivares and the Crown, reaching into a future where the anti-Semitic fear would continue to perpetrate a historical injustice.

The House as Synagogue: Crypto-Judaism and Sacrilege

During the two years that most members of the Las Infantas Street families spent in jail, they were interrogated on a regular basis until they confessed what officials of the Inquisition wanted to hear. Miguel Rodríguez and Hernán Báez confessed immediately in front of Cienfuegos and Cristóbal de Ibarra, officers of the Toledo Tribunal (Pulido Serrano 2002, 129). Moreover, they accused other members of their families, as the testimony of Hernán Báez against his wife Leonor and daughters María and Isabel shows:

> And that with his wife, named Leonor Rodríguez, he followed the law of Moses, as did his daughter, named María Rodríguez, and her husband, Enrique López. That they had communicated and observed the law of Moses for 34 years. His daughter Isabel Rodríguez has too, because he has seen them keep the Sabbath and they have dealt with things related to their rites and ceremonies, and it must be six years now since they got married (she and Manuel Fernández) and in that space of time they have done the aforementioned, and communicated and dealt with those things. And that they keep the Sabbath, they put on clean shirts and their best clothes, and observe the law of Moses. (*Proceso de fe de Leonor y María Rodríguez*, 2–3r)[8]

The transcription reveals how Hernán Báez confesses to observing Judaism and accuses other family members of joining him in the practice. The Holy Office saw a particular threat from Portuguese women, because they were seen as the faith carriers of Judaism after the expulsion of the Jews in 1492. Most of the accused members of Las Infantas Street families were women. Moreover, after the burning and destruction of synagogues in Spain, the house was viewed as a new place of cult for crypto-Judaizers (Levine Melammed 1999, 3). The house in the crypto-Judaic tradition became the domestic synagogue, the safe place of prayer and devotion.

Although evidence of the practice of Judaic traditions, found in the testimony of Hernán Báez, ran afoul of the Inquisition, that evidence alone was perhaps not enough to motivate the desired anger in the larger population. Therefore, Inquisitor Ibarra and General Prosecutor Bartolomé Guijarro focused on the extraordinary element of the story that concerned the desecration of Christ. A six-year-old boy described this violent action, Andresillo, Miguel Rodríguez's son, and he was supported by Ana Rodríguez, his twelve-year-old sister (Pulido Serrano 2002, 131–33). The narrative of the sacrilegious act was also located in the domestic realm, inside the house on Las Infantas Street. These narratives would influence the painters who created a visual memory for the convent.

For the Inquisition, the Las Infantas house became a powerful anti-Christian symbol that had to be destroyed. Therefore, two days after the auto de fe, it was demolished with the help of violent citizens who tore down the house with their own bare hands:

> As soon as the street cry was over, according to the order given, the soldiers' drums sounded the alarm, and the foot-soldiers, officers, and foremen stormed the house, knocking down doors, windows, walls, and roofs, and generating so much dust, confusion, and noise that the sky seemed to come down. And as the demolition began, the escort went back to the Inquisition, providing its ministers with axes; and they helped until they brought down their factory, which at nine o'clock at night, no longer showed signs of a building, because the people, who had no tools, tore out bricks and stones from the foundations with their own hands. A large crowd gathered, which forced the presence of a guard to defend the entrance into streets from people, cars, and horses. (Gómez de Mora 1632, 431)[9]

The violence of the house attack perpetrated by the people of Madrid on July 6, 1632, mimicked the distant anti-Jewish riots of 1391 in Castile and Aragon, where sacred Jewish institutions were destroyed, hundreds of Jews were killed, and many others were forced into conversion. A view had been formed that the center of the crypto-Jewish world was inside that house, in that domestic space where women became the rabbis who would pass on their faith, rituals and traditions, such as "kindle lights on

Friday evening, prepare Sabbath meals, baked *matzah,* observe the dietary laws, and the like; now these observances were to become the major symbols of crypto-Judaism" (Levine Melammed 1999, 31). The house also came to be seen as the gathering space to meet other crypto-Jews who kept their Judaic traditions secretly. Michael Scholz-Hänsel remarks that "it gives us the impression that this was the objective from the beginning, stemming from the notion of building a church to venerate the crucifix on the very site of the destroyed house" (1999, 688).[10] Its destruction was therefore a symbolic destruction of the synagogue, which in turn symbolized Judaism. The subsequent construction of the monastery was a symbolic triumph of Ecclesia (Church), or Christianity as whole. Moreover, the paintings hanging on the monastery's walls became one of the most extraordinary—and effective—propagandistic actions of the Spanish Inquisition.

The Role of Crypto-Jewish Women in a Domestic Environment: From Sacrilege to Miracle

When Miguel Rodríguez and Isabel Núñez Álvarez were arrested in the summer of 1630 and taken from Madrid to Toledo, their youngest son, Andresillo, was left behind and later found by neighbors who took him to their house. When the neighbors asked him about his parents, Andresillo reportedly surprised them by saying that the Inquisition had taken them because they used to whip an image of Christ. Frightened by the accusations, the neighbors supposedly took Andresillo to make a declaration in front of Inquisitor Agustín de Vergara in September of 1630:

> They caught them because they would not eat bacon, which he had heard somewhere. Also, that they caught them because they whipped an image of Christ and that, in order to do so, they locked themselves in the kitchen of their house and hung the Christ from a rope, leaving it hanging there while they whipped him with some thorns, and that his father would grab the Christ by the feet and his mother by the head and they passed him by the fireside [. . .] he would put one eye to a hole in the door of the said kitchen, and through it he could see everything. (Pulido Serrano 2002, 134–35)[11]

It is not surprising that Isabel and Miguel had a figure of Christ in their house since New Christians were obliged to have religious images to promote the Catholic faith at home (Pereda 2011, 264). What is surprising is that a six-year-old boy would retell an anti-Semitic legend that Christians had propagated since the Middle Ages. Pereda argues that "the crime of Las Infantas Street dovetails with a large and legendary tradition of desecration of images that harks back to the high Middle Ages, and that had even left a feast day in the liturgical calendar, that of the Passio Imaginis Christi" (2017, 221–22).[12] Andresillo was most likely pressured by inquisitional officers to compose his narrative and to adapt it to the anti-Semitic perception of Jews as Christ killers.

It is important to note that medieval legends of Jews as desecrators of Christ only involved men as the actively sacrilegious (Mann 2010 and Arciniega García 2012). However, the case of the house on Las Infantas Street blames both men and women as active participants in the crime. The setting of the story as told by Andresillo has a specific domestic component, the kitchen, a female place where Andresillo's mother, Isabel, would have spent time cooking Sabbath meals with other women from the neighborhood. While the narrative of the story was influenced by the anti-Semitic tradition of portraying Jews as Christ killers, Andresillo's story added a new component of crypto-Jewish women as Christ killers. There are previous instances of women accused during the Inquisition of desecrating Christ, but the auto de fe of July 4, 1632, marks the first time that such accusations against women were featured in a public trial and the first time they were the subject of paintings commissioned by the Inquisition.

Andresillo's sister Ana was arrested in September 1631, a year after Andresillo made his statement in front of the Inquisition. As Pulido Serrano observes, Ana had spent most of the year with her brother and knew what he had told Agustín de Vergara, the inquisitor who took his testimony (147). Ana made her statement in front of Inquisitor Ibarra and appears to corroborate Andresillo's story about the desecration of Christ, but provides more details:

> We were in the patio of that house and Beatriz Núñez, a widow who has testified, and her two daughters, Violante Méndez and Victoria Méndez,

came to the house. And Hernán Báez and his wife Leonor Rodríguez, who were staying in the same house, also came, and they all met in a room he had "in that courtyard." The said Fernando Báez, Leonor Rodríguez, Beatriz Núñez, Violante Méndez and Victoria Méndez and Miguel Rodríguez, "Samuel" Núñez Alvarez, her parents, and her sister Beatriz Enríquez all together, she saw that they were whipping a statue of Christ of about half a bar in length and that Fernando Báez was holding in his hands, as were all the people mentioned above. (Testimony of Ana Rodríguez, 6v)[13]

Ana's story involves more people than Andresillo's story, as she reportedly accuses her parents, her sister, and the other two Portuguese families that had been arrested the previous year. The location of her narrative is set in one of the chambers by the courtyard, creating a similar domestic environment to that in Andresillo's statement, but bringing it to a broader space so that everybody would fit in. The scene is overwhelmingly feminine—with seven female family members actively whipping the figure of Christ—reinforcing the agency of women in the sacrilegious act. It is suspicious that the stories evolve, bringing more women into the doubtful acts, thereby broadening the scope of sacrilegious behavior.

The inquisitors used Ana's story to add the accusation of sacrilege to the case files of all members of the Portuguese families involved in the testimony. Most of the prisoners confessed to the crime of sacrilege, providing more details of the act and adding an extraordinary element, which is the miracle of the figure of Christ speaking—"¿por qué me maltratáis?" ("why do you mistreat me?")—and bleeding (Pulido Serrano 2002, 150–51).[14] The "miracle" after the desecration provided inquisitors with the justification to destroy the house where the sacrilege had been committed and to build in its place the Convent of the Capuchins de la Paciencia de Cristo, where the miracle had occurred. Antonio de Contreras, member of the Order of Calatrava, was made responsible for the construction of the convent and the commission of the paintings. As Pereda points out, "it seems obvious that it was Contreras who gave the criminals' exact number, age, and sex to the artists. Their names would have been lost by then (the chronicler could not track down the child who had discovered the evil deeds, as by then he had been forgotten); the invented images took their place instead" (2017, 250).[15] Francisco Rizi's *Familia*, in particular, exhibits an extraordinary amalgamation of influences— the agency of women in the desecration, the domestic environment, the miracle—that contributed to the propagandistic message of the story as a collective truth.

Francisco Rizi's *Familia de herejes*

There are many dubious historical records that contributed to the propa- ganda of the case, such as the official account by Juan Gómez de Mora, the architect who had been responsible for creating the stage for the auto de fe. Although Mora had the exclusive rights to publish the account (at least for two years), there were many non-official news pamphlets, letters, loose sheets, prayers, and the like that were distributed after the auto de fe and validated its popularity, "allowing the Inquisition to communi- cate with all segments of society" (Pulido Serrano 2002, 223).[16] Francisco de Quevedo, Gabriel Bocángel, Lope de Vega, and Calderón de la Barca also contributed to the propaganda through their works.[17] However, the paintings became a more efficient medium of communicating the anti- Portuguese and anti-Jewish message of the Inquisition. Four paintings narrate the scenes of desecration of the Christ by the Portuguese families, and a fifth colossal painting by Rizi, *Cristo de la Paciencia*, relates the des- ecration to the original crucifixion and resurrection of Christ. Together, these works encompass an impressive production of Catholic imagery intended to communicate the event to the masses and to sow fear among New Christians. As Brown has argued, "the paintings represent a kind of encyclopedia of Inquisitional iconography and a triumphant defense of the validity of punishment (justice) in the practice of the faith" (Brown 1991, 52).

There were no direct previous visual references portraying Jewish women as Christ killers for the four artists—Francisco Camilo, Francisco Fernández, Andrés de Vargas, and Francisco Rizi. In the first three paint- ings by Camilo, Fernández, and de Vargas, the symbolism is ordinary and appears to follow the wishes of Antonio de Contreras, who had commissioned them. The two paintings by Rizi, *Familia* and *Cristo de la Paciencia*, are different and filled with far more subtle imagery that presents this anti-Semitic story with a richer power. In *Familia*, Rizi draws upon previous portrayals of Jewish biblical women, Jewish women shown in the desecration scenes as passive witnesses, and the allegory of Synagogue as a representation of Judaism through the figure of women. Drawing upon these familiar elements, Rizi provides for the first time a depiction of Jewish women as active Christ killers, imbuing the scene with great symbolic meaning.

Rizi's *Familia* represents the moment of sacrilege supposedly committed by the Portuguese family against Christ. The location of the scene, a chamber by the courtyard, coincides with the testimony of Ana Rodríguez, which expanded the original story to incorporate more people in the crime. The painting thus portrays six women (Leonor Rodríguez, Beatriz Núñez, Violante Méndez, Victoria Méndez, Isabel Núñez Álvarez, and Beatriz Enríquez), three men (Miguel Rodríguez, Samuel Núñez Álvarez, and Hernán Báez), and one female child (Ana Rodríguez) all participating actively in Christ's desecration. Two of the three men in the painting are identified as Jews because of the pejorative marks of their physiognomies, such as long and pointed noses, while the third one wears a tzitzit in his left hand as a reminder of the Laws of God (fig. 1).

Male Jews in Christian art prior to Rizi's *Familia* were portrayed with specific pejorative and stereotypical signs such as pointed hats, long noses, red hair, grotesque skin, badges, or yellow clothing. Christian imagery of male Jews in Spain portrays them as ugly, old, and evil, which Rizi maintains in his portrayal. This was, of course, a propagandistic scheme that sought to portray Jewish men as Christ killers. Rizi took pains to paint the families in ways that would draw forth the ire of his audience. In reality, the families of Las Infantas Street were poor and almost all of them were illiterate. Nonetheless, the painting portrayed them as the despised bankers that Olivares had invited into the country and common Spaniards wanted to kill.

Rizi's portrayal of Jewish women is more nuanced, and in many ways more powerful. In contrast to the overwhelming history of anti-Semitic and ludicrous imagery portraying male Jews, there was no history of pe-

FIGURE 1. Francisco Rizi, *Profanación de un crucifijo o Familia de herejes azotando un crucifijo*, 1651. © Archivo Fotográfico Museo Nacional del Prado.

jorative images for Jewish women in Spanish Christian art prior to 1651.[18] Jewish women were usually portrayed as passive agents, accompanying their fathers or husbands. Take, for example, Jaume Serra's *Altarpiece of the Virgin Mary* (1367–81), representing the first chronicled Christian depiction of an allegation of a Jew desecrating the host (1290). The plot of the painting is similar to the one found in the Las Infantas Street case. The painting depicts a Jewish family in a domestic environment where an elderly Jewish man struck at the sacred host—the holy "bread" that is the body of Christ according to the Catholic dogma of transubstantiation. The holy bread remained intact and started to bleed, symbolizing the death of Christ. Finally, the Jew threw the holy bread into a pot of boiling water. The blood turns the water red, and from the boiling pot the child

FIGURE 2. Jaume Serra, *Altarpiece of the Virgin Mary,* Monastery of Santa María de Sigena, Huesca. 1367–1381. Detail, *Desecration of the Host.* © Museu Nacional d'Art de Catalunya, Barcelona.

Jesus Christ emerges as a miracle. The legend behind the painting tells the story that a crucifix emerged from the boiling water (Rubin 1999, 41). The desecration resulted in a miracle. The Jew was accused for his act of sacrilege and sent to death at the stake. The difference in this earlier story is that his family was not killed, detained, or punished as in the Las Infantas case, but rather they converted to Christianity after they witnessed the miracle. This could explain the passivity of the woman depicted in the painting, and the admiration of the child in front of the miracle. Coincidentally, the Jew's house was confiscated, destroyed and a chapel was built in its place (Rubin 1999, 44). The scene of desecration leading to a miracle and the elements of Catholic triumph serve as precursors to the Las Infantas case and possible influences for Rizi's portrayal (fig. 2).

As Miri Rubin has observed in her study of narratives detailing assaults against Jews in late Medieval Europe, "Men and men alone were the culpable parties in the host desecration accusation" (1999, 71). She continues, "Jewish women rarely appear as abusers of the host and were often punished only by implication and by association with the guilt of their menfolk. When agency is imputed to them this takes the form of more innocent or simple-minded transgressions" (76). Rizi's painting advances a new version of the anti-Semitic narrative by portraying crypto-Judaic Portuguese women as active sinners and a threat to Christianity. The Portuguese women are central to the story of the families from Las Infantas Street, and it is interesting that Rizi's depiction of these women is far more nuanced than the stereotypical portrayal of the Jewish men and involves a subtle use of beauty that draws upon traditions in Christian art but also breaks new ground.

Jewish women depicted in Spanish biblical art during the Renaissance and Baroque are typically young, beautiful, and sensuous, but are also presented with a sense of perversion. Artists following this tradition would draw upon a set of standard "marks" that would tell the audience how to place the women in a biblical context. Biblical Jewish women such as Esther, Ruth, Judith, and Salome are depicted as young and beautiful, but also as pale and dangerous; in Lipton's words, as "lethal in act but visually benign" (Lipton 2008, 214). These portrayals reflect sensual women, dressed in luxurious clothes, adorned with expensive jewels, who seduce and deceive their Christian companions so that they can commit their sinful act. Salome, for example, in Amishai-Maisels's words, "epitomized evil sensuality for medieval man since her lascivious dance led to the death of John the Baptist" (1999, 57). What is more, these women were compared to animals, as seen in the portrayal of Salome given by Petrus Chrysologus, bishop of Ravenna in the fifth century:

> She moves like a tiger, not a woman; [. . .] she shakes her mane, not human hair; she bows and stretches her body; she grows with increasing fury, rising over the mass of men in her horribleness [. . .] A serpent was hidden in this woman, whose unholy gift overflowed her whole body and dominated the guests, so that their bodies and souls thrilled madly; she turned them into beasts who longed to eat human flesh and drink human blood. (Quoted in Amishai-Maisels 1999, 57)

This incongruous perception of Salome made her an important precursor to the later female Christ killer. John the Baptist fulfills the role of Christ in this scene and Salome, concealed by her sensuality, turns out to be his assassin.

Rizi's painting draws from this tradition of a sensuous portrayal of Jewish women and reveals subtle messages that would provoke admiration in the viewer while at the same time garnering acceptance of the story. Rizi places the bleeding upside-down Christ at the center of his painting, emphasizing the sacrilege and subsequent miracle in the salvation of Christ. A young female figure is placed behind and she is actively whipping the figure of Christ. This woman is understood to be Beatriz Enríquez, described as a sixteen-year-old maiden in the *Auto de Fe,* one of the beautiful daughters of Miguel Rodríguez, and Ana's sister. Beatriz is wearing a silk dress and extravagant earrings, feeding the Christian prejudice that Jews lived in abundance, and contributing to the false propagandistic message that the male subjects are bankers. In dressing Beatriz this way, Rizi is portraying her as an impious woman, since "Franciscan moralists insisted the Jewish women be forced to wear earrings as signs of Jewish difference; they also began to associate the adornments with luxury, lust, and prostitution" (Lipton 2008, 230). Beatriz's youth and beauty remind viewers of other Jewish biblical characters, such as Judith, who had embodied virtue but was later portrayed as a *femme fatale,* or Salome, whose seductive dance and beauty had disguised her true self, but was later portrayed as a fallen woman, ready to kill (Amishai-Maisels 1999, 57).

The symbolic element of the "fallen Jewish woman" in Christian representations dates back to the ninth century. Christian art had portrayed the "fallen Jewish woman" as a female personification of Synagogue juxtaposed against larger Christian scenes, which decorated the altars of churches and cathedrals. The allegory of Synagogue was usually exhibited next to the allegory of Ecclesia, representing the triumph of Christianity over Judaism. Ecclesia is frequently depicted carrying the cross and collecting the blood or body of Christ in a chalice, symbolizing the death of Christ on the cross and the miracle of his resurrection. But Synagogue carries the Tables of Law or the Torah, the symbolic knife for circumcision and a broken spear. Her eyes are covered by a blindfold that symbolizes the blindness of Jewish people who are unable to see the true God in Christ (García García 2013, 13). These representations of Ecclesia and Synagogue were popular and continued to be commissioned well into the sixteenth century.

In most of these depictions, there is a striking juxtaposition between Ecclesia and Synagogue in terms of their age. Fernando Gallego's altarpiece *Christ Blessing* (1494–96) reflects this apposition clearly (fig. 3). While Synagogue gives the illusion of being young and beautiful from far away, the reality is quite grotesque. A closer look reveals that she is old and ugly; her yellow dress that, from afar looked elegant, up close looks ragged and dirty, blending with the yellowness of her torn banner and exposing her Judaism; her inclined posture, rather than reflecting a playful gesture, on closer inspection appears distorted and unbalanced, symbolizing the vanquished faith of Judaism. Gallego portrays Synagogue as a fallen woman and, with her demise, proposes the idea that Judaism will tumble. By contrast, Ecclesia is portrayed as a young, beautiful figure who looks down on Synagogue, representing her power, stability, and victory. The symbolic elements of the laurel wreath, the flag of victory, the chalice with the Host and her red dress contribute to the triumph of Christianity over Judaism with the sacrifice of Christ's blood and subsequent miracle of resurrection.

FIGURE 3. Fernando Gallego, *Christ Blessing*, 1494–1496. © Archivo Fotográfico Museo Nacional del Prado.

Rizi would certainly have been familiar with such depictions of Synagogue and Ecclesia and he used their symbolic imagery in his painting. The artist juxtaposes female youth and old age, contrasting Beatriz Enríquez's youth and beauty with the ugliness of an old female character sitting at the foreground of the canvas. The subject matter of the old woman is common in Rizi's paintings. We see the old woman in both of his paintings of *Presentación de Jesús en el Templo*. However, Rizi hides the old woman, locating her behind other subjects, almost outside the frame of the paintings, as if she were unimportant. In his other paintings, the old woman is portrayed as a negative of her opposite young self and becomes the marginalized subject.

What is extraordinary about Rizi's *Familia* is the prominence given to this particular old woman. The old woman is shown in the foreground and receives most of the light beaming horizontally across the painting from right to left. She is shown as one of the protagonists of the scene. This old character is probably Beatriz Núñez, the widow and matriarch of the Portuguese families. It is interesting to note that Rizi appears to juxtapose the two Beatrizes and plays off the contrast between what might be seen as young and old versions of the same woman. In so doing, Rizi draws upon the tradition of Ecclesia and Synagogue, but in his *Familia* painting he is using the device to new ends. In Beatriz Núñez's old age, Rizi has caricatured her as a "recognized" Jewish woman: her features are sharpened, and her nose is longer and hooked. Her clothes are old and dirty, and she is the only one sitting on a wooden structure because, as Synagogue, she does not have the stability to stand up. Viewers see old Beatriz organizing the thorns and sticks to whip the figure of Christ. This reflects her power and active performance in the sinful act. She represents the fallen woman, the allegory of Synagogue, the personification of Judaism.

Following the historical Christian pattern, one might think that young Beatriz could in turn represent Ecclesia. However, Rizi cleverly plays with this imagery, reflecting the objectives of his new propagandistic mission. Rizi portrays young Beatriz as an illusion; her beauty and youth do not reflect who she is in reality. She is like Synagogue from far away, a fallen woman who will become old Beatriz. Her figure in the painting is in full movement, almost theatrical, but her face reflects a static posture. The passivity of her expression reminds viewers of the stereotypical image of the Jewish women in Christian art, such as the wife in Gallego's *Desecration of the Host*. Rizi and Gallego both show Jewish women who are self-absorbed, looking inward, and oblivious to those who are looking at them.

Rizi uses structure and light in the painting to establish the relationship between the young and old women. The wash of light that flows from right to left creates a relationship between old Beatriz and the inverted Christ, emphasizing the active role of the old lady in the sacrilegious act. The light also links old Beatriz with young Beatriz, who is standing just behind the Christ figure. Young Beatriz is looking toward the right and seems to be gazing at both Christ and old Beatriz. The two women are presented as young and old representations of Synagogue and are united in their collusion against Christ. Both women were ultimately defeated at trial as the young Beatriz was sentenced to life in jail while old Beatriz was sentenced to death at the stake.

Rizi's *Familia* strikes new ground with the depiction of Jewish women as killers of Christ. His painting serves the propagandistic interests of his patrons, creating a powerful image that continues to tell lies that are drowned in prejudice. However, it is Rizi's conniving use of traditional imagery that is most powerful. By drawing upon the depictions of Ecclesia and Synagogue, he presents clues that are familiar to his audience. However, his replacement of the female Ecclesia with the illusionary vision of Beatriz as young Synagogue is particularly pernicious. In Rizi's painting, there is no Ecclesia to ensure the future of Christianity. Rather, the painting presents an apocryphal scene where the Jewish faith is a threat to all Christians. It is a powerful call for the existence of the Inquisition. With no Ecclesia to provide comfort to his audience, Rizi is presenting the Inquisition as the ultimate defender of his faith and protector of his land.

With his paintings for the Convent of the Capuchins of Cristo de la Paciencia, Rizi continued a very successful career as an ambassador for the propagandistic mission of the Inquisition. Later in his career, as a royal painter and architect for Carlos II, Philip IV's heir, he was commissioned to paint the *Auto de fe de la Plaza Mayor de Madrid* (1683)

(277 × 438 cms.), which became the most grandiose painting ever commissioned by the Inquisition. In Rizi's career, art was carefully aligned to power. Against the power of this history, we must recover the true stories of those who suffered under the false presentation of the Christian faith.[19]

NOTES

1. This case has attracted the attention of many scholars; see, among others, Caro Baroja (1975, 65–70; 1986, II, 445–47), Yosef Hayin Yerushalmi 1989 (66–75), Bethencourt 1992, Alpert 1997, Scholz-Hänsel 1999, Rose 2001, Pulido Serrano 2002, Gitlitz 2003, Bustillo 2010, and Pereda 2017. According to Pereda, some scholars have ignored the anti-Semitism involved in the case and have assumed the desecration as a true fact (221, n. 31). See, for examples of this, Mesonero Romanos (1881, 104); Amador de los Ríos 1860–64, v3, 33); Palomino (1947, 1016); and more recently, Urrea (1994, 90). For an excellent study on the anti-Semitism involved in the case, see Pulido Serrano. It is worth noting that none of these studies focuses on the representation of women in the paintings and their symbolic importance.

2. The convictions can be found in Mora 1632 (12r and 14v–14r). They also appear in a manuscript archived in the Rare Book and Manuscript Library of the University of Pennsylvania with the title "List from auto de fe held in Madrid, Spain on July 4, 1632."

3. "Los lienzos constituyen la única prueba de lo ocurrido: el punto de entuentro entre el testimonio y la ficción, el lugar donde el testimonio se hace engaño y el desengaño, ficción."

4. According to Fernández García, "in the seventeenth century, the Holy Office's activities were aimed to repress the Portuguese crypto-Jews. This repression was provoked by the economic situation. In Granada, between 1600 and 1691, the Holy Tribunal condemned 379 Portuguese for practicing 'the law of Moses'" (1995, 481). ("En el siglo XVII la actividad del Santo Oficio estuvo dirigida a la represión de los marranos portugueses. La coyuntura económica es la que marca la actividad represora. En Granada el Santo Tribunal condenó entre 1600 y 1691 a 379 personas por la 'ley de Moysen'").

5. Juana de Silva was murdered in 1632 (Pulido Serrano 2002, 125).

6. The accusation of desecration was made later, on December 13, 1630. It was based on the testimony of Miguel Rodríguez's son, Andresillo, a six-year-old child who said that "[they] put a noose [around his neck] and there they beat him with some thorns, and afterwards, they would push him in the fire, and then pull him out to beat him again, and keep him in a trunk, and many Portuguese women and men would congregate at his house. [. . .] He would peek through a hole in the aforementioned kitchen door and see everything" ("poniendo una soga y allí lo azotaban con unos espinos, y que luego lo

metían en el fuego y lo volvían a sacar y lo azotaban y guardaban en un cofre, y que a
su casa acudían muchos portugueses y portuguesas [. . .] se ponía por un agujero que
está en la Puerta de la dicha cocina y por allí lo veía todo") (Pulido Serrano 2002, 134).
See Pereda's "Falso testimonio" (2017) for his analysis on the perspective of the paintings
through Estebanillo's testimony.

7. "Luego se mudaron a la calle de las infantas frontero de la casa *donde se vende la
sal* y estando en dicha casa estos y su hermano y los hijos de su cuñado Enrique Méndez
que también se mudaron con estas a la misma casa a la qual iban algunas veces esta y
su madre Beatriz Núñez y su hermana Seraphina." Unless otherwise stated, all English
translations of the Spanish quotations are mine. For the purposes of this article, I have
modernized the style, prioritizing the meaning and intended function of the originals.

8. "Y que con su mujer que se llama Leonor Rodríguez seguía la ley de Moisés y
también su hija que se llama María Rodríguez, y su marido Enrique López. Que habían
comunicado y guardado la ley de Moisés por 34 años. También su hija Isabel Rodríguez
porque les ha visto guardar los sábados por fiestas y han tratado cosas de sus ritos y cer-
emonias, y ya habrá seis años que están casados (con Manuel Fernández) y en espacio de
este tiempo han hecho los susodicho y comunicado y tratado. Y que guardan los sábados
por fiesta, se ponen camisas limpias y ropas mejoradas y observan la ley de Moisés."

9. "Al punto que se acabó el pregón, conforme la orden dada, las caxas de los Sol-
dados tocaron a rebato, y los Peones, Oficiales, y Maestros de obras, dieron asalto a la
casa, derribando las puertas, ventanas, paredes, y tejados, siendo tan grande el polvo,
confusion, y ruido, que parecia vernirse el cielo abaxo. Y aviendose empeçado el derribo,
bolvió el acompañamiento a la Inquisición, dexando Ministros della con hachas; que
asistieron hasta poner por el suelo su fábrica, que al punto de las nueve de la noche, ya
del edificio no parecía señal, porque la gente, que no tenia herramientas, con las manos
arrancaba ladrillos y piedras de sus cimientos. Fue grande el concurso que acudió, que
obligó poner guarda, que defendiese las bocacalles de la gente, coches y caballos."

10. "Nos da la impresión de que este era el objetivo desde el principio, nació de la idea
de construir una iglesia para la veneración del crucifijo en el solar de la casa arrasada."

11. "Los prendieron porque no comían tocino, que así lo ha oído decir y que también
los prendieron porque azotaban un Cristo, y que para azotarlo se encerraban en la cocina de su casa y colgaban el Cristo de una soga, y estando colgado lo azotaban con unos
espinos, y que su padre tomaba el Cristo de los pies y su madre de la cabeza y lo pasaban
por la lumbre [. . .] él se ponía por un agujero que está en la Puerta de la dicha cocina y
por allí lo veía todo."

12. "El crimen de la calle Infantas encaja en realidad en una larga y legendaria
tradición de profanación de imágenes que se remonta hasta la Alta Edad Media y que
había dejado incluso una fiesta en el calendario, la Passio imaginis Christi." Pereda creates
a parallel with the Cristo de Berito (Christ of Beyrouth) in Valencia: "produced also by
some Jews in the interior of a house that had belonged to a Christian; probably due to a

collective ceremony, the crucifix had also bled at the moment of desecration" ("producido también por unos judíos en el interior de una casa que había pertenecido a un cristiano; también se habría tratado de una ceremonia colectiva; también había sangrado en el momento de profanarla") (2017, 222).

13. "Estabamos en el patio de dicha casa y vinieron a ella Beatriz Núñez, viuda, quien tiene declarado y sus dos hijas Violante Méndez y Victoria Méndez y también vinieron Hernán Báez y Leonor Rodríguez su mujer que posaran en la misma casa de sus padres desta y juntandose en un aposento que tenia en 'aquel patio.' Los dichos Fernando Báez, Leonor Rodríguez, Beatriz Núñez, Violante Méndez y Victoria Méndez y Miguel Rodríguez, 'Samuel' Núñez Alvarez padres desta y su hermana Beatriz Enríquez todos juntos vio esta que tenian azotando a un cristo de bulto que seria de cerca de media barra de largo y que tenia en sus manos Fernando Báez y todos los demas susodichos."

14. Andresillo's testimony was the first to include the miracle. Other testimonies that followed included reference to the miracle, but Miguel Rodríguez, Isabel Núñez Álvarez, and Beatriz Enríquez denied the miracle to the end. The three were condemned to death at the stake (Pulido Serrano 2002, 152).

15. "parece evidente que Contreras adoctrinó a los pintores sobre el número exacto, edad y género de los criminales. Sus nombres habrían de perderse (el cronista no pudo ya dar con el niño que había descubierto las maldades, para entonces ya había caído en el olvido); su lugar lo ocuparon sus imágenes fabricadas."

16. The auto de fe's *Relación* reads, "[He was] given license to publish it, for the duration of two years, with the proscription that no one else could publish or sell it without license, under the penalties stated in the laws and decrees of these realms, which he should sign to give faith. In Madrid, October 9, 1692" ("se le dio licencia para podella imprimir, por tiempo de dos años, con prohibicion, que otro ninguno la pueda imprimir, ni vender sin su licencia, so las penas contenidas en las leyes, y pragmaticas destos Reinos, y en fe dello lo firme. En Madrid nueve de Octubre de este año de mil y seiscientos y treinta y dos años") (3r).

17. See "Poetas, poesía y antijudaísmo" in Pulido Serrano 2002, 257–65, and Pereda 2017, 212 (note 11).

18. See, for example, Lipton 2008 on the representations of Jewish women in the *Cantigas*.

19. I am grateful to Mary Ellen Whiteman, Roger Berry, Lisa Fiore, Clara Eugenia Ronderos, Marta Mateo, and María Jesús Zamora Calvo for their insightful comments and helpful suggestions.

WORKS CITED

AHN (Archivo Histórico Nacional). Inquisition, 140, file 4g, 1629–1632. Proceso de fe de Beatriz Rodríguez.

————. Inquisition, 140, file 4a, 1630–1633. Proceso de fe de Beatriz Enríquez.

————. Inquisition, 140, file 4f, 1630–1633. Proceso de fe de Elena Núñez.

————. Inquisition, 140, file 4b, 1630–1632. Proceso de fe de Fernán Báez.

————. Inquisition, 178, file 11, 1630–1632. Proceso de fe de Guiomar Rodríguez.

————. Inquisition, 140, file 4e, 1630–1632. Proceso de fe de Isabel Núñez Álvarez.

————. Inquisition, 189, file 26, 1630–1632. Proceso de fe de Leonor y María Rodríguez.

————. Inquisition, 140, file 4c, 1630–1633. Proceso de fe de Miguel Rodríguez.

————. Inquisition, 140, file 4d, 1630–1632. Proceso de fe de Violante Méndez.

Alpert, Michael. 1997. "Did Spanish Crypto-Jews Desecrate Christian Sacred Images and Why? The Case of the *Cristo de la Paciencia* (1629–32), the *Romance* of 1717 and the Events of November 1714 in the *Calle del Lobo.*" In *Faith and Fanaticism: Religious Fervour in Early Modern Spain*, ed. Lesley K. Twomey, 85–94. Aldershot, Hampshire: Ashgate.

Amador de los Ríos, José. 1860–64. *Historia de la villa y la corte de Madrid.* Madrid: Establecimiento tipográfico de M. López de la Hoya.

Amishai-Maisels, Ziva. 1999. "Demonization of the 'Other' in the Visual Arts." In *Demonizing the Other: Antisemitism, Racism, and Xenophobia*, ed. Robert S. Wistrich, 44–72. Amsterdam: Harwood Academic.

Arciniega García, Luis. 2012. "La *Passio Imaginis* y la adaptativa militancia apologética de las imágenes en la Edad Media y Moderna a través del caso valenciano." *Ars Longa* 21:71–94.

Bethencourt, Francisco. 1992. "The Auto da Fé: Ritual and Imagery." *Journal of the Warburg and Courtauld Institutes* 55:155–68.

Blázquez Miguel, Juan. 1988. *Inquisición y criptojudaísmo.* Madrid: Kaydeda.

Brown, Jonathan. 1991. *Painting in Spain.* New Haven, CT: Yale University Press.

Bustillo, Martha. 2010. "The Episode of the Cristo de la Paciencia and Its Influence on Religious Imaginary in Seventeenth-Century Madrid." In *Imaginary, Spirituality and Ideology in Baroque Spain and Latin America*, ed. Martha Bustillo and Jeremy Roe, 59–70. Cambridge: Cambridge Scholars Publishing.

Camilo, Francisco. 1651. *Ultrajes al Crucifijo o Cristo de las Injurias.* Oil on canvas. 209 × 230 cms. Madrid, Prado Museum.

Carducho, Vicente. 1979. *Diálogos de la pintura: Su defensa, origen, esencia, definición, modos y diferencias*, ed. Francisco Calvo Serraller. Madrid: Turner.

Caro Baroja, Julio. 1986. *Los judíos en la España moderna y contemporánea.* Madrid: Istmo.

————. 1975. "La sociedad criptojudía en la corte de Felipe IV." In *Inquisición, brujería y criptojudaismo*, 11–180. Barcelona: Ariel.

De Salvatierra, Francisco. 1632. *Relación verdadera, en la qual se da cuenta y declara el Auto de Fe.* Granada: Imprenta de Bartholome de Lorençana y Antonio René de Lezcano.

Elliott, J. H. 1986. *The Count-Duke of Olivares: The Statesman in an Age of Decline.* New Haven, CT: Yale University Press.

Fernández García, María de los Ángeles. 1995. "Criterios inquisitoriales para detectar el marrano: los criptojudíos en Andalucía en los siglos XVI y XVII." In *Judíos, Sefarditas, Conversos: La expulsion de 1492 y sus consecuencias,* ed. Ángel Alcalá, 478–502. Madrid: Ámbito.

Fernández, Francisco. 1651. *Herejes maltratando un crucifijo.* Oil on canvas, 171 × 296 cms. Madrid, Prado Museum.

Gallego, Fernando. 1494–96. *Christ Blessing.* Panel. Mixed Method. Madrid, Prado Museum.

Gállego, Julian. 1984. *Visión y símbolos en la pintura española del Siglo de Oro.* Cátedra: Madrid.

García García, Francisco de Asís. 2013. "Iglesia y Sinagoga." *Revista Digital de Iconografía Medieval* 9:13–27.

Gil, Juan. 2007. "Los conversos de Sevilla (siglos XV y XVI)." In *La memoria de Sefarad: Historia y cultura de los sefardíes,* ed. M. Piñero Ramírez, 139–71. Seville: Fundación Sevilla NODO y Fundación Machado.

Giles, Mary E. 1998. *Women in the Inquisition: Spain and the New World.* Baltimore: Johns Hopkins University Press.

Gitlitz, David. 2003. *Secreto y engaño: La religion de los criptojudíos.* Valladolid: Junta de Castilla y León, Consejería de Cultura.

Gómez de Mora, Juan. 1632. *Auto de fe celebrado en Madrid este año MDCXXXII.* Madrid: Francisco Martínez.

León de Pinelo, Antonio de. 1971. *Anales de Madrid (desde el año 447 al de 1658),* ed. Pedro Fernández Martín. Madrid: Instituto de Estudios Madrileños.

Lipton, Sara. 2008. "Where Are the Gothic Jewish Women? On the Non-Iconography of the Jewess in the Cantigas de Santa María." *Jewish History* 22, no. 1/2: 139–77.

———. 2014. *Dark Mirror: The Medieval Origins of Anti-Jewish Iconography.* New York: Metropolitan Books.

"List from auto de fe held in Madrid, Spain, on July 4, 1632." Manuscript. Rare Book & Manuscript Library University of Pennsylvania. Ms. Coll. 218.

Lowe, Ben. 1994. "Body Images and the Politics of Beauty: Formation of the Feminine Ideal in Medieval and Early Modern Europe." In *Ideals of Feminine Beauty: Philosophical, Social, and Cultural Dimensions,* ed. Karen A. Callaghan, 21–36. London: Greenwood Press.

Mann, Vivian B., ed. 2010. *Uneasy Communion: Jews, Christians, and the Altarpieces of Medieval Spain.* New York: Museum of Biblical Art.

Melammed, Renée Levine. 1999. *Heretics of Daughters of Israel? The Crypto-Jewish Women of Castile.* New York: Oxford University Press.

Méndez-Silva, Rodrigo. 1649. *Epítome de la vida de Fernando de Cordoba Bocanegra.* Madrid: Coello.

Mesonero Romanos, Ramón de. 1881. *El antiguo Madrid.* Madrid: Oficinas de la Ilustración Española y Americana.

Orfali, Moisés. 2007. "Del lujo y de las leyes suntuarias: Ordenanzas sobre la vestimenta femenina en su contexto social y halájico." In *La mujer judía*, ed. Yolanda Moreno Koch, 161–79. Córdoba: El Almendro.

Palomino, Antonio. 1947. *El museo pictórico y escala óptica*. Madrid: Aguilar.

Pereda, Felipe. 2007. *Las imágenes de la discordia: Política y poética de la imagen sagrada en la España del 400*. Madrid: Marcial Pons Historia.

———. 2011. "Through a Glass Darkly: Paths to Salvation in Spanish Painting of the Outset of the Inquisition." In *Judaism and Christian Art: Aesthetics Anxieties from the Catacombs to Colonialism*, ed. Herbert L. Kessler and David Nirenberg, 263–90. Philadelphia: University of Pennsylvania Press.

———. 2017. "'Falso testimonio': El testimonio como engaño, el engaño como ficción." In *Crimen e ilusión: El arte de la verdad en el Siglo de Oro*. Madrid: Marcial Pons Historia.

Pérez Sánchez, Alfonso E. 1986. *Carreño, Rizi, Herrera y la pintura madrileña de su tiempo (1650–1700)*. Madrid: Museo del Prado.

Pérez Sánchez, Alfonso E., et al. 1991. *Museo del Prado: Inventario general de pinturas: Tomo II, El museo de la Trinidad (Bienes desamortizados)*. Madrid: Espasa Calpe.

Pérez-Villanueva, Sonia. 2017. "Misericordia y justicia: La representación del cuerpo de la mujer en la Inquisición." In *Mulieres inquisitionis: La mujer frente a la Inquisición en España*, ed. María Jesús Zamora Calvo, 147–76. Vigo: Academia del Hispanismo.

Portús Pérez, Javier. 1998. *La sala reservada del museo del Prado y el coleccionismo de pintura de desnudo en la Corte española (1554–1838)*. Madrid: Museo del Prado.

Pulido Serrano, Juan Ignacio. 2002. *Injurias a Cristo: Religión, política y antijudaísmo en el siglo XVII*. Madrid: Universidad de Alcalá.

Rizi, Francisco. 1647–51. *El Expolio de Cristo o Cristo de la Paciencia*. Oil on canvas, 527 × 352 cms. Madrid, Prado Museum.

———. 1647–51. *Profanación de un crucifijo o Familia de herejes azotando un crucifijo*. Oil on canvas, 209 × 230 cms. Madrid, Prado Museum.

Rojas, Francisco de. 1634. *Vespertinas de los oprobios de la Passion de Cristo*. Madrid.

Rose, Constance H. 2001. "El Madrid inquisitorial en la España del Siglo de Oro." *Revista de Dialectología y Tradiciones Populares* 56, no. 1: 129–46.

Rubin, Miri. 1999. *Gentile Tales: The Narrative Assault on Late Medieval Jews*. New Haven, CT: Yale University Press.

Scholz-Hänsel, Michael. 1999. "Sor Juana Inés de la Cruz y la Inquisición: Amenazas reales y espacios libres en las artes plásticas y la literatura en el Siglo de Oro." In *La creatividad femenina en el mundo barroco hispánico*, II, ed. Monika Bosse et al., 687–718. Kassel: Reichengerger.

Serra, Jaume. 1367–81. *Altarpiece of the Virgin Mary*. Tempera, gold leaf and metal plate on wood, Barcelona, Museu Nacional D'Art de Catalunya.

Simón Díaz, José, ed. 1982. *Relaciones breves de actos públicos celebrados en Madrid de 1541 a 1650*. Madrid: Nilo.

Urrea, Jesús. 1994. *Pintores del reinado de Felipe IV.* Madrid: Museo del Prado/Caja de Ahorros de Navarra.

Vargas, Andrés de. 1991. *Martirio del brasero del Cristo de la Paciencia,* 1647–51. Oil on canvas, 171 × 296 cms. *El museo del prado: Inventario general de pinturas II. El Museo de la Trinidad.* Madrid: Espasa Calpe.

Yerushalmi, Yosef Hayin. 1989. *De la corte española al gueto italiano: Marranismo y judaísmo en la España del siglo XVII.* Nashville: Turner.

✠

Catalina Mateo

Portrait of a Witch in Sixteenth-Century Castile

MARÍA JESÚS ZAMORA CALVO

The Hispanic witch, particularly in the early modern period, was forged from singularities that differentiate and set her apart from her representations in Europe. She was characterized as being a malicious agent, often dedicated to the murder of young children. She possessed the extraordinary ability to enter chambers through windows, doors, or small cracks. She also possessed amazing metamorphic powers, the ability to fly, frighten men, turn off house lights, urinate in people's houses, and destroy crops: an entire host of ancient stereotypes that crystallized as never before during this time (Bonomo 1985; Levack 1995; Campagne 2002 and 2009). According to Pedro Ciruelo,

> The things that witches or *xorguinas* [a Basque term for witches] can do are so marvelous that they cannot be attributed to natural causes: that some smear themselves with ointments and utter certain words and jump out from the chimney or through a window and fly through the air and rapidly go to lands far away, and return hastily to relate the affairs happening there. Others, as soon as they slather the ointment and utter those words, fall to the ground as if dead, cold and unconscious; although they are burned or cut, they do not feel it, and after two or three hours, arise quite swiftly, and tell many things from lands and places they claim to have visited. (1538, 9v)[1]

Despite the power attributed to her in the early modern period, she was paradoxically condemned to the same scorn with which other old and widowed women were frequently treated by society. Fifty-year-old

Catalina Mateo, for example, was accused by sixteen witnesses of having killed four or five infants. In this essay, I propose to shed light on this case in order to address the marginalization suffered by poor women in sixteenth-century Castile because of their age, which subjected them to a state of loneliness and helplessness. Numerous mechanisms were put in place to be rid of these elderly women, who, although perceived as useless, nevertheless aroused social fears.

Catalina Mateo, "widow, resident of Casar, age fifty," was arrested by the Vicariate of Alcalá, along with Juana la Izquierda ("the Left-handed") and Olalla Sobrino.[2] The neighbors were suspicious of them because they lived alone, lacked male protection, and attempted to survive thanks to the knowledge and skills that life and oral culture had given them. They raised all sorts of suspicions, which is why they were considered responsible for the death of several local children. The three were subjected to torment and because of the violence she suffered, Catalina conceded to what the people wanted to hear:

> The aforementioned Catalina Mateo said it was true that perhaps four or five years prior, Olalla Sobrino had asked her if she wanted to be a witch, offering that the demon would do obscene things to her and that it was a good occupation, and that one night, through the aforementioned Juana Izquierda, she had beckoned her to her home. When all three were there, the devil had appeared and manifested himself as a goat and had spoken to each separately, first he had embraced the aforementioned Olalla and Juana, and later the aforementioned Mateo, because they had told him she too wanted to be a witch. And that the devil had requested something from her body and she had offered a nail of the middle finger of her right hand, and rejoicing in the accord they had made with him, he had lain carnally with each in the presence of all three. (AHN, Inq. Book 91, file 1)[3]

It is odd that she was not the one who resorted to her close friends to request entrance into the conclave, as both Juana and Olalla were widows twenty years older than Catalina. However from their own experience, they knew that she was suffering and took advantage of her fragility, offering her a means of earning a living and certain sexual encounters they knew to be "awkward," by which they meant filthy and evil customs.

Why was being a witch regarded as a "good occupation"? In a patriarchal society in which most women were submitted to male authority from birth, whether father, brother, husband, or son, when a woman mainly of the lower classes became a widow, was already of a certain age and poor, perhaps a foreigner and in bad health, she often found herself in an impossibly vulnerable position. If she had children, they were likely unable to afford to help her. These older women often were in the first stages of senile dementia, demonstrably ill-tempered, grumbling, and rude. They seemed to live in a world apart, disconnected from reality, and as they usually slept fewer hours, they kept abnormal schedules that gave rise to all kinds of suspicions and mistrust. The poet Francisco de Quevedo y Villegas satirizes the appearance of old women and their desire to look younger in the following sonnet:

> **Vieja vuelta a la edad de las niñas**
> **(An Old Woman Reverts to a Young Girl's Age)**
>
> Why try to persuade us you are a young girl?
> Does it matter if you can catch and die from smallpox?
> For lack of teeth and molars,
> A matronly mouth garnishes you in old age.
>
> You do battle with your age, standing firm,
> Appealing, old girl, to those yet to be born,
> trilling with a dotard beak,
> and declaring your skirts a diaper.
>
> Your mouth, once open sore, now a funnel,
> conceals the staleness of yesteryears,
> And tries to pass its dribble for gruel.
>
> Big girl, here's to achieving your deceptions,
> That you possess few years, I have no doubt,
> If those few years are all you have left.
> (Quevedo y Villegas 1981, 392)[4]

These are elderly, poor, and abandoned women, who used to be in close contact with one another. In the face of helplessness, scorn, and isolation, driven by the natural impulse to survive, what some of these women did was to foster—to the extent possible—a reputation as witches. Thus, their mere presence would inspire fear in their neighbors, and they would come to them with a certain respect seeking protection, remedies, trysts, love, money, health (Bonomo 1985; Ginzburg 1989; Berti 2010). They made the witch stereotype their own, claiming magical abilities they certainly lacked, but that allowed them to play with this deception in order to live comfortably. Therefore, both Juana *la Izquierda* and Olalla Sobrino convinced Catalina Mateo to become a witch, since by doing this she would have clothes, food, and drink in abundance. Castañega himself acknowledges that "from experience we see every day that poor women and needy, greedy priests, profess to be conjurers, sorcerers, necromancers, and seers, in order to support themselves and eat copiously" (1529, 7v).[5]

The need was pressing, and Catalina was simply carried away, "You will be one, even if you do not wish it,"[6] they said. One night, Juana beckoned her and the three met at Olalla's house, where there appeared "the devil as a goat [. . .] and he had lain with all three in the presence of each other."[7] The orgy had already materialized, being one of the most widely spread myths surrounding witchcraft in the western world (Ortiz 2015). However, intercourse with the devil was not always linked to pleasure. On another occasion, Catalina confessed to having been the victim of a rape,

And that a few days later after the mentioned occasion, the aforementioned goat had gone to her house one night and, finding her in bed, forced himself on her and made some typical comments, and he had done the same thing in the prisons of the vicar. And that after a few days, at the aforementioned Olalla's house, she had been given a knife, and with it she had cut the fingernail she was told to cut, and gave it to him.[8]

A woman in this time was attractive in the eyes of men only while she was in her fertile years, that is to say, while she was healthy and young and could conceive children. As soon as she reached menopause, unless she was wealthy or of independent means and thus still marriageable, she became useless to society and remained isolated in her own home: "This is more so with the old and poor women than with the young and comely because, when old, men neglect them, so they resort to the devil to satisfy their appetites, especially if they were so inclined and prone to the vices of the flesh when young" (Castañega 1529, 13r–v).[9] Indeed, women allegedly continued to have sexual desires that husbands no longer satisfied. In the face of this situation, older women became teachers of young and inexperienced boys who had no need to remain virgins until marriage. If they wanted to demonstrate their virility, they should have skill and experience in consummating the sexual act (Roper 1997; Culianu 1999; Stephens 2002). As the years passed and her body aged, the woman resorted to masturbation, for which she usually used what was readily on hand: a broom. Hence, Remy considered "All those who have maintained sexual commerce with incubi or succubi unanimously declare that it is difficult to imagine or describe something more repugnant and unpleasant [. . .]. According to witches, demons' virile organs are so large and hard that penetration is impossible without excruciating pain" (Culianu 1999, 203). To seal the demonic covenant, the goat required a token from Catalina's body, and she offered him a fingernail from her right hand. Why a fingernail? A hard, corneous matter growing from the extremities of the hands, fingernails symbolized deception and theft. The pact with the devil was the fundamental crux of witchcraft that gave it a heretical essence and placed it within the Inquisition's jurisdiction. It entailed the rejection of God and the establishment of a link with Satan in exchange for various earthly favors (Castiglioni 1993). There were two types of pacts: the explicit and the implied. According to Castañega:

> The specific pact that the devil makes with his recruits is twofold: one is so explicit and clear that they, with clear and formal words, reject their faith and profess vows to the devil in his presence, who appears to them in the form and figure that he wants to take, promising him obedience and offering him their souls and bodies. [. . .] Others have explicit and express pacts with the devil, not because they have ever spoken with him or seen him in a recognizable figure, save with other ministers of his, who

are other conjurers, sorcerers or witches and take the same profession as the first; or though they never speak with others or the devil in another figure have they seen, they themselves make such covenant and promise to the devil, granting him the worship they had conferred to Christ, and celebrating ceremonies that other sorcerers celebrate or the devil has inspired in them and teaches. (1529, 11v–12r)[10]

In the pact, the witch promised loyalty to the devil in an indirect way, by way of another witch. And he is the one Catalina Mateo embraced.

The implicit or secret pact is also twofold. Some have a secret covenant with the devil when, without denying or apostasizing or losing the Catholic faith in their opinion, they have and believe and celebrate the same ceremonies and recite diabolical invocations; and have hidden and secret pacts with the devil, because hidden and virtually, in that belief and trust they have in such ceremonies and superstitions, is enclosed the apostasy of the faith of Christ. [. . .] These are commonly called sorcerers. (Castañega 1529, 12r)[11]

This second covenant is more typical of sorceresses, not of witches. Guaccio collects the common aspects of the demonic pacts and categorizes them in eleven points. In the eighth he says, "prollicentur sacrifica, et quaedam striges promittunt se singulis mensibus, vel quindenis vnum infantulum strigando" (Guaccio 1624, 40), that is to say, they promise to offer sacrifices to the devil, and some witches even vow to strangle or suffocate a small creature.

Catalina Mateo was aware of the danger that her life was in if she confessed to having had some pact with the devil; therefore, in her statement made before the vicar of Alcalá, she denied "having had any other, explicit or tacit, covenant with the devil besides the one she had mentioned."[12] She thus minimized its significance, trying to reduce the appropriate sentence. She also confessed that, to complete the union, they went flying out the window in search of creatures while saying, "from beam to beam with the wrath of Santa María" (López-Ridaura 2013, 37–58).[13]

There were sixteen witnesses from El Casar who, highly suspicious, accused Catalina Mateo of being a witch because "in the village, during four years to the date, four or five creatures had died a violent death, which was impossible without witches."[14] Infanticide was a crime associated with witches, especially in Spain (Tausiet 1998, 61–83; Sánchez Ortega 2004, 125–39; Campagne 2009, 151–223). In the case of Catalina Mateo, under torture she confessed that

> that night, the aforementioned Olalla had smeared the joints of her toes and hands and, in the company of that goat, had gone to a house and carrying embers in a cloth, had entered through a window at midnight. And, making the parents fall asleep by placing poppy seeds and other herbs under their pillows, she had taken one of the daughters out of bed. Squeezing her chest, they had choked her and lighting a fire with the embers, they burned her buttocks and broke her arms, and the noise had awakened the parents and both left with the goat through the air to Olalla's house, where they had dressed and gone each to their own house and that they had flown back and forth naked.[15]

The torture they had inflicted on the girl, such as burning her buttocks, breaking her arms, choking her, all triggered stupefaction, rejection, and hatred toward witches, who had to be punished for the harm and evil they caused. Binomially linking the terms "death" and "infant" together, the mob became violent and irrationally attacked whoever they thought was to blame. It was a public lynching of someone who had raised fear by not being under the auspices of a man. Catalina took this collective imaginary as her own and confessed what the Inquisition wanted to hear. She was aware that this would hopelessly condemn her, but she did not want to be subjected to physical torture. She began a series of confessions, each one bloodier than the last, with the purpose of ceasing the torment that her body was suffering. She therefore admitted to taking part in several events: "That other nights she had smeared herself at the home of the aforementioned Olalla and in the company of the goat went to another house and choked a child and ripped off his private parts. Later, she went to two other houses on different nights and choked two other children and that she invoked the devil only once by saying 'Devil, come hither.'"[16]

At another time she admitted that "after disrobing and with disheveled hair, they both went to the house of an apothecary who lived in El Casar."[17] On this occasion the devil, in the form of a goat, accompanied them and took them through the air and helped them enter through a low window. "The two of them dragged a child the parents had that was in bed and killed him and pinched him all over and before this, they had suffocated him, squeezed his chest with their bare hands and, having done this, put him back in the same bed."[18]

She also recalled that "around three or four years before that, having all three gathered in that house and having stripped while in the company of said devil in the form of a goat,"[19] they went to the house of Juan García, a professional farrier: "There was a child on the bed so they dragged him and they all suffocated him and broke his feet and arms and ripped out his private parts and, having done this, they left the child in a corner of the chamber and then left with the devil."[20]

These murders were ratified by the witnesses of the trial against Catalina Mateo. They were the ones who described in detail the crimes committed by her. On one occasion she asked a neighbor for a little flour. The neighbor refused, but it awakened fear in her husband, since they had a young and particularly handsome child. In the evening they heard noises on the roof and sank into a deep sleep. Upon awakening they found their dead son near the fireplace, "arms and kidneys split, his face twisted, and his privates ripped out, and many other things done to him, so cruel as to break one's heart."[21]

The methods used for their infanticide were based on pinching, biting, maiming, and brutally beating children, practices also documented in proceedings against other women in the area accused of being witches. In the mid-sixteenth century, in the triangle formed by the towns of Cuenca, Guadalajara, and Alcalá de Henares, an obsession with witches was unleashed. This kind of psychosis was driven largely by an increase in the number of infants who had died in the night and were found smothered and with bruises on their bodies. The cause was more than obvious, as we will discuss later, but society had to find a culprit to be held accountable for the pain inflicted, and who better than a witch to accuse of infanticide? Even the Church itself augmented this fear, both in sermons and proclamations, in which people were encouraged to denounce any behavior that did not conform to the "normal" conduct of the time (Pastore 1997; Bravo 2002). The witch hunt began with the purpose of monitoring and reining in society more than for the sake of supposedly protecting its children. Upon seeing that the ecclesiastical hierarchy itself acknowledged the existence of witches, panic spread among the townsfolk, who already believed in ointments, night flights, covens, demonic pacts, destruction of their fields, and so on.

On June 20, 1519, the first complaint was recorded regarding a certain Juana, a townswoman from Villalba de Huete (currently Villalba del Rey), who blamed the witches for having killed one of her daughters sixteen years before and for again trying to kill, this time a newborn infant (ADC 230–2902). This accusation took more shape when, shortly after, the carpenter's son, Sancho de Francos, was found dead with clear signs of violence (ADC 230–2902). These two cases gave rise to the persecution of any elderly, widowed woman who was known to apply natural remedies, to mend maidenheads, to restore male sexual prowess, and/ or to unite forbidden lovers: in short, any woman who survived through secret knowledge in a society that isolated her because she was perceived as useless and ugly. The fear the deaths caused spread so quickly that no day went by without an accusation (Clark 2009).

Mari Martínez de la Canal, mistress of the inquisitor Juan Yáñez, testified on the death of her son at the hands of *xorguinas* (ADC 230–2902). Mateo Muñoz, cloth beater, said that witches had murdered two of his sons who, one morning, were found full of bruises (ADC 230–2902). Teresa López said that La Illana was a witch and had killed many children. Inés López also ratified the existence of old murderous women. Pedro Vidal accused La Illana of also using his daughter's body to make ointments during Lent. In the same liturgical period, the wife of Francisco de Yanguas confessed that on Holy Monday, while she was alone at home, an elderly woman knocked on her door to ask for fire. The next morning, her daughter was lifeless. Juan de Lorca, hosier, testified that one night they had put their six-month-old daughter to sleep beside her mother on one side of the bed and that when they woke up, they found the baby dead. Quiteria Martínez accused La Lorenza of choking a foreign child that she was nursing. Francisco de Rojas blamed La Illana once again for having murdered his daughter, whom he found "with her throat bruised and her lips torn, and bleeding through her ears and nose and the legs covered in welts and dark bruises."[22] Diego Hernández de Parada; Violante, Mata's wife; Leonor Rodríguez, Luis Vidal's wife; Juana López; Sancho Molina; and others all blamed witches for the death of their infants and young children. Because of these complaints, women such as La Lorenza (ADC, book 76, file 1108), La Illana (ADC, book 75, file 1095), Águeda de Beamud (ADC, book 79, file 1147), María de Moya (ADC, book 77, file 1130), La Ansarona (ADC, book 99, file 1441), "La Roa" (ADC, book 199, file 2248), among a long list of accused women, were arrested and imprisoned in the secret dungeons of the Inquisition (Cordente 1990, 23–82).

The deaths of young children in Castile were so frequent that even the inquisitors of the Cuenca Inquisition court opened a special record for these cases in 1519:

> In the city of Cuenca, on the twentieth day of the month of November, one thousand and five hundred and nineteen years, the reverend lord inquisitors Pedro Gutiérrez de los Ríos and Juan Yáñez stated that because it has come to their attention that in this city of Cuenca and elsewhere in the bishopric some children have been found dead, from which it is suspected they have been killed and wounded by *xorguiños* and *xorguiñas,* they should *ex officio* be given all information found about the aforementioned, which they said in my presence, Francisco Ximénez, notary of the secret. (ADC, book 230–2902)[23]

But what was behind so many children's deaths, especially in this period? It was a means of population control exercised consciously or involuntarily. María Monja, better known as La Lorenza, argued in her defense that the cause of so much infanticide was the poverty in which the parents lived, which pushed them to drink wine to keep warm. Sometimes the mothers ingested more than they should have, lay down in bed drunk with their children, and, without meaning to, smothered them. She mentioned herself as an example, confessing that at a wedding she "drank more wine than was necessary."[24] She fell asleep next to her newborn son and if not for her husband, who woke her up angrily, he would have been smothered because she had put her elbow covering the mouth of the infant (ADC, book 76, file 1108). This was one of the most widely used methods of killing children who, for any reason, were not wanted. In the morning, the children were found with purple blotches and bruises, and with blood in their mouth, nose, and ears.

The trials revealed data indicating that the Iberian witches, especially those living close to vineyards, drank wine; in their night flights and after killing the young, they went readily through the cellars and wineries in the houses. Juana la Izquierda stated that in winter, when the nights were longer and colder, they drank in the storerooms where the wine was kept. María Manzanares and Ana de Nieva, townswomen from Miraflores de la Sierra, confessed to having finished three jars of wine in Tor de Laguna.

Another reason that could explain the high number of infanticides occurring at this time relates to the abuse women suffered at the hands of their husbands. Some, in revenge, stopped breastfeeding their children. At other times the beatings and consequent mood of the mother influenced the quality of her milk, "an upbringing with little love, in sum, was deemed as a cause of some child deaths by the same protagonists of the facts" (Tausiet 2004, 429).[25] Mothers also often tried to rid themselves of unwanted children or those born from a rape. On other occasions, vengeful older children fabricated allegations against their mothers, accusing them of being witches. While growing up, these children had been ill-treated by their mothers and, in reprisal, had gone to the Inquisition to liberate themselves from them. "The poor nutrition, premature withdrawal from breastfeeding, neglect, and indifferent parenting, in sum, were responsible for causing abundant deaths by starvation, dehydration or lack of care that newborns required" (Tausiet 1998, 77).[26] Other factors included climate, disease, and the high cost of raising a child, the latter responsibility falling especially to the mother, which resulted in a heavy burden that not all were willing or able to assume (Harris and Ross 1987; Bideau 1987; Dejardins and Pérez Brignoli 1987).

That infanticide was a widespread practice did not mean it was accepted as normal. In the face of a child's death, parents always sought a culprit and in early modern society, where fear permeated through all levels, witches became responsible for a situation they had not brought about (Delumeau 2002).

But let us return to Catalina Mateo, at the moment when she confirmed the truth of what she had confessed to the Vicar at Alcalá, who sent her along with Olalla Sobrino and Juana la Izquierda to the Inquisition of Toledo (Cuevas 1980, 25–92; Dedieu 1989, 325–27;[27] Sierra 2005, 129–31). There the three begged for mercy and Catalina said everything declared in Alcalá was false and that she testified in order not to be subjected to torture. The inquisitor requested an investigation be made in El Casar:

> On what [Catalina] had said for fear of torment, and 16 witnesses having been interrogated in El Casar, she claimed it was true that these children had been killed and were found dead and abused in the same manner and form that the aforementioned Mateo had confessed to and, having substantiated her case, she was put to torment. The sentence having been pronounced, she was taken to the chamber for execution, and reprimanded before undressing, she claimed everything she had said before the Vicar of Alcalá was true and indeed confirms this in substance, although in some instances she changed some things, saying that much was true, both in how she had confessed and how she had sworn under oath.[28]

On the basis of the evidence and testimonies, the inquisitors condemned Catalina Mateo to appear at the auto de fe held on June 9, 1591, which Philip II himself attended:

> And after the time allowed, [her statement] was ratified in her confessions, and in other audiences subsequently held with her. Afterward, she repeated the same and denied knowing what the ointments were made of, or having had another covenant, explicit or tacit, with the devil other than what she had previously stated. She gave the reasons she had for taking revenge on the parents through the death of their children, which are the same that the parents had testified to when they suspected that the women had killed them. Their cause was substantiated and voted on, subjecting them to an auto with abjuration *de levi* [mild]; and to wearing a *coroza* [conical paper hat worn with the *sambenito*, or Inquisition gown]; receiving two hundred lashes, and imprisonment for a time they deemed suitable.[29]

Catalina was nothing more than a scapegoat for a series of murders for which she was not responsible. A solitary, sullen, distrustful woman, possibly marked by psychological disorders caused by her alcoholism, and disoriented by anxiety and isolation, she decided to dress as a witch, to immerse herself in an imaginary dimension in which she inspired the respect, fear, and suspicion of society. Even the inquisitors realized that she lived in an unreal universe. They knew she was no murderer, only a woman who could not escape her ungrateful fate, an old woman in a world that no longer had need of her other than to instigate fear.

NOTES

1. "[. . .] las cosas que hazen las bruxas o *xorguinas* son tan maravillosas que no se puede dar razón dellas por causas naturales: que algunas dellas se untan con unos un-güentos y dizen ciertas palabras y saltan por la chimenea del hogar, o por una ventana y van por el ayre y en breve tiempo van a tierras muy lexos y tornan presto diziendo las cosas que allá pasan. Otras destas, en acabándose de untar y dezir aquellas palabras, se caen en tierra como muertas, frías y sin sentido alguno; aunque las queman o asierran, no lo sienten y, dende a dos o tres horas, se levantan muy ligeramente, y dizen muchas cosas de otras tierras y lugares adonde dizen que han ydo."

2. It is likely that this nickname indicated Juana's left-handedness. During the Modern Age left-handers were considered servants of the devil, as blessings could be dispensed only with the right hand, while the left was used in black masses. The devil is also often described as being left-handed.

3. "la dicha Cathalina Mateo dijo que era verdad que podría haber cuatro o cinco años que Olalla Sobrina la había dicho si quería ser bruja ofreciéndole que el demonio tendría con ella acceso torpe y que era buen oficio y que una noche por medio de la dicha Joana Izquierda la había llamado a su casa a donde estando todas tres había entrado el demonio en figura de cabrón y hablado aparte primero con las dicha Olalla y Joana las había abrazado y después a la dicha Mateo porque ellas le habían dicho que tan bien ella quería ser bruja y que el dicho demonio le había pedido alguna cosa de su cuerpo y ella había ofrecido una uña de un dedo del medio de la mano derecha y que por regocijo del concierto habían hallado con el dicho cabrón y él se había echado carnalmente con todas tres en presencia de todas."

4. "¿Para qué nos persuades eres niña? /¿Importa que te mueras de viruelas? /Pues la falta de dientes y de muelas /boca de taita en la vejez te aliña. /Tú te cierras de edad y de campiña, /y a que están por nacer, chicota, apelas; /gorjeas con quijadas bisabuelas, /y

llamas metedor a la basquiña. /La boca, que fue chirlo, agora embudo, /disimula lo rancio en los antaños, /y nos vende por babas el engrudo. /Grandilla, porque logres tus engaños /que tienes pocos años no lo dudo, /si son los por vivir los pocos años."

5. "Por experiencia vemos cada dia que las mugeres pobres y clerigos necessitados e codiciosos, por officio toman de ser conjuradores, hechizeros, nigromanticos y adeuinos por se mantener e tener de comer abundosamente."

6. "Serlo habéis, aunque no queráis."

7. "el demonio en figura de cabrón [. . .] y él se había echado carnalmente con todas tres en presencia de todas."

8. "y que de allí a pocos días el dicho cabrón había ido una noche a casa de la dicha Mateo y hallándola acostada la había forzado y tenido cuenta carnal con ella diciendo en esto algunas particularidades y lo mismo había hecho en las cárceles de dicho vicario y que al cabo de algunos pocos días en casa de la dicha Olalla le habían dado un cuchillo y con él se había cortado la uña que le habían mandado y se la había entregado."

9. "E mas son de las mugeres viejas e pobres que de las moças e ricas porque como después de viejas los hombres no hazen caso dellas, tienen recurso al demonio que cumple sus apetitos, en especial si cuando moças fueron inclinadas e dadas al vicio de la carne."

10. "El pacto expresso que se haze al demonio de sus familiares es dos maneras: vno es tan expresso y claro que con palabras claras e formales, renegando de la fe, hazen nueua profesion al demonio en su presencia que les aparece en la forma e figura que el quiere tomar, dandole entera obediencia y ofreciendole su animo y cuerpo. [. . .] Otros tienen pacto explicito y expresso con el demonio, no porque ayan hablado alguna vez con el o le hayan visto en alguna figura conocida, saluo con otros ministros suyos, que son otros encantadores, hechizeros o bruxos y hazen la mesma profession que los primeros; o aunque nunca con otro hablen o al demonio en alguna figura ayan visto, ellos mesmos hazen tal pacto y promessa al demonio, apostando de la fe de Christo e hazen las cerimonias que los otros hechizeros hazen o las que el demonio les inspira y enseña."

11. "Pacto implicito o oculto es tanbien de dos maneras. Unos tienen con el demonio pacto oculto quando, sin renegar ni apostatar ni perder la fe catolica a su parecer, tienen e creen y hazen las mesmas cerimonias e inuocaciones diabolicas; y estos tales tienen pacto oculto e secreto con el demonio, porque oculta e virtualmente, en aquella creencia e confiança que en los tales execramentos cerimonias y supersticiones tienen, se encierra la apostasia de la fe de Christo. [. . .] Estos se llaman comúnmente hechizeros."

12. "[. . .] haber tenido otro pacto explicito ni tácito con el demonio más del que había dicho."

13. "de viga con la ira de Santa María."

14. "en la dicha villa de quatro años a esta parte abian muerto quatro o cinco criaturas de muertes violentas, que era imposible aberlas hecho sino bruxas."

15. "[. . .] aquella noche la dicha Olalla la había untado las coyunturas de los dedos

de los pies y manos y en compañía del dicho cabrón habían ido a una casa y llevando unas brasas en una tela, habían entrado por una ventana a las doce de la noche y echando sueño a los padres con unas dormideras y otras hierbas puestas debajo de la almohada les habían sacado una niña de la cama y apretándola por las arcas la habían ahogado y encendido lumbre con lo que llevaban y le quemaron las partes traseras y quebrantado los brazos y que al ruido habían despertado los dichos padres y ellas se habían vuelto con el dicho cabrón por el aire a casa de la dicha Olalla, a donde se habían vestido y ido cada una a su casa y que a la ida y vuelta iban por el aire desnudas."

16. "[. . .] otras noches untándose en casa de la dicha Olalla y en compañía del dicho cabrón había ido a otra casa y ahogado a un niño y arrancándole sus vergüenzas y después otras dos casas en diferentes noches y ahogado otras dos criaturas e que una sola vez había invocado al demonio diciéndole 'Demonio, ven allí.'"

17. "abiendose desnuda en cueros y descabelladas tanto se fueron en casa de un boticario que viue en el casar."

18. "sacaron las dos dellas un niño que tenían los padres en la cama y le mataron y ahogaron a pellizcos y primero que le pellizcasen le hayan ahogado aprentándole las arcas con las manos y echo esto le tornaron a meter en la mesma cama."

19. "abrá tres o quatro años poco más o menos que aujéndose juntado en dicha casa todas tres y auiéndose desnudado estando yo conellas en compañía del dicho demonio en figura de cabrón."

20. "estando un niño en la cama se le sacaron y todas juntas le ahogaron por las arcas e le quebranron los pies y los brazos e las vergüenzas le arrancaron y hecho esto dexaron el dicho niño en un rincón del aposento y se fueron cada una y el demonio con ellas."

21. "quebrados los brazos y por los riñones, torçidos los rostros y arrancadas sus vergüenzas, y hecha otras muchas crueldades en él, que era para quebrar el coraçón."

22. "con la garganta amagullada e todos los labios rompidos e por los oídos e por las narices echaba sangre e todas las piernas las tenía llenas de pellizcos y negros."

23. "En la cibdad de Cuenca a veynte e un días del mes de noviembre de mil y quinientos e diez e nueve años los reverendos señores inquisidores Pedro Gutierrez de los Rios e Juan Yañez dixeron que porque a su noticia es venido que en esta cibdad de Cuenca y en otros lugares de su obispado se han hallado algunos niños muertos e señalados de golpes de donde se tiene sospecha ser muertos y heridos de *xorguinos* e *xorguinas* que debían de oficio rescibir toda la información que acerca de lo susodicho hallasen los qual dixeron en presencia de my Francisco Ximenez, notario del secreto."

24. "bebió más vino del que era menester."

25. "una crianza poco amorosa, en suma, era juzgada como causa de algunas muertes infantiles por los mismos protagonistas de los hechos."

26. "La mala alimentación, el retiro prematuro del pecho, la crianza descuidada e indiferente, en suma, se encargaban de provocar abundantes fallecimientos por inanición, por deshidratación o por falta de la atención que los recién nacidos requerían."

27. After numerous consultations at the AHN (National Historical Archive – Spain) we have found that the catalog number assigned to this case in Dedieu's book does not correspond to any inquisitorial case and that the French translation is, at the very least, quite free, as can easily be seen.

28. "lo cual había dicho por miedo del tormento y habiéndose examinado dieciséis testigos en el Casar contó ser verdad que los dichos niños habían sido muertos y se hallaron de la misma manera y forma muertos y maltratados que la sobre dicha Mateo lo había confesado y habiéndose sustanciado su proceso fue puesta a cuestión de tormento y habiéndose pronunciado la sentencia y abajadola a la cámara para ejecutarse antes de desnudarse habiendo sido amonestada, dijo ser verdad todo lo que había dicho ante el vicario de Alcalá y en efecto lo ratifica en sustancia aunque en algunas circunstancias mudaba alguna cosa asegurando mucho ser verdad asi en la manera del confesar como del jurarlo."

29. "y pasadas las horas del derecho se ratificó en sus confesiones y en otras audiencias que con ella se tuvieron después dijo lo mismo negando saber de qué fue hechos los dichos ungüentos ni haber tenido otro pacto explicito ni tácito con el demonio más del que había dicho y dijo las causas que había tenido de vengarse de los padres en la muerte de sus hijos que son las mismas que los padres testificaron donde sospecharon que ellas se los hubiesen muerto y sustancióse su causa y votose, auto con coroza, levi, doscientos azotes y reclusa por el tiempo que pareciere."

WORKS CITED

ADC (Archivo de la Diócesis de Cuenca). 230–2902.
———. Book 199, file 2248. Trials of Ana La Roa and María Parra.
———. Book 75, file 1095. Trial of Illana de Peñalver.
———. Book 76, file 1108. Trial of María Monxa, a.k.a. La Lorenza.
———. Book 77, file 1130. Trial of María de Moya.
———. Book 79, file 1147. Trial of Águeda García de Beamud.
———. Book 99, file 1441. Trial of Francisca "La Ansarona."
Archivo Histórico Nacional (AHN). Inquisition, record 92, file 1, 197 h.
Berti, Giordano. 2010. *Storia della stregoneria: Origini, credenza, persecuzioni and rinascita nel mondo contemporaneo*. Milan: Oscar Mondadori.
Bideau, Alain, Bertraud Dejardins, and Héctor Pérez Brignoli, eds. 1987. *Infant and Child Mortality in the Past*. Oxford: Clarendon Press Oxford.
Bonomo, Giuseppe. 1985. *Caccia alle streghe: La credenza nelle streghe dal secolo. XIII al XIX con particolare riferimento all'Italia*. Palermo: Palumbo.
Bravo, Elia Nathan. 2002. *Territorios del mal: Un estudio sobre la persecución europea de brujas*. Ciudad de México: Universidad Nacional Autónoma de México/Instituto de Investigaciones Filológicas/Instituto de Investigaciones Filosóficas.

Campagne, Fabián Alejandro. 2002. *Homo Catholicus. Homo Superstitiosus: El discurso antisupersticioso en la España de los siglos XV a XVIII*. Buenos Aires: Miño y Dávila.

―――. 2009. *Strix hispánica: Demonología cristiana y cultura folklórica en la España moderna*. Buenos Aires: Prometeo libros.

Castañega, Martín de. 1529. *Tratado de las supersticiones y hechizerias y de la possibilidad y remedio dellas*. Logroño: Miguel de Eguía.

Castiglioni, Arturo. 1993. *Encantamiento y magia*. Ciudad de México: Fondo de Cultura Económica.

Ciruelo, Pedro. 1538. *Reprovación de las supersticiones y hechizerías: Libro muy útile y necesario a todos los buenos christianos*. Salamanca: Pedro de Castro.

Clark, Stuart. 2009. *Vanities of the Eye: Vision in Early Modern European Culture*. Oxford: Oxford University Press.

Cordente Martínez, Heliodoro. 1990. *Brujería y hechicería en el obispado de Cuenca*. Cuenca: Diputación Provincial.

Cuevas Torresano, Ma. Luz de las. 1980. "Inquisición y hechicería: Los procesos inquisitoriales de hechicería en el Tribunal de Toledo durante la primera mitad del siglo XVII." *Anales Toledanos* 13: 25–92.

Culianu, Ioan P. 1999. *Eros y la magia en el Renacimiento, 1484*. Madrid: Ediciones Siruela.

Dedieu, Jean-Pierre. 1989. *L'Administration de la Foi: L'Inquisition de Tolède (XVIe–XVIIIe siècle)*. Madrid: Bibliothèque de la Casa de Velázquez.

Delumeau, Jean. 2002. *El miedo en Occidente (Siglos XIV–XVIII): Una ciudad sitiada*. Madrid: Taurus.

Ginzburg, Carlo. 1989. *Historia notturna*. Torino: Giulio Einaudi Editore.

Guaccio, Francesco Maria. 1624. *Compendium Maleficarum: Ex quo nefandissima in genus humanum opera venefica, ac ad illa vitanda remedia conspiciuntur*. Milan: Collegio Ambrosiano.

Harris, Marvin, and Eric B. Ross. 1987. *Death, Sex and Fertility: Population Regulation in Preindustrial and Developing Societies*. New York: Columbia University Press.

Levack, Brian P. 1995. *La caza de brujas en la Europa Moderna*. Madrid: Alianza Editorial.

López-Ridaura, Cecilia. 2013. "*De villa en villa, sin Dios y ni Santa María*, un conjuro para volar." In *La ascensión y la caída: Diablos, brujas y posesas en México y Europa*, ed. Claudia Carranza, 37–58. San Luis Potosí: El Colegio de San Luis.

Ortiz, Alberto. 2015. *El aquelarre: Mito, literatura y maravilla*. Barcelona: Ediciones Oblícuas.

Pastore, Federico. 1997. *La fabbrica delle streghe: Saggio sui fondamenti teorici e ideologici della repressione della stregoneria nei secoli XIII–XVII*. Pasian di Prato: Campanotto Editore.

Quevedo y Villegas, Francisco. 1981. *Obras completas*, ed. Felicidad Buendía. Madrid: Aguilar Ediciones.

Roper, Lyndal. 1997. *Oedipus and the Devil: Witchcraft, Sexuality and Religion in Early*

Modern Europe. London/New York: Routledge.

Sánchez Ortega, María Helena. 2004. *Ese viejo diablo llamado amor: La magia amorosa en la España Moderna.* Madrid: UNED Ediciones.

Sierra, Julio. 2005. *Procesos en la Inquisición de Toledo (1575–1610): Manuscrito de Halle.* Madrid: Editorial Trotta.

Stephens, Walter. 2002. *Demon Lovers: Witchcraft, Sex, and the Crisis of Belief.* Chicago: University of Chicago Press.

Tausiet, María. 1998. "Brujería y metáfora. El infanticidio y sus traducciones en Aragón (s. XVI–XVII)." *Temas de Antropología Aragonesa* 8:61–83.

———. 2004. *Ponzoña en los ojos: Brujería y superstición en Aragón en el siglo XVI.* Madrid: Turner Publicaciones.

II

WOMEN
AND THE
INQUISITION
IN THE
NEW WORLD

✠

Toward an Inquisitorial History of Binding Spells or Ligatures

The Case against María de la Concepción, a Gypsy in New Spain

ALBERTO ORTIZ

And those [books] wherein there are spells, sorcery, omens, auspices, cursed incantations, and superstitions banned by the aforementioned index, under the censures and punishments contained therein, are forbidden to be read or in any way retained by all Christians, who should turn them over to the bishops and locals, or present and remand them to the inquisitors.

Y aquellos, en que haya sortilegios, hechicerías, agüeros, auspicios, malditas encantaciones, y supersticiones en el dicho índice vedados, debajo de las censuras y penas en él contenidas leerse de cualquier cristiano, o de alguna manera detenerlos, debiendo darlos a los obispos, y a los ordinarios de los lugares, o presentarlos, y consignarlos a los dichos inquisidores.

—PAPAL BULL OF POPE SIXTUS V, 1586

The Workings of the Enchantment Called Amarre or Ligadura (Ligature)

Throughout the history of human culture, part of the collective imagination has endowed language with alleged magical abilities. Special expressions are used to exert a chimerical power at a distance by one person over another, be it to injure, heal, convince, reject, drive away, or attract. These are usually short texts, wishful prayers that are meant to command express lyrical and emotional attributes. This magical and superstitious tradition entails a hermetic immanence of language, a secret power from beyond this earth encouraged or revealed through precise words, recited at the same time that complex rituals are performed. In the field of semantics of western magic, the speech forms have been called incantations, conjurations, and spells, among other commonly accepted terms. The catalog of these magical formulations is very broad, despite their brevity and reiterated format, thanks to the hundreds of years during which this western magical thought has been accumulated, repeated, adapted, and renewed. Among such formulas those deployed for erotic purposes stand out, in accordance with their own superstitious tradition.

From Athens, third century CE, comes the following fragment of a magical prayer:

[. . .] Powerful Beptu, I deliver to you Leosthenes and Peios, who frequent Juliana, to whom Marcia gave birth, so you may freeze them and their intentions, so that they may not speak to each other or walk together, take a seat at Juliana's brothel, or send messages to Juliana, or to Leosthenes or Peios. And also freeze those who bring them together in your gloomy atmosphere. Chain them to the unilluminated atmosphere of oblivion, freeze them, and do not allow Proclus, Leosthenes or Peios to have sexual intercourse. (López Jimeno 2001, 90)[1]

Here the utterance comes from a woman. By contrast, the following example of a formulaic mandate, written during the fourth century CE, seems to be designed for male use:

Arise to serve me, whoever you may be, male or female, and go forth to every place, down every path, into every dwelling, and bring and bind her. Induce (insert the name of the petitioner's loved one), whose identity you possess, to love me (insert the name of the petitioner), son of (the petitioner's father); that she not have sex either from the front or from behind, or seek pleasure with any other man but me (the petitioner). Make it so that she may not eat, drink, love, suffer, or enjoy health; that she may not be able to sleep without me (the petitioner); because I conjure you, by the name of the most terrible and fearsome, whose name when pronounced will open up the earth, whose terrible name when heard will fill demons with panic, whose name when heard will destroy the rivers and stones.

I conjure you, demon of death, [. . .] that on the contrary, you drag (the petitioner's loved one) by her hair, her insides, her soul, toward me, (the petitioner), at every moment of her life, night and day, until at last she comes to me (the petitioner), and remains inseparably united with me (the petitioner). (Luck 1995, 131)[2]

For practical purposes for the facilitator or conjurer and the concerned complainant or petitioner, conjurations such as the previous ones do not employ gender. They are prefabricated like a mold; a one-size-fits-all format or a general template to which the names of the petitioner and the target are to be inserted. Therefore, in the first example, a restraining spell, it would not be an exaggeration to state that the names of the targets, the regular attendants to Juliana's brothel, Leosthenes and Peios, were added in later. The "freezing" referred to implies the incapacity to exercise any sexual activity with other women besides the issuer. The second magical conjuration exhibits a format that in fact still exists in books of love magic or grimoires to this day: the main statement remains basically the same and it is only necessary to add the names of each suitor and desired person for each petition.

There is a notoriously strong intentional charge from the petitioner, as he or she aims to achieve—without the protocol of formal courtship, family pact, religious license, mutual agreement, or even courteous romancing—total domination of another's affections, the desired one, who has neither voice nor decision in the face of the supposed strength of the amatory spell. The spell, for its part, expresses a demand for control, thus becoming utilitarian and turning the subjectivity of amatory feeling into a pragmatic matter. At the center of its meaning is the forced exclusivity, which the other must obey without hesitation. It is not only about achieving love through the magical verbal spell; it is just as important to prevent the desired person from making contact with one's competitors or obtaining pleasure from other bodies. Hence the insistent craving for exclusivity, which comes from possessive demand and works within the magical illusion for the hope of nullifying the other's will and imposing the spell caster's personal and intimate desire.

This seemingly delusional demand for erotic control, with the pretense of exclusivity over the body of the desired subject, by means of a conjuring formula and, at the same time, precluding the pleasant exchange in amatory affairs with other people, is called *ligadura* (ligature), *atadura* (tether), or *amarre* (binding spell); these terms accord with the defining lexicon of magical semantics described and censored by demonologists in the treatises that dealt with magic, the devil, and witchcraft that were written in the Renaissance and Baroque periods.

The terms may be used as synonyms; the differences between them are very minor and their meanings are regularly confused. One of those small differences lies in *ligadura* being often mentioned in cases and discussions regarding magical involvement with an overtly sexual nature, whereas the term *amarre* appears repeatedly in inquisitorial trials occurring in New Spain: "the *ligadura* is a state of impotence, produced by sorcery, which is generally carried out by making knots in threads or skeins [*licia* in Latin] and also by administering potions" (Robbins 1991, 370).[3]

If anything characterized the early modern myth of witchcraft it was an ability to increase, or better said, overflow its own narrative boundaries. The editorial and legal success of scholarly treatises, written to denounce and combat a supposed witch infestation within Christian villages, involved inserting lurid details in the popular imaginary surrounding devil worship and the threats to Christian morality and order.

Amatory bonding had taken place in medieval love stories, as exemplified in the theater, chivalric romances, poems, and novels, by way of a sensual enchantment, far removed from diabolical overtones, although necessarily close to erotic magic. Such an idea of love was typical of court poetry and exercised amidst the codes of the perfect gentleman and the courtier lover. Tristan and Isolde and Calisto and Melibea are archetypal examples from medieval literature.[4] The passionate bond, then, depended on an amatory case acknowledged by literature: the *philocaptio.*

Witchcraft inherited from the inquisitorial jurisdiction this possibility of influencing human passion as, in the end, erotic love was seen as a disease, an outburst, an alienation, a violence against reasoning, a detour from the straight path traced by God and His representatives. Therefore, all manifestations of overwhelming, violent passions, subject to sensuality, were abhorred and associated with sins because they drove the subject away from spiritual purification and closer to the corruption of the body. In addition, Church doctrine stated that if human flaws caused greater evils and culminated in capital sins such as vanity, pride, and lust, amid scandal and immorality, they must be fostered by the lord of lust, the devil.

Legal treatises helped to modify the perspective of love, already constantly related to the notions of sin and heresy. *El manual de los inquisidores* (The Inquisitors' Manual), written circa 1376 by Nicolau Eimeric but printed in 1503, and then reissued and expanded by Francisco Peña in 1578, asserts the traditional view that those demon worshipers who make love philters deny they contain special powers, and maintains that these potions cannot induce love. This can only happen when someone resorts to the devil to materialize their carnal desires (Eimeric and Peña 1983, 83–84). Thus, innocuous natural means, such as the traditional use of herbs such as sage to prepare love philters, without external authority, are acknowledged to induce love; the problem for the Church arises when diabolical intervention is suspected.

When the witchcraft myth was at its height—during the sixteenth, seventeenth, and part of the eighteenth centuries—the alteration of consciousness to sin through the senses shifted from human functioning to the sphere of the diabolical attack. What was once a sensual game, more or less governed by licentious but not evil practices, became a threat to procreation, that is to say, to the continuity of the work of God, who, according to biblical discourse, ordered humanity to "be fruitful and multiply." The *philocaptio* changed from bonding two lovers to separating them. Henceforth, the ligature no longer consisted in achieving only the sudden infatuation of a woman or a man through philters or the natural powers of the fascination for beauty. According to the expanded witchcraft myth, a ligature's purpose was also to prevent intercourse between husband and wife, seeking to thwart conception, thereby turning them into impotent, sterile beings. Within this patriarchal and phallocentric framework, the man was the main target and the woman the main conspirator.

Demonological Theory and "Truthful" Examples
in Relation to the Ligature

Heinrich Kramer and Jacob Sprenger's *Malleus Maleficarum* devotes at least five sections to initiate reprobations on magical activities against male potency and procreation that witches supposedly performed.[5] We should recall the broad societal, political, religious, and cultural impact this book had on Catholic Europe, thanks to the first publication and to the endless list of reissues, glosses, references, and confirmations it received during the more than two hundred years in which this work constituted the authority on the subject.

According to Kramer and Sprenger, the movement toward sins related to sexuality comes from diabolic instigation and human weakness; given that the devil can influence people's emotions, despite having no influence upon one's free will, it can also incite unbridled eroticism through persuasion and direct means: demons, visible or invisible, give harmful advice to men and present and promote erotic fantasies to excite them. In this process of diabolical temptation, a first binding takes place; the gripping of the man's instincts and imagination: "It follows that it is not strange that, with divine permission, demons may constrain the use of reason; and these men are called delirious, because their senses have been snared by the devil. And they do this with or without the cooperation of the witches" (Kramer and Sprenger 2016, 130).

That said, when the witches are those who promote acts of lust, they do not do so independently from the participation of demons, since according to the consistent affirmation of Kramer and Sprenger, a witch is precisely a witch because of the implicit or explicit pact with the devil, so that all their activities depend on that particular contract. Apart from that, the authors recall a case in which a witch killed three abbots and drove another mad through erotic spells, so that they would not stop loving her. Kramer and Sprenger regret the fact that despite her own confession, they could not take her to trial. "And she still lives," they warn.

Among their questions about the matter is how to define "ligature" according to the witchcraft myth. They ask:

> Is it Catholic to state that witches can infect the minds of men with a burning love for unknown women, to the point of inflaming their hearts

so that no scandal, reprimand, word, or action would compel them to desist from such love?; and that, likewise, they can sow such hatred among couples that they cannot consummate the procreational function of marriage, even, in the silence of the night, to travel great distances in search of inappropriate male and female lovers? (2016, 131)[6]

The inquisitors themselves recognize that this is a question difficult to clarify because, on the one hand, the theology of the time ensured that human will was free and could not be governed by someone who was not God; but on the other, ligature necessarily entails an intrusion on one's passions and intimate decisions. However, they point to a solution, as the devil and his acolytes can surely coerce the faculties of the body by influencing the senses: inoculating desires, clouding one's reason, deceiving, and arousing perversions.

As indicated above, the ecclesiastical and societal concern surrounding the issue focused on the magical impediments to conception. Following canonical norms, it was not only considered murder, but what was worse, a sacrilegious crime; an attack on the divine work that should be punished with death.

The witchcraft myth laid several main conditions for the allies of evil, one of which was swearing to the devil to prevent procreation through enchantments, potions, spells, and tricks; they carried out this oath at a specific time in the coven. Therefore, the *Malleus* devotes a section to discuss "whether witches can prevent the power of gestation and hinder the venereal act" (2016, 137). The cumbersome but interesting scholastic disquisition concedes a logical "yes" based on its own judgment and on that of Petrus Paludamus:[7] demons and sorcerers can prevent some people from sexual practice and encourage it in others. Even God gives them more permission to interfere in this matter than in other human activities, because it is the means to challenge sin. It can drive bodies closer or further apart, to rouse or suppress desire, to make a woman or a man repugnant or attractive to their spouse, to cause erectile dysfunction in the male member and inhibit movement during intercourse, and, lastly, to impede the flow of semen by closing the seminal ducts, as well as other resources (2016, 139).

Based on St. Bonaventure and Petrus Paludamus, Kramer and Sprenger state that the sorcery of a ligature spell is achieved in such a way as to disable a man and even inculcate disgust when he copulates with a woman, but allows him to have a normal appetite to do so with other women, because the devil affects

> [. . .] men's genital function, not intrinsically, through an injury of the organ, but extrinsically, rendering it inoperative. Therefore, as [the spell] is an imposed rather than natural impediment, it can render a man impotent with one woman, but not with others, blocking the passion he feels for one, but not for others, through its own power, by way of some herb, a stone or other surreptitious natural means. (2016, 140–41)[8]

In an unusual display of logical reasoning, Kramer and Sprenger accept that the causes for the lack of sexual potency may reside in natural diseases, given that demons cannot influence or physically disrupt the organs because they do not have control over matter and they themselves do not possess a physical body: "When the member is not in any way aroused and cannot consummate intercourse, it is a sign of the frigidity of nature; but when it is stirred and aroused, and still cannot perform, it is a sign of sorcery" (2016, 141).

Starting from the reiterated assertion that all the evil things concerning this matter are real and happen to both married and unmarried couples—in such an obvious way that anyone who says otherwise is guilty of disloyalty and suspect of heresy—the authors of *Malleus Maleficarum* point to some variables that accompany the phenomenon, namely, women can also suffer from a ligature, which hampers conception, provokes miscarriages, and forces them to look for lovers when they cannot bear the physical closeness of their husbands due to the spell. However, this occurs more commonly in men because, first, the effect operates on the male member and seminal ducts, and second, because most of the conjurers are considered to be spiteful women, instigators of adultery, who hate married couples.

Men's phallocentric concern regarding binding is evidenced in the curious, and even humorous, section on "whether witches can produce an illusion to make the virile member seem entirely detached and separate from the body" (2016, 144). The inquisitors are convinced of that danger and also of the possibility that demons and witches will in reality or in effect remove the reproductive organs. The male fear of castration rears its anxious face at this feature of the witchcraft myth, of a piece with the belief in the vagina *dentata* that mutilates penises.

The stated opinions of the *Malleus Maleficarum* were a constant referent in the subsequent disquisitions on witchcraft, to such a degree that, as the book inaugurated the genre of demonological treatises and reinforced the tradition of inquisitorial manuals, it put in place a theoretical-methodological line, almost a style of credulity, regarding the world of witchcraft and the constant influence of the devil in the lives of men, and it sought to silence contrary opinions by branding the skeptics as wicked. The notorious theologian Martín Antonio del Río adheres to that line of magical beliefs and defense of the operational existence of witchcraft. He calls the ligature *ligamen,* or impediment, and includes it in the first part of the third book of his *Magical Disquisitions,* which means to explain and describe the curses in two special essays, "Amatory Spell" and "Hostile Spell." In the first, he explains what they are, how amatory philters work, and their allowed antidotes, all of which he views as part of everyday practice in his own time, the early seventeenth century. Del Río agrees that the love-spell ligature, being a diabolical trap, cannot force free will, but can compel bodily desires and cause disease (Del Río 1991).[9]

One of the argumentative weapons of all specialists was the example—along with descriptions of symptoms, analysis, reprimand, and censure—which is usually included in stories that are presumed to verify them. As a result, there are many narratives of almost all the possibilities of the ligature spell. Francesco Guazzo, author of the *Compendium Maleficarum,* recounts the case of a knight who was ligated by Venus, since as a newlywed, he placed his wedding ring on a finger of a statue of the goddess of love. When he attempted to retrieve it, the hand was closed. He went away and returned that night, but the ring had disappeared. Later, when he tried to consummate his marital obligations on his honeymoon, this proved impossible for him because something stood in between the bodies. Then he heard the goddess say that she was his wife because he had given her the ring. Faced with the logical complaints of his human spouse, he asked for advice from his parents, who sent him to Palumbus, a necromancer priest, who made him undergo a ritual that combined the road to hell, the parade of sinners, and the presence of the demon, so he could, in the end, retrieve the ring and compel Venus to undo the ligature. With this, he also recovered the freedom to sleep with his wife and consummate their love (Guazzo 1988, 164).[10]

In this case both the ideas that remained about the Greco-Latin past, that is, the demonization of Olympic deities and their admixture with medieval demonologic theory and beliefs, are clear. Yet although Venus acts the role of sorceress, there is no woman sorceress present who, with evil intentions, becomes the third party in discord and undermines the couple's joining for procreational purposes. However, the female character in opposition to a couple does appear in the following example: in exchange for money, a woman disrupted a marriage. After a failed attempt,[11] she succeeded in awakening extreme hatred between the spouses by making them eat a cheese with magical writing and half of a black chicken. She offered the other half to the devil, whose participation and help to the witch were crucial in securing the ligature (Guazzo 1988, 165–66).[12]

As stated above, the woman can also suffer the effects of a binding. Guazzo also summarizes the case of the Neapolitan Jacopo, who could not approach his wife without her reacting with fury, terrorized by his presence. This caused them to live apart, without sexual contact. A priest visiting the husband wished to question the wife. The husband hid and had his wife brought in. When asked the reasons for her aversion toward her husband, she stated that she did not know why; simply that when they were apart she loved him very much, but when he approached her, she imagined hideous monsters that took on his appearance, so she would rather die than be by his side. The priest ordered two women to tie her to the bed, arms and legs apart, then asked the husband to do his job as lover. "The wife, in her desire for her husband, let herself be tied and asked that her husband be let in, but when he entered, never such a fury had ever been seen. No wild beast has ever been more fierce or full of madness and rage as that woman, as she foamed at the mouth, ground her teeth and rolled her eyes, while her whole body seemed agitated and possessed by demons" (1988, 166–67).[13] So the husband, tired of fighting and compassionate when he saw there was no remedy, had to leave.

Another variable concerning Guazzo's characters' participation in the accounts of ligatures consists in having the witch or the sorcerer make use of enchantment for their own erotic benefit:

> In the city of San Gimignano in Tuscany, a young man fell so desperately in love with a witch that he left his beautiful and faithful wife and their children and, forgetting all about them, lived with his lover until his wife, convinced that his behavior was on account of witchcraft, covertly sought the spell that had caused his acts. She found it in a jar under his bed, a frog with its eyes sewn shut. She took the frog, opened its eyes, and then burned it; immediately thereafter her husband, as if awakened from a slumber, remembered his family and with this, came back to his wife and children. (1988, 167)[14]

Another example, this time of a man, is the case of the Frenchman Louis Gaufridy, who, according to the demonologist Pierre de Lancre, gave his soul to the devil in exchange for the power to captivate women. The devil agreed and gave him the power to "inflame" any woman he wished, just by exhaling his breath directly into her nose (Lancre 2013, 153–54).

Examples such as these abound. In each case, the main factor that concerns theologians and inquisitors is the challenge to religious dogma because they assume that what is to be found behind ligature enchantments is the subversive plans of the devil, the great enemy of Christianity.

An Inquisitorial Case in New Spain

Inquisitorial records in New Spain are an important source of research for scholars. Despite the vicissitudes of time and the partial abandonment by the governing authorities, Mexico has rich archives, documentary repositories, and libraries acknowledging past events that forged the criteria, imaginary, and idiosyncrasies of its settlers. One topic in these collections attests to the transmission of demonological, magical, and superstitious ideas that impregnated the mentality and imagination of colonial society. With regard to this transitional period, specialists speak more of a continuity than of a new perspective in terms of instructions to regulate the faith. As Jiménez Rueda rightly affirms: "The religious unrest is manifest in the colony. There is hardly any shade of European dogmatic differences which is not represented in the history of our heterodox believers" (1946, IX).

However, in magic and witchcraft, differences with Catholic Europe, although minimal, were significant. As is well known, the territory of New Spain did not witness the massive and spectacular autos de fe that served to exhibit penitents, apostates, witches, heretics, and so on, with the possibility of their suffering a violent death penalty before the public. Diabolical pacts recorded in the cases, as fantastic as those of Europe, were few and contaminated by other factors or by the inquisitorial insistence, whose wish it was to find demons where there had only been manifestations of pre-Hispanic reminiscences or outright ignorance. The witch was more of a *yerbera* (herbal healer), more a daughter of traditional indigenous and African rituals than a voluptuous mistress of Satan. The few covens that existed did not share the motley myth; attendants did without flying goats, turkeys to ride, or walks toward a vague meeting. The infestation of demons such as those that possessed the beleaguered bodies of the cloistered nuns in Loudun, Louviers, and Madrid was not acknowledged. The popular, satirical, mocking or mocked devil, companion of adventurers, fallacious friend inclined to gab and imbibe alcoholic beverages, gets the upper hand over the scholastic devil described by experts; he seems to be more of a *nahual,* the mythical Mesoamerican shapeshifter. And there are virtually no demonological treatises written in America, despite their potential publishing success and doctrinal importance.

However, since amatory ailments are ascribed human motivation, men of New Spain, like any others of the time, resorted to prohibited and magical remedies to achieve the materialization of their desires. In the face of passion, the discourses of the doctrinal system time and time again reproached the weaknesses of the flesh while extending the justification to sin through the offer of forgiveness. It is no coincidence that most of the inquisitorial records against magical practices, both in America and Europe, refer to conflicts related, directly or indirectly, to eroticism.

In the social sphere the witch must have an ambiguous image; this perception among her neighbors and outlanders consists in the game of acceptance and rejection, repulsion and condescension, which is set in motion every time the user goes into a crisis and requests her services. For her part, the witch must show, or at least feign, her possession of secrets, forbidden wisdom, dominion of otherworldly entities, and her belonging to an ancient magical tradition. This last aspect is reinforced by the real or invented exoticism of the witch's or sorceress's lineage. When the requirements are met, the common people rely more on a foreign witch that stands out, both to blame her for their common maladies and to consult her on their concerns, ailments, and needs.

The western collective imaginary has endowed Gypsies or Roma with the same magical qualities. Loved and feared as a people of uncertain origin, the Gypsies carry with them, from time immemorial to the present, the stigma of a special race, among whom magic, divination, and prophecy pass from generation to generation as family legacy.[15] To this we must add the prejudices of the period that branded them as immoral and dissipated and as tricksters and thieves.

The stereotype already existed in seventeenth-century New Spain. In 1668, the Court of the Holy Office of Mexico opened a trial and prosecution of crime against the faith on María de la Concepción (Flores and Masera 2010, 133–36).[16] She was questioned during the month of November. She was old, widowed, poor, unemployed, superstitious, and Portuguese, that is to say, a foreign and female Gypsy; in short, she met an almost perfect combination of discriminating factors that designated her as a propitious victim, according to the ideas of persecution at the time.

In the port of Veracruz, a man accused her of having bound him at the request of another woman with whom he had previously had sexual encounters. According to the complainant, for this purpose, María de la Concepción had used "superstitious and demonized means." She defended herself by arguing and demonstrating with prayers and signs that she was a Catholic, and she even showed a bull of the Holy Crusade, something that must have been in response to the judges, given that the recitation of the four basic prayers was a mandatory procedure in these cases. She also claimed to be the victim of false testimony by a *mulata* woman from Veracruz who had asked for her help, because María knew how to cure erysipelas and the evil eye, skills she learned while living in Cartagena de Indias.

According to her testimony, the true story was as follows: she had gone to a house when invited to do so by the *mulata* woman. There she met a man, Portuguese also, who complained to her because a woman there had told him she "had bound him." She denied having done so to the accuser, but it was useless. The Portuguese called a bailiff and she was taken to jail. It is ironic that her name was *Concepción* (conception) when, in witchcraft myth, one of the main purposes of a ligature was indeed to prevent it.

But the truth as assumed by complainants, witnesses, and inquisitors told a different story, especially after she was subjected to torment in 1699. According to their version, two years prior María de la Concepción had sought and told Pancha Montes, the woman pursued by the Portuguese man, to accept him because he had money, telling her that she was young and could benefit from the relationship. At this stage, the poor woman seems to play solely the role of an intermediary. In this sense, the accused would be guilty only of matchmaking; unfortunately for her, however, witnesses argued that she had used oral incantations and rituals to ensure the cohabitation of the lovers.

Under the inquisitorial version, the mediation turned to diabolical unlawfulness. She had supposedly promised to guide the maiden and gave her a "remedy" so the Portuguese man would love and please only her. Days after asking for money without saying what she wanted it for, she went back to Montes and directed her in a ritual using an orange tape that she knotted three times while both repeated "Matheo Andrés [the Portuguese man's name], I hereby bind you, I hereby enthrall you, with the Virgin and the Holy Spirit" (Flores and Masera 2010, 134) and other, unintelligible prayers.

Forced to confess, María de la Concepción pleaded guilty, "bad and sinful," accepted that she had indeed bound the man by making three knots with the ribbon and saying "Matheo Andrés, I hereby bind you, I hereby tie you, by the power of God" (2010, 135). But she made clear she had not said "here I enthrall you," as she knew that binding and uttering incantations were sins and contrary to the faith, although she had used them owing to economic necessity.

Everything shows that, based on warnings and advice, she conjectured that issuing words of enchantment and spells implied a pact with the forces of evil, or, at least, would cause a harsher sentence, so she tried to dispel the suspicions of witchcraft.

Until this moment, the trial would seemingly conclude in a reprimand and a slight penance. Regrettably for the poor woman, between the hearing and her torment, either a lawyer well versed in demonological theory, a judge, a consultant, or a prosecutor must have influenced a change in the defendant's declaration so that she responded with what the inquisitors wanted to hear:

And when asked if she could bind men with what she had done with that ribbon and with those words, she replied that she could not, except by summoning sin, which was what she had done when she uttered those words. And when asked who the summoned sin was when those words were uttered and what the name of the sin was, she responded that the sin summoned was the devil, and when she summoned him, she would utter:

Devil, come and bind so-and-so.

When told to speak all the words she had said to bind that man, she replied that the words she had said were:

Matheo Andrés, I hereby bind you, I hereby tie you, by the power of God and the Holy Spirit. Devil, bind Matheo Andrés so he will have nothing to do with any other woman except with this Pancha Montes; come Devil, and bind Matheo Andrés.

And with this, the Devil came and bound him. And when she made the knots, that was the moment she summoned the Devil, because that is when he should be summoned to perform the ligature. (2010, 135)[17]

It is possible that at some point during the deliberation, the judicial decision might have been to agree on the sentence, that is, the death penalty, but even to the harshest judges the woman, in case all of the above were true, had clearly been driven by self-interest, seeking her means of subsistence and ignoring the theological implications of her purported magical acts. In 1670, María de la Concepción, a Portuguese Gypsy, poor, old, widowed and a procuress, abjured *de vehementi* (under strong suspicion of heresy); she was sentenced to be publicly humiliated by wearing the marks of penitent and witch, to receive two hundred lashes, and to serve in a hospital for ten years.

Impotentiam Ligaturam

Less than forty years before the Portuguese Gypsy's inquisitorial trial in New Spain, a priest from Aragon, Gaspar Navarro, brought to light in 1631 his demonological treatise, *Tribunal de superstición ladina* (Tribunal of Ladino Superstition), condemning all superstitions. It was updated "in an easy and common language" citing the authorized verdicts on a wide range of magical, diabolical, and superstitious phenomena, so that ordinary people besides the spiritual directors, priests, and lawyers could know what was right and wrong regarding magic, divination, prophecies, spells, enchantments, etcetera, and thus defeat the devil, who by these malicious means tries to usurp space and veneration from the divine. The sins of superstition, Navarro says, are a small and malicious enemy that nevertheless undermine the Church and "with a mask of virtue and religious worship deceive so many souls, [...] To repair this damage comes this booklet [...] compassionate love put the pen in my hand and encouraged me to conclude my attempt, which is only to put in clear terms, set the common people straight from the all too frequent error that remains in many superstitions as being exempt by virtue of devotions" (1631).[18]

One of Navarro's chapters, "Dispute 22," is dedicated to the spell of impotence, or marriage ligature, which he defines as a curse performed by conjurers through words, poisons, and signs that they know thanks to their pact with the devil. It causes impotence in a man or woman in a conjugal relationship. He adds a relevant detail: the ligature is an affront to Christian charity, to Christ's mandate to "love one another," and to natural law, which asks that you not do unto others what you do not want done unto yourself (1631, 57v–60v). This specific ideological approach, turned into a legal tool, is similar to those that the inquisitors applied in the case of María de la Concepción; the proximity in time between the book's publication and the conclusions of the case gives a very precise idea as to the notions held by the judges on the diabolical and justifies its mention here.

If we consider amorous ligature as a symptom of the *pathos* that protects the women from being viewed as malignant, Navarro's arguments also reflect male concerns and weaknesses: the deep fear of sexual impotence; the double standard of guilt from infidelity placed on a third party, usually a witch; the natural erotic differences between male and female that translate as a silent lack of virility to another's demands, the wife or lover unable to achieve carnal satisfaction for their alleged inclination to sensuality; the trend, shared by both, to victimize the different, the weak, and the defenseless through a cathartic scheme that requires a scapegoat and depends on violence, blood, and death to renew the sense of community life, as René Girard (1986) has explained.

In conclusion, it is clear that the Catholic system reiterated its varied methods against superstition in theory and practice. This line of specialized disquisitions contained several internal disputes and mistakes, particularly in its application. For example, the inquisitorial apparatus was bureaucratic, heavy, complex, and slow; but it built a discursive tradition with which the most-recognized authors necessarily concurred with Catholic dogmas and precepts of the papal hierarchy. Expert demonologists and inquisitorial judges were instrumental in the constant attempt to unify the inner and outer life of the subject as only in this way was there a chance the soul could be saved. What now seems injustice, repression, and censorship was a legitimate and desirable attempt at eternal salvation for the early modern mentality.

The witchcraft myth has been interpreted as a feverish venting of repressed anxieties; it is likely that the limitless possibilities of expression within their essential components: coven, possession, covenant, enchantment, and so forth, brought balance to the official system, based on dogmatic demands and admonitions in face of the weaknesses and diabolical temptations.

Behind the ludicrous fantasy of the binding spell, or ligature, can be glimpsed the erotic concerns of an earlier western society governed by religious doctrine. The use of one's own body and those of others, the control of their natural instincts and inclinations, the balance between virtue and vice were challenges for the inquisitorial trial. Accepted authority as well as scholarly opinion guided this complicated fabric of justice, theology, and gullibility.

NOTES

1. "[. . .] poderoso Beptu, te entrego a Leóstenes y a Pío, los que frecuentan a Juliana, a la que parió Marcia, para que los congeles, a ellos y su entendimiento, para que no puedan hablar juntos, ni pasear, que no puedan ir a sentarse en el burdel de Juliana, ni enviar mensajes a Juliana, ni Leóstenes ni Pío, y en tu oscura atmósfera y a sus intermediarios. Encadénalos a la iniluminada atmósfera del olvido, congélalos, y no permitas a Proclo, Leóstenes y Pío tener relaciones sexuales."

2. "Levántate para servirme a mí, quien quiera que seas, varón o mujer, y dirígete a todo lugar, a todo camino, a toda casa y tráela y átala; induce a fulana, cuya identidad posees, a que me ame a mí, fulano, hijo de mengano; que no tenga relaciones sexuales por delante ni por detrás, ni busque placer con otro varón, sino únicamente conmigo, fulano; de manera que fulana no pueda comer, ni beber, ni amar, ni sufrir, ni gozar de salud; que fulana no consiga dormir sin mí, fulano; porque yo te conjuro, por el nombre del terrible y aterrador, cuyo nombre al oírlo la tierra se abrirá, cuyo terrible nombre al escucharlo los démones se llenarán de pánico, cuyo nombre al oírlo los ríos y las piedras se romperán.

"Yo te conjuro demón de muerto, . . . por el contrario, arrastra a fulana por los cabellos, las entrañas, su alma, hacia mí, fulano, en cada momento de su vida, de noche y de día, hasta que venga a mí, fulano, y permanezca inseparablemente unida a mí, fulano."

3. Performing actual or symbolic ligatures is a central part of this magical practice, as shown by the examples included here. See below the case in New Spain of the Gypsy accused of binding a man.

4. *La Celestina* may be viewed as including diabolical participation, depending on whether Celestina is recognized as a witch or a simple procuress; there is no consensus among scholars.

5. See "Question VII. If demons can influence the minds of men to love or hate," "Question VIII. If witches can prevent the power of gestation and hinder the venereal act," "Question IX. If witches can produce an illusion of prestidigitation so that the virile member seems entirely far and removed from the body" (Kramer and Sprenger 2016, 125).

6. "[. . .] ¿es católico afirmar que las brujas pueden infectar la mente de los hombres con un amor ardiente por mujeres desconocidas, hasta inflamar de modo tal su corazón que ningún escándalo, reprimenda, palabra o acción alguna los obligue a desistir de tal amor?; ¿y que, asimismo, pueden sembrar tal odio entre las parejas que les sea imposible consumar las funciones procreadoras del matrimonio, de modo que, en el silencio de

la noche, recorran grandes distancias en búsqueda de amantes masculinos y femeninos irregulares?"

7. Petrus Paludamus was a fourteenth-century Thomist theologian. The authors also refer to St. Bonaventure, St. Thomas Aquinas, and St. Augustine, following patristic authority.

8. "[. . .] la capacidad genital no en forma intrínseca, mediante una lastimadura en el órgano, sino de manera extrínseca, inutilizándolo. Por consiguiente, como se trata de un impedimento artificial y no natural, puede volver a un hombre impotente hacia una mujer, pero no hacia otras: obturando la pasión que siente por ella, pero no por otras mujeres, ya mediante su propio poder, por alguna hierba, una piedra u otros medios naturales subrepticios."

9. The first known edition dates from 1599–1600. There is a partial translation in Spanish (covering book II) by Jesús Moya.

10. Guazzo writes about having taken on the case of Vincent de Bauvais, a monk who lived between the twelfth and thirteenth centuries, author of an extensive work called *Speculum Maius*. Martin del Rio also mentions the case in his *Magical Disquisitions*.

11. On that first occasion she attempted to have both spouses carry a paper with magical writing, that is to say, she used some manuscripts, even reusing them in the spell that was successful. Writing as a magical catalyst was frequently used in amatory practices.

12. Guazzo copied the motif from *Praeceptorium Divinae Legis,* a work published in Cologne, Germany, in 1481, by the Augustinian monk Gotschalcus Hollen.

13. Guazzo took the example from the treatise by the physician Giovanni Battista Codronchi, *De morbis maleficiis.* Codronchi (1547–1628) is considered a pioneer in studies of forensic medicine. In addition, he discussed diabolical possession and its medical aspects. The work to which Guazzo refers is *De morbis veneficis ac veneficiis*, published in Venice in 1595.

14. "En la ciudad de S. Gimignano en Etruria un joven se enamoró tan desesperadamente de una bruja que dejó a su bella y fiel esposa así como a sus hijos y, olvidándolos, vivió con su amante hasta que su esposa, convencida de que su conducta se debía a la brujería, secretamente buscó el sortilegio que lo había causado, y encontró en una jarra debajo de su cama un sapo con los ojos cosidos. Se llevó aquello, le abrió los ojos, y después lo quemó; e inmediatamente su esposo, como si se despertara de un sueño, recordó a su familia y con ello volvió con su mujer y sus hijos." The author takes this case from Codronchi as well.

15. Note that one of the characteristics of witchcraft reiterated by Baroque treatises was that if a woman went to the coven, she had the obligation to bring her children and offer them to the devil as new followers. The daughter or granddaughter of a witch almost necessarily was one too. It was assumed to be a maternal legacy.

16. The file corresponds to the Inquisition branch, vol. 1502, file 4, ff. 1r–21r of the AGNM (Archivo General de la Nación México).

17. "Y preguntada si con lo que hiço en dicha cinta y con dichas palabras se podía ligar y ligaban los hombres, respondió que no, sino llamando al pecado, que se llamaba quando se deçían las palabras. Y peguntada quién es el pecado que se llama quando se deçían dichas palabras y cómo se llamaba al pecado, respondió que el pecado que se llamaba es el Diablo, y que cuando lo llamaba deçía: "Diablo, ven y amarra a fulano. Fuele dicho dijese todas las palabras que havía dicho para ligar a dicho hombre; respondió que las palabras que havía dicho eran: 'Matheo Andrés, aquí te ato, aquí te amarro, con el poder de Dios y del Espíritu santo. Diablo, amarrad a Matheo Andrés para que no tenga parte con otra muger, sino con esta Pancha Montes, venid Diablo, y amarrad a Matheo Andrés.' Y que con esto viene el Diablo y lo amarra. Y que al dar los nudos fue quando llamó al Diablo, porque entonces es quando se ha de llamar para que haga la ligadura."

18. "Prólogo," n.p. The punctuation and spelling in the quotations have been modernized.

WORKS CITED

Del Río, Martín. 1612. *Disquisitionum magicarum libri sex: Quibus continetur accurata curiosarum artium et vanarum supertitionum confutatio.* Lugduni: Ioannem Pillehotte.

———. 1991. *La magia demoníaca.* Madrid: Hiperión.

Eimeric, Nicolau, and Francisco Peña. 1983. *El manual de los inquisidores.* Barcelona: Muchnik Editores.

Flores, Enrique, and Mariana Masera, coords. 2010. *Relatos populares de la Inquisición Novohispana: Rito, magia y otras "supersticiones," Siglos XVII–XVIII.* Madrid: Consejo Superior de Investigaciones Científicas/Universidad Nacional Autónoma de México.

Girard, René. 1986. *El chivo expiatorio.* Barcelona: Anagrama.

Guazzo, Francesco María. 1988. *Compendium Maleficarum.* Alicante: Club Universitario.

Jiménez Rueda, Julio. 1946. *Herejías y supersticiones en la Nueva España (Los heterodoxos en México).* Ciudad de México: Imprenta Universitaria.

Kramer, Heinrich, and Jacob Sprenger. 2016. *Malleus Maleficarum.* Barcelona: Iberlibro.

Lancre, Pierre de. 2013. *Tratado de brujería vasca: Descripción de la inconstancia de los malos ángeles y demonios.* Vizcaya: Txalaparta.

López Jimeno, Amor, ed. 2001. *Textos griegos de maleficio.* Madrid: Akal.

Luck, Georg. 1995. *Arcana mundi.* Madrid: Gredos.

Navarro, Gaspar. 1631. *Tribunal de superstición ladina.* Explorador del saber, astucia y poder del demonio. . . . Huesca: Pedro Bluson.

Robbins, Rossell Hope. 1991. *Enciclopedia de la brujería y demonología.* Madrid: Debate.

✟

Maleficata Impotentia

From Malleus Maleficarum *to the Eighteenth-Century Enchantresses of New Spain*

CECILIA LÓPEZ-RIDAURA

The curse depriving a man of his manhood received thorough treatment in four paragraphs of the Dominicans Heinrich Kramer and Jacob Sprenger's treatise *Malleus Maleficarum* (The Hammer of Witches): Question VIII: "Whether witches can blunt the powers of generation or obstruct the venereal act"; Question IX, "Whether witches may work some prestidigital illusion to make the male organ appear entirely removed and separate from the body"; Chapter VI: "How witches impede and prevent the power of procreation," and Chapter VII: "How they deprive man of his virile member."

In this essay, I briefly review how the approaches by the authors of this most famous manual on witchcraft were consistently reflected later in the testimonies collected by the Inquisition in New Spain. Several scholars have noted that the *Malleus Maleficarum* is primarily a lengthy exposure of the sexual conflicts of its authors, who insist throughout the book that the origin of all evil is women's lustful nature, and an explanation of why they virulently attack all women (Smith 2002, 85–86).[1] Kramer and Sprenger begin from the idea that God gives the devil ample leeway to act on everything related to sex as this is the most corruptive act and agent in the spread of the first sin. Therefore, the loss of manhood is often the result of ending a supposed illicit friendship with either the witch herself or with any woman who seeks revenge after the relationship is ended. Let us read one example provided by the authors of the manual:

A certain high-born Count in the ward of Westerich, in the diocese of Strasburg, married a noble girl of equal birth; but after he had celebrated the wedding, he was for three years unable to know her carnally, on account, as the event proved, of a certain charm which prevented him. In great anxiety, and not knowing what to do, he called loudly on the Saints of God. It happened that he went to the State of Metz to negotiate some business; and while he was walking about the streets and squares of the city, attended by his servants and domestics, he met with a certain woman who had formerly been his mistress. Seeing her, and not at all thinking of the spell that was on him, he spontaneously addressed her kindly for the sake of their old friendship, asking her how she did, and whether she was well. And she, seeing the Count's gentleness, in her turn asked very particularly after his health and affairs; and when he answered that he was well, and that everything prospered with him, she was astonished and was silent for a time. The Count, seeing her thus astonished, again spoke kindly to her, inviting her to converse with him. So, she inquired after his wife, and received a similar reply, that she was in all respects well. Then she asked if he had any children; and the Count said he had three sons, one born in each year. At that she was more astonished and was again silent for a while. And the Count asked her, Why, my dear, do you make such careful inquiries? I am sure that you congratulate me on my happiness. Then she answered, Certainly I congratulate you; but curse that old woman who said she would bewitch your body so that you could not have connection with your wife! And in proof of this, there is a pot in the well in the middle of your yard containing certain objects evilly bewitched, and this was placed there in order that, as long as its contents were preserved intact, for so long you would be unable to cohabit. But see! it is all in vain, and I am glad. On his return home, the Count did not delay in having the well drained; and, finding the pot, burned its contents and all, whereupon he immediately recovered the virility which he had lost. (1971, 98)

This account, which is much more of a story, and almost a tale, than a legal argument, shows the common practice of requesting the services of a professional in magic: an enchantress, to avenge an abuse or a deception. One activity often attributed to the witches is inserted into the complexities of the sacrament of matrimony. Witches cannot only cause miscarriages and infertility in women, but also impotence in men, and all its implications for men's esteem and reputation are one of the greatest fears of all time. The authors of the *Malleus Maleficarum* mention that men's inability to fulfill the sexual function may occur with some women and not with others. This is one sign that impotence is due to a curse and not a physiological problem: the authors separate the intrinsic from the extrinsic generative obstacle, and—following the Thomistic theologian, the Dominican Petrus Paludamus—mention that there are five variants of this spell: the first consists in the devil, with God's permission, taking control of the persons and physically preventing their encounter. The second is by causing a cooling of passion in either of the two, primarily in the man, commonly by making use of special herbs and powders. The third is the devil taking hold of the imagination and causing a change in the man's visual perception so that the woman is unbearable to him. The fourth consists in diminishing the vigor required to consummate the union. And the fifth is obstructing the flow of semen so that the act itself is infertile (1971, 55).

As the spell or hex is an artificial and unnatural impediment, men who suffer from it may be impotent with one woman and not with another (1971, 55). This spell is known as *ligadura* or *ligamento* (ligature).[2] Aguirre Beltrán points out that the term refers to a dual purpose: a positive one of union, which seeks to increase the lover's passion;[3] and a negative one, meant to prevent the accursed person from sexually approaching another (1963, 175–76). Both purposes are often combined or the first implies the second; that is to say, the ligature forces the person it is performed on to fall in love with the petitioner and unable to approach anyone else. One example is the prayer to St. Sylvester, recited by an enchantress of Valencia in the sixteenth century: "Lord Saint Silvester of Montemayor, as you deterred the maiden and the man, deter so-and-so, from the member to the testicles, so that he may not lie with a woman, widow or married, or any other status, but only with me. So-and-so, come, come, and may no one stop him" (Blázquez 1989, 267).[4]

And the following spell, which can still be obtained in markets or shops specializing in herbal medicine and esotericism:

Prayer of the Deaf and Mute Soul. Eternal Father, sovereign God, etc.

Soul, lone soul, who moans and cries through hills and vales: I beckon you and need you to find me nine souls of Limos; nine I require, nine you shall bring me, three dead by hanging, three by firearm, and three by misfortune. These nine souls will writhe in so-and-so's head and again they will turn, and will not let him go by, live or eat, drink, or rest, or pursue any other woman. He will not think of any other but me, he will abhor everything, and will have no power over any other woman, only with me. Until raging like a dog, humble and meek, desperate, and madly in love, only with me, as Jesus Christ had to die on the Cross. In the same way, come to me, so-and-so, come and beg me with all your love, so-and-so, come to me, for I need you. Amen.[5]

Countless cases of both types of ligature appear repeatedly in all cultures and at all times, but I would like to highlight their presence in the inquisitorial testimonies of New Spain with a few examples.

Testimonies of the first type of ligature can be found in a long trial held against many women and some men in Monclova, Coahuila, Mexico, between 1748 and 1752 (Iruegas 2015; Semboloni 2004; López-Ridaura 2011, 2012, and 2014). One such case is that of a Spanish woman named María Josefa de Yruegas, nicknamed La Adaisena, who was interrogated in October 1751 by the Franciscan friar Hermenegildo Vilaplana, a commissioner appointed to deal with the outbreak of witchcraft which had surged in the area. After stating that she was a witch and enchantress, she confessed that when she made a pact with the devil to become a witch, he gave her some powders so men would desire her. She claimed that she sprinkled them on two men, Xavier Barrera and the tailor José Antonio Lazcano, although the powders had effect only on the latter, with whom she then had a sexual relationship. María Josefa de Yruegas also related that when she became an enchantress, two years before becoming a witch, the devil gave her a small fig leaf and some feathers and told her to mix them with cabbage seeds and mushrooms and add them to the food of the man whom she wished to fall in love with her, and he would reciprocate at once. This happened to Miguel de Hoyos, a man with whom she had had an illicit friendship a few years earlier, thanks to her sprinkling his clothes with the powders from the demon. After he abandoned her, an *india* (indigenous woman) from Monclova named Frigenia gave her a series of objects that would make men desire her for "lascivious purposes." According to the woman's instructions, the objects, consisting of an herb, a stone magnet, and a doll with a pin in her head, should be placed in the sun. One day Miguel came to Josefa's home, saying that he did not know why, but that he had been forced to go to her house because of some wheat spikes that clung to his clothes and stung him. What happened to Miguel resembles a story recorded by the authors of the *Malleus Maleficarum:*

> And there was in the town of Mersburg in the diocese of Constance a certain young man who was bewitched in such a way that he could never perform the carnal act with any woman except one. And many have heard him tell that he had often wished to refuse that woman and take flight to other lands; but that hitherto he had been compelled to rise up in the night and to come very quickly back, sometimes over land, and sometimes through the air as if he were flying. (Kramer and Sprenger 1971, 118)

In the Inquisition files of the archive "House of Morelos"[6]—in Morelia, Michoacán, Mexico—we find the case of three free *mulata* women, single and neighbors of the ranch of Purépero: a grandmother, an aunt, and a granddaughter who, in Zamora, Michoacán, in 1743, put a curse on a Spanish thirty-year-old mule driver named Antonio de Melgosa, who was married.[7] The victim reported that due to his debility, after marrying Juana de la Cerda, he had maintained an unlawful friendship for a month with the *mulata* Ana Serafina de Melgosa, granddaughter of Sebastiana de Melgosa. After Antonio put an end to the affair and left the girl, he felt he was bound ("ligado") and could not have relations with his wife. To verify if Ana Serafina had caused the damage, he sought her out again and found that he could have intercourse, so he was not impaired with her, only with his own wife. The facts were that his impotence was selective and that the girl; her mother, María Guadalupe de Melgosa; her aunt, Petrona de Melgosa; and her grandmother Sebastiana were known enchantresses; in addition, it was rumored that María Guadalupe, the mother, had left another man impotent and that she herself had healed him. For these reasons, the mule driver was convinced that Ana Serafina had hexed him (AHCM, box 1235, file 5, ff. 8r–8v).

Although it is less common, women can also suffer this hex and be unable to have sexual relations. In the same case above, the *mulata* Ana Serafina—the granddaughter—is also accused of killing the wife of Luis Martínez, a former lover. Martínez, a twenty-five-year-old Spanish mule driver, testified before Francisco Bernal de Pinavero, commissioner of the Holy Office of Zamora, Michoacán, that he had had an affair with Ana Serafina Melgosa, but that "after realizing the seriousness of his action, he tried to distance himself from such an illicit friendship" and decided to marry the Spaniard Juana Gertrudis Duarte, whom "the aforementioned Sebastiana and her granddaughter resented greatly" and on whom they threatened to take revenge. Sometime later, a few days after giving birth, Juana Gertrudis became seriously ill and said that she was being torn apart inside. In her delirium, the afflicted woman said that Ana Serafina and Sebastiana had appeared before her and wanted to force her to grab the tail of an animal. In view of the severity of Juana Gertrudis's ailment, her family sent for a *curandera* (healer) named María Beltrán, nicknamed *La Morellona*. She was a *mulata* about fifty years of age who lived in Tla-zazalca, Michoacán, where Luis Martinez's wife had given birth. Thinking that the woman might have suffered injury during childbirth, the healer examined her and found that "she did not seem a woman because her *ve-renda* (private parts) was closed up." Shortly after, Juana Gertrudis Duarte died and soon the rumor spread that the Melgosa women had put a curse on her (AHCM, box 1235, file 5, ff. 3r–3v).

After these complaints were received by the Holy Office in Mexico City, the prosecutor responsible for the case, Diego Mangado y Clavijo, ordered the inquisitors to imprison the three women, berate them severely in front of the people of the ranch, and give them twenty-five lashes. In the file, only the statements and ratifications of the witnesses are recorded, and we do not know if the punishment was carried out.

Twelve years later, in 1755, one witness in this case, Antonio Magaña, accused some other Melgosa women—Isabel, Micaela, and Dionisia—as well as a friend of theirs, Gertrudis de Orozco, in a clear reiteration of the case of his friend Antonio de Melgosa and his wife, of having bound him. Antonio Magaña, "considered a Spaniard," forty years old and married to Rita Báez, testified before Agustín Francisco de Esquivel y Vargas, the commissioner of the Holy Office of the town of San Sebastián de la Piedad, in the jurisdiction of Tlazazalca, Michoacán, that fifteen years prior—three years before the previous case had been submitted—although he was already married, he had a brief affair with Isabel Melgosa, a mestiza woman, unmarried, resident of the Purépero ranch. He left her soon after and, even though she tried to hold him, ignored her.

One night in February 1753, Antonio was talking with Bernardo, the tailor, when Isabel Melgosa approached him accompanied by a mestiza woman named María Antonia. Rita, Magaña's wife, had gone to a nearby town for a family affair. Calling Magaña over, Isabel told him she had brought the mestiza woman for his pleasure. He replied that he had not asked for anyone and that he was not interested; however, the women began to mock and ridicule him, saying that he would lie with a stone rather than part with a *real*. In the end "his debility got the best of him" and he agreed to have relations with María Antonia, but when he tried, "he found himself entirely impotent and unable to penetrate her." Furious, Antonio swore at the two women for mocking him. From that day on, he began to feel ill: he was sick to his stomach and felt a great weakness in his legs that prevented him from leaving the house.

In the meantime, on the way back to Purépero, his wife suddenly began to feel terribly nauseated. Later that night, when he wanted her to perform her conjugal duty, he found her "quite bound and impotent." As he could do nothing else, Antonio was forced to confess to his wife the episode with Isabel Melgosa and María Antonia. Rita Báez immediately sought out Melgosa and struck her, calling her an enchantress for the damage that she had done to them. But this worsened Rita's ills; her belly began to grow as if with child. Nine months later, convinced that this was no pregnancy, she prayed to San Antonio and her belly went flat, but she remained constantly nauseous and sick to her stomach. A *curandera* confirmed that this had been caused by hexes Isabel and her sisters had put on her. Antonio Magaña said that "[since he was] ever eager and always longing for his wife's health, someone advised him to approach and grat-

ify Isabel; and not finding another way or thinking it the most effective
way, he had illicit relations with her about four times, caressing her, so
she would heal his wife."[8] According to Antonio, Isabel asked if, when he
became a widower, he would marry her and he responded negatively. At
the time of the case, which in the end was dismissed by the Holy Office
in Mexico, the complainants still could not lead a marital life (AHCM,
box 1236, file 39).

Another case kept in this archive deals with a black woman, María
Manuela Chavira, accused by her mistress of putting a curse on her husband, who was left sick and bound. Margarita de Alvarado, the mistress,
related that in 1750 she had traveled to Valladolid, now Morelia, to find a
cure for a disease that she suffered, and while there, she was sent a black
girl, a virgin, to be hired as a maid. She accepted and asked her husband, Tomás Ortiz, to go find her and take her to the town of Tarímbaro,
where they lived. At night, the husband went to fetch the new maid and,
on the way, "as a man, he was tempted"—he said that he had attempted
to seduce her and that she accepted, but he changed his mind and did
nothing. A few days later the man fell ill with fever that kept him awake
and, according to the wife, although they lay in bed together, they were
"as siblings." Margarita asked her husband what was wrong and he would
not respond, but when she asked in front of the black girl, he pointed to
her and said that only she could cure him. Then he was forced to confess
to his wife what had happened that night he brought the black girl to the
house. Margarita searched María Manuela and discovered a small wax
doll wrapped in rags among her clothes. Then, voluntarily—Manuela assured she was threatened with being hanged from a tree—the black girl
confessed not only to having put a curse on her master for leaving her
"wanting or aroused," but others as well; for example, she had also bound
an *indio*, Matías, whom she had courted, yet he had rejected her saying
he "did not need any dirty blacks." Manuela, offended, bound him. Manuela was forced to heal the *indio* Matías: she took a stalk of maguey on
which there were some figures scratched that, she confessed, represented
the man, and scratching with her fingernail the area corresponding to the
genitals, said that he was cured. The town priest took the black girl into
custody. The next day her master "flew" ("dio un volido") from his bed,
hit himself on a door frame, and died.

Manuela was never prosecuted, the priest died, and everyone forgot about her. It was not until 1762, twelve years later, that Pedro Jaurrieta, the provisional judge of the Diocese of Michoacán, during a visit to the House for Repentant Women in Valladolid, found her and discovered there was not the slightest documented trace of her case (AHCM, box 1238, file 63).

The men affected in these cases meet some of the conditions that make them prone to this curse, according to the authors of the *Malleus Maleficarum:* they are adulterers or fornicators (1971, 60). Again and again, the authors speak of "illicit friendship" that "fragile" men had with women considered to be enchantresses and who took revenge upon being abandoned. In other cases, such as the previous one, men can be punished, not for having sinned, but for *not* sinning with the enchantress.

Sometimes neither the devil nor the witches are content only with impotence and prefer mutilation. Kramer and Sprenger assert that there are two ways in which the devil, through the witches, causes the loss of manhood: one is real and true, and the other illusory. As the reality of the virile member is perceived through the senses of sight and touch, the devil can alter the victim's perception of reality so they cannot perceive more than a smooth surface, even if it is not one. However, they assure that "there is no doubt that certain witches can do marvelous things with regard to male organs, for this agrees with what has been seen and heard by many" (1971, 58). To support this assertion, the authors refer to two similar stories:

In the town of Ratisbon [Germany], a certain young man who had an intrigue with a girl, wishing to leave her, lost his member; that is to say, a spell was cast over it so that he could see or touch nothing but his smooth body. In his worry over this he went to a tavern to drink wine; and after sitting there for a while, he got into conversation with another woman who was there, and told her the cause of his sadness, explaining everything, and demonstrating in his body that it was so. The woman was astute and asked whether he suspected anyone; and when he named the girl, she said: "If persuasion is not enough, you must use some violence to induce her to restore to you your health." So, in the evening the young man watched the way the witch was in the habit of going, and finding her, begged her to restore his body's health. And when she maintained that she was innocent and knew nothing about it, he fell upon her, and winding a towel tightly about her neck, choked her, saying: "Unless you give me back my health, you shall die at my hands." Unable to cry out, and with her face already swelling and growing black, she said: "Let me go, and I will heal you." The young man then relaxed the pressure of the towel, and the witch touched him with her hand between the thighs, saying: "Now you have what you desire." And the young man, as he afterwards said, plainly felt, before he had verified it by looking or touching, that his member had been restored to him by the mere touch of the witch.

A similar experience is narrated by a certain venerable Dominican,[9] well known in the order for his chaste life and learning. "One day," he says, "while I was hearing confessions, a young man came to me and, in the course of his confession, woefully said that he had lost his member. Being astonished at this, and not being willing to give it easy credence, since to the wise it is a mark of frivolity to believe too easily, I had proof when the young man removed his clothes and I saw nothing where the member should be. Then, using the wisest counsel, I asked whether he suspected anyone of having so bewitched him. And the young man said that he did suspect someone, but that she was absent and living in Worms. Then I said: 'I advise you to go to her as soon as possible and try your utmost to soften her with gentle words and promises'; and he did so, for he came back after a few days and thanked me, saying that he was whole and had recovered everything. And I believed his words, but again I proved them by the evidence before my own eyes." (1971, 119)

About three centuries after the *Malleus Maleficarum* was published, across the Atlantic we find an account that similarly describes the same condition. In the same long record on the witches of Monclova referred to earlier, we find four cases of magical castration. In January 1751, the soldier Joaquín de la Garza,[10] married, fifty-five years of age, indicated that he had gone to the home of a Spanish woman named María de Hinojosa, to fetch the food she was sending to her husband, also a soldier. But the woman asked him to show her the food for another companion, Pedro Javier Ramón. When Joaquín refused, the woman thrust herself upon him; he stopped her with his arm, dodged her and left. But, soon after, when he came to the river bank, he had the urge to urinate; he stopped, dismounted his horse and then discovered "that he was as a woman": his member had completely disappeared, although in another statement he said that, instead, it had become a little button the size of a hazel-nut. There were several eyewitnesses to his body's appearance: his wife, Rosa García, Lieutenant Felipe Joaquín de Yruegas, and the notary of the Holy Office Juan Ignacio de Castilla y Rioja, who stated that Joaquín de la Garza came to his house to confess what had happened to him. The notary, as was the case with the Dominican in the *Malleus,* asked him to show proof, which is why he alleged he was eyewitness to what Joaquín said and it was true. When the soldier was asked if he was bound while the illness lasted, about two and a half months, he responded in the affir-mative in terms of the activity, but not in terms of desire.

María de Hinojosa was no stranger to the commissioner Vilaplana: just a few weeks earlier the commissioner had arrived in Monclova with the mandate of prison and sequestration of property for her and four other women and two men in dealing with the celebrated case that José Toribio Medina called "the complicity of Coahuila" in his *Historia del Tri-bunal del Santo Oficio de la Inquisición en México* (History of the Tribunal of the Holy Office of the Inquisition in Mexico) (2010, 377). The proceed-ings involving the accused reflect the European witch stereotypes, which included making pact with the devil, night flight, attending the coven— not for being lesser in size was it less heretical—and casting spells. The witch hunt began when María de Hinojosa dropped a bag with hexes, among which there was a lodestone wrapped in hair and other bundles intended to attract the soldier Pedro Javier Ramón. As she did not get the other soldier's food from Joaquín de la Garza, in revenge, she caused the accident described.[11]

Loss of the virile member is not the only effect mentioned in the case of the Monclova witches. The cashier for the governor, Manuel Andrés del Moral y Zevallos, states that one day his private parts became as when he was a child and, unlike Joaquín de la Garza, he had also lost sexual drive. The notary Juan Ignacio de Castilla y Rioja wrote in the certification that he was eyewitness to the fact that Manuel Andrés del Moral was without "man's natural function" for over three years. Manuel Andrés del Moral said that at first, he did not suspect it was a curse, but while imprisoned, the *india* Frigenia, one of the important protagonists of this case, assured him it was a curse that she herself had put by request of the *mulata* Felipa Guevara. The *india* told him that the spell consisted of a few powders, and that just throwing them on the victim was enough to have them take effect. Initially, the *mulata* wanted the curse to harm another man she was already living with, but this man was away from Monclova and Felipa had a brief affair with the cashier. When he abandoned her, Felipa requested the spell from the *india,* who gave her some powders dissolved in the chocolate that she offered Andrés. The notary Castilla y Rioja ordered the *india* Frigenia to heal the man. The *india* led the notary to a hill to search among the bushes for a small red fruit known as *capul.* This fruit, crushed and mixed with warm water, was given to the cashier to drink, and fifteen days later he had recuperated (AGN, Inquisition, vol. 827, file 2, ff. 112r–113r and vol. 935, file 1, ff. 94v–95r).

There is a third case in Monclova in the mid-eighteenth century: Manuela Salvadora, mestiza, married, twenty-eight years of age, hexed her *compadre,* Alonso Muñiz, making him as a woman, because he left her (AGN, Inquisition, vol. 827, file 1, f. 66v). Lastly, Lucrecia de la Garza left the soldier Nicolás Cadena without his virile parts over a quarrel they had had (AGN, Inquisition, vol 827, file 2, f. 143v).

We cannot know how much is truth and how much is fiction in these four cases,[12] but the insistence with which different men claim to have been victims of the loss of their virile member shows us that the belief in witches' power to cause this type of damage was very much alive, and how easy this belief spread among the people.

Moira Smith emphasizes that the appeal of the stories in the *Malleus Maleficarum* has caused readers to lose sight of the framework of skepticism that surrounds them. She observes that the authors claim that the devil can make those who suffer the curse, and those who witness it, see something that in reality is not there, because the devil can circumvent the external senses of sight and touch, and, although it cannot intervene in the internal senses—fantasy and imagination—these can be influenced by the external, so that particularly those who do not have a clear conscience may see and feel things different from what they really are (1971, 119–20).

Indeed, according to Kramer and Sprenger, this occurs when the devil acts by means of witches; however, they end by saying, "And it may be asked, if the devil by himself and without any witch removes anyone's virile member, whether there is any difference between one sort of deprivation and the other. First, in addition to what has been said in the First Part of this book on the question, 'Whether witches can remove a member,' he does actually remove it, and it is actually restored when it has to be restored. Second, just as it is not removed without injury, so it is not restored without pain" (1971, 122). Noting that some authors consider absurd the belief that the virile member can be amputated temporarily by magical means, Smith quotes Richard Kieckhefer, who in his book *European Witch Trials: Their Foundation in Popular and Learned Culture, 1300–1500* opines that this image is absent from popular culture and therefore must be the product of the authors' disorderly mind. She counters, however, that these stories are evidence that fear of magical impotence is widespread in popular culture from antiquity to the present (Smith 2002, 92).

Now, when the penises are stolen, what happens to them? Kramer and Sprenger end their thoughts on the subject of magical castration with the following unusual narration:

And what, then, is to be thought of those witches who in this way sometimes collect male organs in great numbers, as many as twenty or thirty members together, and put them in a bird's nest, or shut them up in a box, where they move like living members, and eat oats and corn, as has been seen by many and is a matter of common report? It is to be said that it is all done by devil's work and illusion, for the senses of those who see them are deluded in the way we have said. For a certain man tells that, when he had lost his member, he approached a known witch to ask her to restore it to him. She told the afflicted man to climb a certain tree, and that he might take the one he liked from the nest in which there were several members. And when he tried to take a large one, the witch said: You must not take that one; adding, because it belongs to a parish priest. (1971, 121)[13]

Many researchers have tried to find an explanation for this narrative's appearance in a book that, given its content and scope, has been deemed the most infamous on the subject. Smith points out that several reasons have been proposed, from Kramer having a pathological obsession with sex that allowed him to believe such stories, which he must have heard many times, to his suffering from a crisis of faith that needed to be reinforced with supernatural stories supported by tradition (2002, 110).

The story is, of course, burlesque. On the one hand, the association of the penis with birds appears in many cultures: Smith shows how in the slang of various languages terms semantically related to birds are used to refer to the virile member (98). On the other hand, the story's reference to the priest's large member belongs to the tradition of anticlerical mockery that deals with the sexual immorality of priests and friars and highlights their reputation as excellent lovers, both for their wealth and for their virile potency (Alzieu 1984, 107). The theme, recorded in Stith Thompson's *Motif-Index of Folklore-Literature* as "Recognition of monk by his large organ" (H79.7), appears in medieval and Renaissance tales and popular poems, as in the following medieval Spanish poem:

> The ladies have much love
> For the father prior,
> Because he carries a long
> Do-re-mi-fa-sol.
> (Frenk no. 2635)[14]

The following Spanish folk song refers to sexual relationships between friars and nuns as well as to organ size:

> Fifty friars depart
> From Seville
> With staffs of great length
> And large saddlebags.
> Fifty nuns
> Depart from Toledo
> In search of the friars

And their saddlebags.
(Frenk no. 2638)[15]

However, we must ask, what is an anticlerical joke doing in a book written by priests for priests? For Smith, the explanation is that the treatise is addressed to the inquisitors, that is, men of the same ecclesiastical hierarchy as the authors, and that the joke is intended to make fun of lower-ranking priests. Kramer's sense of humor allowed a tongue-in-cheek gesture in his otherwise very serious manual (Smith 2002, 106–8).

The *Malleus Maleficarum,* like many subsequent treatises, is full of popular accounts, short stories with a long life in the oral tradition. The authors have apparently adapted these narratives, reformulating them and incorporating them as examples of their theoretical approach. Over time and through the dissemination of the content of these manuals, whether by priests at mass, or by the authorities at the trials, these stories—more entertaining than the theories they exemplified—were recontextualized and transmitted within popular culture. Their themes and motifs, therefore, circulated widely across cultures and remain popular to this day.

Gustav Henningsen speaks of a "black gospel" when referring to the popular beliefs that crossed the Atlantic along with the missionaries who brought Christianity to the New World. A wealth of beliefs, superstitions, and rites was introduced in New Spain and rapidly disseminated and syncretized with indigenous beliefs and practices, shaping them into a common system (Henningsen 1994, 10). The inquisitorial testimonies included here demonstrate how, in eighteenth-century New Spain, magical impotence became part of the cultural heritage. Therefore, when there arose this kind of a sexual problem, whether due to some physiological or psychological malaise, the people did not doubt its cause and testified that it resulted from a curse.

NOTES

1. Esther Cohen states, "In many ways, it could be said that the *Malleus* is a treatise on the weaknesses of the body, an inordinate attack against sexual pleasures of the so-called witches, who do nothing but to expose the pleasures of women in general, but even

more specifically, the *Malleus* unmasks the erotic fantasies of the men who described them" (2003, 27). However, Kramer and Sprenger were not the initiators of these ideas: as asserted in the treatise, everything has been taken from different authorities: the Bible, Aristotle, the Patristics, and collections of decrees, among other sources.

2. Moira Smith says that the "technical term for the practice in English is *ligature* (French, *nouer l'aiguillette;* German, *Nestelknüpfen*), because the most common method for casting this spell involved tying knots in a cord or string, sometimes accompanied by the pronunciation of various spells" (2002, 92–93). That is also why a ligature meant to unite two people is called in Spanish *amarre* or *atadura* (binding or tying). This type of spell, examples of which can be found in all times and places, persists to this day.

3. The authors of the *Malleus Maleficarum* dedicated Chapter III to this topic,: from Question II: "Remedies prescribed for those who are Bewitched by being inflamed with Inordinate Love or Extraordinary Hatred" (1971, 170–73).

4. "Señor sant Silvestre del Montemayor, ansí como encortaste la doncella y el varón, así me encorteis a fulano, desde el miembro hasta el compañón, que no pueda tratar con mujer viuda ni casada ni de ninguna manera de estado, sino conmigo. Fulano, venga, venga y que nadie le detenga." Juan Blázquez Miguel relates that the Decrees of Burchard, bishop of Worms, already mention the peasants' fear of being rendered impotent by a curse which consisted in tying three knots in a handkerchief or rope. Blázquez says that, even in the 1950s, at weddings, family members on the groom's side kept an eye out for any female guest tying knots in her handkerchief (1989, 268, n. 50).

5. "Oración de la ánima sorda y muda. Padre Eterno, soberano dios, etc. Anima, ánima, ánima sola, que gimes y lloras por montes y valles: yo te llamo y te necesito para que me vayas a buscar nueve ánimas de Limos, nueve necesito, nueve me has de traer, tres ahorcadas, tres arcabuceadas y tres muertas desgraciadas. Estas nueve ánimas retorcerán en la cabeza de _____ y otra vez se volverán, y no lo dejarán pasar, vivir ni comer, ni beberá, ni descansará, ni enamorará a ninguna otra, no volverá a pensar [más que] en mí, todo aborrecerá, ni con otra tendrá poder, sólo conmigo. Hasta que rabiando como un perro, humilde y manso, desesperado y loco de amor, solo por mí, como Jesucristo tuvo que morir en la Cruz. Así tú ven _____, ven a rogarme con todo tu amor _____ ven que te necesito. Amén."

6. AHCM (Archivo Histórico Casa de Morelos). All cases are from the Diocesan Fund, Justice Section, Inquisition Series; only the docket and the record are indicated. The documents stored in this archive belong to the Bishopric of Michoacán.

7. It should be noted that when the gentilic "Spanish" appears in the documents, it refers to both the Peninsular and the Criollo.

8. "Deseoso siempre y anhelando por la salud de su mujer, hubo quien le aconsejara que procurara gratificar y llevarse bien con Isabel; y no hallando otro modo o pareciéndole el más eficaz, la trató ilícitamente y reincidió con ella unas cuatro veces, acariciándola al fin de que le sanara a su esposa."

9. According to André Schnyder, the reference was to Kramer himself (Smith 2002, 89).

10. Fray Hermenegildo Vilaplana writes in the margin of the statement he took from Joaquin de la Garza seven months later: "He is held as a man of honor and truth, and gave statement with plenty of shame."

11. The statements pertaining to the condition of Joaquín de la Garza are found in the following records of the Inquisition branch of the AGNM (Archivo General de la Nación México): vol. 827, file 2, ff. 111v–112r; vol. 935, file 1, ff. 104v–105r and 119.

12. There exists a psychiatric disorder known as "genital retraction syndrome," or *koro*, characterized by fear or the feeling that the genitals are shrinking or retracting into the body. While primarily occurring in southeast Asia, China, and west Africa, cases have also been reported in Europe and the United States. According to Moira Smith, following Robert E. Bartholomew, "In areas where belief in *koro* and related maladies is common, there may be outbreaks of mass rumor-panics or collective delusions, where hundreds or even thousands of sufferers are afflicted at once in a relatively short time" (2002, 95–96). This could explain why so many men in Monclova exhibited the same disorder.

13. See Smith (2002) for the long tradition where this image is inserted.

14. "Mucho quieren las damas /al padre prior, /porque tiene muy largo /su re-mi-fa-sol" (Frenk 2003, No. 2635).

15. "Salen de Sevilla / cincuenta frayles / con bordones de a palmo / y alforjas grandes. / De Toledo parten / cincuenta monjas, / a buscar los frayles /y sus alforjas" (Frenk 2003, No. 2638).

WORKS CITED

Aguirre Beltrán, Gonzalo. 1963. *Medicina y magia: El proceso de aculturación en la estructura colonial*. Ciudad de México: Instituto Nacional Indigenista/Secretaría de Educación Pública.

Alzieu, Pierre, Robert Jammes, and Iván Lissorgues, eds. 1984. *Poesía erótica del Siglo de Oro*. Barcelona: Crítica.

Blázquez Miguel, Juan. 1989. *Eros y Tánatos: Brujería, hechicería y superstición en España*. Toledo: Arcano.

Cohen, Esther. 2003. *Con el diablo en el cuerpo*. Ciudad de México: Universidad Nacional Autónoma de México.

Frenk, Margit. 2003. *Nuevo corpus de la antigua lírica popular hispánica (Siglos XV a XVII)*. Ciudad de México: Universidad Nacional Autónoma de México/El Colegio de México/Fondo de Cultura Económica.

Henningsen, Gustav. 1994. "La evangelización negra: Difusión de la magia europea en la América colonial." *Revista de la Inquisición* 3: 9–27.

Iruegas, Gustavo. 2015. *La complicidad de Coahuila.* Coahuila de Zaragoza: Secretaría de
    Cultura, Gobierno del Estado de Coahuila de Zaragoza.

Kramer, Heinrich, and Jacob Sprenger. 1971. *The Malleus Maleficarum,* ed. Montagne
    Summers. New York: Dover.

López-Ridaura, Cecilia. 2011. "Las brujas de Coahuila: Realidad y ficción en un pro-
    ceso inquisitorial novohispano del siglo XVIII." PhD diss., Universidad Nacional
    Autónoma, Ciudad de México.

———. 2012. "Las brujas de Coahuila, un proceso emblemático del norte de la Nueva
    España." In *Espejo de brujas: Mujeres transgresoras a través de la Historia,* ed. María
    Jesús Zamora Calvo and Alberto Ortiz, 115–33. Madrid: Abada Editores/Universidad
    Autónoma de Zacatecas.

———. 2014. "La caza de brujas en la Nueva España: Monclova." *e-Humanista: Journal of
    Iberian Studies* 26: 234–63.

Medina, José Toribio. 2010. *Historia del Tribunal del Santo Oficio de la Inquisición en
    México.* Ciudad de México: Consejo Nacional para la Cultura y las Artes.

Semboloni, Lara. 2004. "Cacería de brujas en Coahuila, 1748–1751: De Villa en Villa, sin
    Dios ni Santa María." *Historia Mexicana* 66, no. 2: 325–64.

Smith, Moira. 2002. "The Flaying Phallus and the Laughing Inquisitor: Penis Theft in the
    Malleus Maleficarum." *Journal of Folklore Research* 39, no. 1: 85–117.

Thompson, Stith. 1955–58. *Motif-Index of Folk-Literature: A Classification of Narrative El-
    ements in Folktales, Ballads, Myths, Fables, Mediaeval Romances, Exempla, Fabliaux,
    Jest-Books, and Local Legends.* Bloomington: Indiana University Press.

✝

Midwives, Folk Medicine, and Magic in Early Modern Mexico

ROBIN ANN RICE

In early modern Mexico, midwives were, practically speaking, the only caregivers available to assist mothers during childbirth, and this remained true well into the nineteenth century. In fact, "male professionals did not actually attend women giving birth on either side of the Atlantic until before the seventeenth century," and even after that, the number was negligible (Jaffary 2016, 48). In general, these midwives were not European, as proven by the fact that the majority of those who were tried by the Inquisition between 1566 and 1888[1] were listed as mulatto or "African-Mexican." Further, the majority of midwives during this period were middle-aged or older, and normally widowed or single—only in a few cases were midwives married (Jaffary 2016, 48–51).

In New Spain, midwifery did not exactly lead to prosperity, but it paid better than other female professions. In the different studies on the range of activities covered by midwives who were tried by the Inquisition, it is apparent that this type of caregiving was not just about delivering children. Steeped in Pre-Columbian folk medicine combined with medieval European superstitious practices, pseudoscientific cures and magic had no bright-line distinction between them. Midwives gained the trust of their patients and many times were pushed beyond their limit of expertise by their very clients. But the key to understanding the complicit relationship between the midwife or healer and her clients is the stories revealed in the Inquisition records, in which Europeans and locals normally acquiesced to the midwives' recommendations and antidotes for a whole range of ailments related not only to birthing but also to love woes, bad luck, and loved ones' waning interest. When the cures did not work, disgruntled clients were more likely to consider an accusation. Some studies, such as those of Nora Jaffary or Úrsula Camba, allege that clients and the generally devout-minded public were more likely to denounce mulatto or Afro-Mexican midwives than they were to denounce those of other races.

The purpose of this study is to review the extent to which New Spain medical conventions possibly encouraged not only women, but specifically mulatto and Afro-Mexican women, to involve themselves in this line of patient care. Moreover, the types of problems that pregnant and birthing women had might have been metaphorically extended to other human existential problems. The cures used combined medieval Christian superstition with Pre-Columbian and African folk medicine. Besides reviewing these traditions, this essay will study several cases presented before the Inquisition to illustrate the accuseds' possible misunderstanding or misinterpretation of early modern Mexican midwifery.

As early as the middle of the sixteenth century, Mexican society became more complex with the introduction of African slaves and a growing mestizo population. Economic codependence among this racially and socially blended viceroyalty caused very porous borders, which allowed constant interchanges between the various echelons. According to Pilar Gonzalbo, as the number of unemployed, vagabond Spanish settlers increased in New Spain, social status based on race became nebulous (2013, 50). As race became more ambiguous, elements such as family origins and social reputation became more important to determine community respect than were ethnic and physical traits (54). Race was not everything and values based on social-cultural strata made the biggest distinction. For that reason, it should not surprise us that the black, mulatto, and mestizo midwives and healers discussed in this work had alliances, clients, and confidantes from all walks of life. They were important, respected members of their local communities and in many cases, they were the primary caregivers.

In the seventeenth century, Mexican medical practices were divided into two types. On the one hand, the European elite were normally, but not exclusively, attended by doctors whose core beliefs belied an emotional, religion-based medical tradition that was mixed with certain scientific experimental practices. However, much of the population was treated using medieval folk medicine, brought to Mexico from Spain, that consisted of rational practices interwoven with gospels, magic spells, and exorcisms (Aguirre 1973, 35) combined with indigenous traditional medicine. To give us an idea of how widespread nonconventional, semi-superstitious medicine was, we need only look at population. In 1646, the total population in Mexico was 1,712,615, of which 1,269,607 (74.1 percent) were indigenous, 277,610 mestizos (16.2 percent), 151,618 blacks and mulattoes (8.8 percent), and only 13,780 Europeans (8 percent) (Lagunas 2010, 96). It is apparent from these numbers that most people were treated using folk medicine.

Spanish professionals, university-educated and trained in western medicine, were scarce and thus unable to attend to the needs of the small European population, which leads us to believe that the indigenous, black, and mixed races had to fend for themselves. In one of his letters to the emperor, Hernán Cortés insisted on the futility of importing European doctors to the New World because he considered their medicine to be on a par with that of the natives (Aguirre 1973, 80). The situation apparently had not improved after several centuries, since to exemplify this Jaffary cites a 1788 Jesuit medical treatise printed in Mexico that stated women's labor could be facilitated by "drinking the urine of their husbands when they were on the point of giving birth" (2016, 179). The Spanish and New Spain *Boticario general,* widely endorsed by European medical sources, recommended a "solution of horse manure diluted in wine" that supposedly helped desperate women in labor give birth more speedily (Jaffary 2016, 179). Later on, when certain invaluable, indigenous medical scripts had been recovered, they were quickly suppressed and censored. Indigenous, mestizo, black, and mulatto healers incorporated Christian magic, indigenous medicine, and African science to form a new corpus of medicine to treat the 99 percent of the population left unattended by European doctors (Aguirre 1973, 81). Old World and New World traditions believed in amulet sashes from which hung common trinkets such as "deer's eye seeds, *azabache* hand charms, crocodile teeth" (Jaffary 2016, 181) for birthing women.

Many folk cures used bone fragments, skin, umbilical cords, and blood. These folk cures were closely analogous to Christian beliefs that put great faith in the same bodily components of saints to perform miracles under the guise of relics. Besides that, the Holy Office was very aware of the perception that Christianity put great store in what could appear to be the magical powers of spells and prayers (Aguirre 1973, 267). Mestizo medicine was very receptive and thus was enriched by new and constant indigenous, black, and Spanish healing developments (Aguirre 1973, 276). At the beginning, the Inquisition established that the Spanish should set an example for the newly converted castes; however, that did not work. Instead the Spanish transmitted medieval magical thinking, thus contaminating the natives' already ensorcelled system with "misconstrued beliefs and superstitions" (Behar 1987, 35). As the population grew and urban gentrification became more hybrid, the various belief systems became even further interwoven.

For many reasons, mulatto, black, and mestizo women in New Spain were physically and socially freer than their indigenous or Spanish counterparts. When women were of a certain age and widowed, they obtained even more autonomy. Spanish women, especially those who were of a certain social standing, were protected and locked away in their households or convents, while indigenous women were safeguarded in their communities or Indian villages. Female African slaves frequently worked as maids and could eventually buy their freedom. One example is María de la Cruz, who was allowed to have part-time jobs and thus was able to buy her freedom from her owner (Camba 2008, 16). Once emancipated, these former slaves sometimes had small businesses such as inns and *pulquerías* (bars serving *pulque,* an alcoholic drink) that gave them income to live more comfortably. In 1650, Veracruz had a population of six thousand people, five thousand of which had African origins (Roselló 2014, 231). Widows had a special status: while young girls were under parental custody, others were tied to marital or clerical authority. Widowhood seemed to be an ideal state and could have allowed for independence and upward economic mobility (Camba 2008, 18).

One of the most interesting cases of this aspirational frame of mind combined with pseudoscientific job skills is that of Josepha de Zárate, nicknamed "Mother Chepa," a mestizo or mulatto widow of roughly forty years of age who was tried by the Inquisition in the second decade of the eighteenth century.[2] In the documentation on the case, the woman is alternately called mestizo and mulatto. She is referred to in the files using both denominations, which she herself might have encouraged to take advantage of whichever caste suited her according to the situation; in seventeenth-century Veracruz, it probably was not very easy to know the difference. Although originally from the Tuxtlas, where her mestizo father owned a ranch, her productive life was carried out in the port city of Veracruz, where she was taken to live at the age of twelve after marrying a mestizo man. Between 1721 and 1723, she was accused of, and then charged with, superstition and witchcraft. As a sign of her mercantile mentality, Josepha had a boarding house that catered to recently anchored Spanish sailors who frequently arrived sick after the long expedition across the ocean. In fact, she was known as the mariners' protector.

By 1713, Veracruz boasted of a booming business providing lodging, meals, health care, and other services to the travelers arriving at its port. Inns were always under suspicion. Indeed, they often fostered brothels due to the high traffic of foreign sailors. Veracruz was one of the most important ports through which merchandise and humans entered New Spain. Mother Chepa knew how to take advantage of the situation: she was a midwife and also cured people with what seems to be a very typical kind of folk medicine (Camba 2008, 17–18). She was also quite popular, which gave her the opportunity to come into contact with many people in the community. The precarious health system, coupled with the already porous social and racial perimeters, gave women like Mother Chepa access to European private living quarters in order to provide their services.

One of her boarders was a Spanish sailor by the name of Francisco Juan Salas. One day he came home incredibly angry because he had lost money at gambling. As he was very distraught, Mother Chepa told him that she had a remedy that could bring him financial luck. The antidote was a lodestone and powders that she prepared for him in a packet to carry around. The good-luck charms did not work, though, and he continued being angry and disappointed. One day Francisco ran into a fellow sailor and countryman named Pablo Ferrer and he recommended that he obtain lodging at Josepha's. After living there for a few days Pablo realized that he could not afford the place. When he commented on this to Mother Chepa, he claimed, the widow gave him a paper relic that contained a small piece of a newborn's placenta and a wrapper holding thin, dried-up skin. The woman allegedly assured him he would achieve maritime safety, success in his endeavors, and a guarantee that he would never be held prisoner and he would have financial good fortune. He said she told him to take the package and its contents to the local Jesuit church, place it under the altar, and leave it there until three masses had been said surreptitiously over it. His friend Francisco Salas accompanied him to the church to see if the good luck might rub off on him. However, Pablo Ferrer became ill and had to be hospitalized. He alleged that instead of having good luck, he constantly felt as if he had a stone in the pit of his stomach, light-headedness, and anxiety. Even though he followed the innkeeper's instructions to take the relics to the church and have masses said over them, none of his wishes was granted. Their friend Juan Flores found out what Francisco and Pablo had done and scolded them, but they insisted that nothing could have gone awry because the cure had involved masses and the church.

Mother Chepa had no problems with the men until the spell did not work and they became scornful of the woman. The contemptuous men accused her of being a conjurer and a sorceress. True to the thinking of his times, Pablo never imagined that his actions reeked of superstition probably because church and masses were involved. Of course, Mother Chepa denied everything and insisted that Spaniards were bad people, steeped in vice and addicted to gambling. Besides, according to the woman, it was Francisco himself who offered to do tricks to change everyone's luck (Camba 2008, 19). Indeed, Mother Chepa's income was based on benefits coming from tending to the sailors but also from her services as a midwife and curing all types of afflictions: physical, emotional, and economic. When she was interrogated about the dried-up skin, she affirmed that she was a midwife and a healer and that it was from a snake and was used for side aches, fever, and scorpion bites.

The Inquisition qualifiers determined that Josepha should be judged and three years after being denounced, she was condemned to public humiliation and was banned from Veracruz, Mexico City, and anywhere within six leagues around for ten years. The first four years she had to be secluded in a shelter for fallen women in Puebla called the Recogimiento de la Magdalena y Santa María Egipciaca. But Mother Chepa was a shining example of upward mobility. In the inventory of her goods seized by the Inquisition, we find that she kept a slave woman and her small son, evidence that, as in other cases of mulatto women in Veracruz, she earned enough to have servants and to support them. She had people to serve her, her own house, an important job, and she enjoyed living with imported commodities even if they were timeworn.

The forty-year-old was accused of being maleficent, superstitious, and a master of witchcraft. The qualifiers suspected that she had a pact with the devil because of the magic means she used to acquire riches through gambling and other ways. Based on these charges, the Holy Office functionaries determined that her goods should be embargoed and that she should be locked up in the inquisitorial qualifiers' jail in Mexico City. The day she was imprisoned, she wore a rosary with a Saint Benito bronze medal around her neck as part of her penitence. (While the saint is identified with the Inquisition, he was also revered among blacks and mulattoes in Veracruz.) However, she was also wearing some gold-and-pearl earrings and a straw hat. When Mother Chepa arrived to be jailed, how she was dressed and what she had packed were indicative of her enterprising frame of mind and a marked upwardly mobile attitude. Besides the jewelry that she was wearing, she had on a shawl made of satin from China, a fawn-colored apron skirt from Ceylon, a petticoat, a white waistcoat from Brittany, a very old linen blouse with lace on the sleeves, and knit stockings. To afford herself some comfort during her prison time, she brought with her an old striped silk mattress and two old sheets from Brittany. Her dress and accessories are indicative of many things. First, she was very careful to make a good impression by dressing up even if it were to go to jail. As a woman who had an important role and status in her community, appearances were important, especially for professional purposes. After all, as a midwife she went in and out of her patients' houses, and she also had foreigners staying at her inn, which served as a makeshift infirmary. Her work had been an important vehicle to forge her reputation, prestige, and social respect. Second, she herself was a mixture of cultures and races, and she came in contact on a regular basis

with humans from all walks of life who disembarked at the Veracruz sea-
port. Luxury goods and exotic foreign products arrived at Veracruz from
abroad and were redistributed throughout New Spain. Her dress was em-
blematic of someone who wanted to show that she too was an eager recip-
ient of these foreign sumptuary goods. She had probably pulled herself up
from nothing and wanted to show where she had landed.

The woman's interactions were with a sphere wider than the Spanish
seamen with whom she dealt. She was, as previously mentioned, a midwife, so her comings and goings had to do with the more intimate and
yet all-encompassing world of everyday female well-being. Therefore, she
was sought out to help with birthing, general health, and love sickness.
She was contacted directly by other women, such as María, who asked her
for an antidote to her husband Martín's lack of interest in her. Juliana de la
Rosa petitioned the woman for a spell to get back at a man who had used
her and then caused her harm. But more importantly, besides her work
in love spells and sorcery, many people pursued her for actual healing.
Mother Chepa took her job seriously and the Inquisition's inventory of her
goods testifies to that. Faithful to the type of medicine frequently practiced in seventeenth-century Mexico, the list included snake skin, an as-
sortment of colored powders, all kinds of water, crystal jars, various types
of elixirs, pieces of deer antler, and other vials with potions that illustrate
Josepha's active and probably daily medical practice. She herself describes
using many of these products to cure blood hemorrhages, sores, and
other physical ailments. Her own great niece testified that she frequently
visited her aunt to borrow a pestle used to grind peppers that Josepha
had recommended to knead and soothe her son's bumps and bruises.

Mother Chepa was very versatile and knew how to market her services to a wide public consisting of both men and women. She was an
elderly widow of unknown lineage who could come into contact with
an ample and varied population without raising suspicions. In a society
in which university-trained doctors were more than scarce and attended
the well-off Spanish and Creole segments of the population, Josepha
must have been a great blessing to foreign sailors, people of color, and
downtrodden Europeans. Deep down, her magical intent to help suffering wives, scorned women, and unlucky, needy gamblers was an early

modern attempt to provide psychological help and hope to an insecure population in an age of flux. To a community that did not know any better, these talismanic, ritualistic verbal formulas and potions could actually seem quite akin to church practices and miracles. Saints' relics, prayers and responses, holy oils and water, ashes could all seem quite analogous to what Mother Chepa was dispensing. Added to that was the fact that some of her charms had to be taken to the church for blessings or masses, which could have easily confused and dumbfounded an already superstitious community.

The midwife probably did not think that she was in the wrong. During her interrogation, she declared that she was a good Christian, had been baptized, confirmed, and went to mass as much as she could, went to confession, and received communion on holy days of obligation. To prove all of this, she showed the inquisitors that she could make the Sign of the Cross correctly and could unerringly recite the "Our Father," "Hail Mary," the "Apostles Creed," and the Ten Commandments. She herself had her faith printed on her body: on her left hand were tattoos of a rosary and an image of Jesus. She frequently used a composite of Catholic symbols and practices to carry out her magic and cures and thus gain community respect. She used Christian symbols in her magic which she herself revered and extolled.

As mentioned earlier, the midwife had a medal of San Benito, whose brotherhood in Veracruz endeavored to have female members in its ranks. It is probable that the midwife had acquired individual and collective agency in this brotherhood because of the appellative "Mother"—an honorific title—that was bestowed on her and other women who had become important and influential members. The female members of this brotherhood were well known for their active role in economic administration and the organization of feast day parties, as well as in relief aid for which the association was famous (Roselló 2014, 84–85). Therefore, for the Inquisition to try for sorcery a "Mother" from the Saint Benito brotherhood could have been shocking to many in her community.

As mentioned earlier, in 1724 the Holy Office found the midwife guilty of superstition and of being a cheat and she was paraded around with those insignias. She was to march around the city of Veracruz while being whipped two hundred times and was exiled for ten years and placed in seclusion in the Magdalena retreat house in Puebla, Mexico. Nevertheless, the midwife had a true belief in what she did, felt that her cures were effective, and was empathetic toward the people who told her their woes. Proof of that is seen in her actions during her reclusion in Puebla. A Spanish woman also imprisoned in the Magdalena asked her for a spell so that her husband would free her from jail. Mother Chepa had her repeat an esoteric incantation five times. The sorceress was reported and threatened and no more is to be found about her fate after that incident.

Other Examples and Considerations

The cases reviewed of black and mulatto women taken before the Inquisition for witchcraft reveal examples of subjects who were openly Catholic practitioners, well known in their communities, and sought out for their expertise. These social groups generally lived in tight quarters where gossip was rampant. Witnesses went before the officials because they themselves were afraid or felt guilty. Many times, the very witnesses were also healers or palm readers or provided the accused with supplies to make their potions. Rhonda Gonzales claims that "these Black and Mulatta women, free and enslaved, participated in dynamic communities that involved complicated relationships that were unbounded by ethnic category" (2013, 4).

One such case is that of María Vásquez, a free black woman living in Salaya, Michoacán, who was called to the attention of the Inquisition in 1614 for her "treatment of a sick child who ultimately died" (Gonzales 2013, 4). Curiously, the child had died six years before the witness— also a healer—stepped forth. From afar, it appears that the elixir had not worked and six years later, the healer was accused of causing the child's death through witchcraft. It all began when María Vásquez was witnessed frequenting the house of a Spanish woman slave owner named María de Torres. A testifier said that she had seen the two women talking and exchanging articles that were used to make remedies that were secretly mixed with the slave owner's husband's chocolate beverages to better his disposition. One of the slave owner's own servants testified against her, saying that she had seen María Vásquez, the supposed sorceress, and the slave owner, María de Torres, whispering together in the presence of the sick child. The child was given a holy card folded in half with a picture of a saint (2013, 4). The women also prayed over an "incense-burning altar" (2013 5). Another time, the Spanish woman sent some "small white bones and wings" which she had received from the healer to be ground up and she then put the concoction in her husband's tea so as "to 'bind' him" to her. On other occasions, the slave owner had sent her servant to the black witch's house to pick up potions that she urgently needed (2013, 5). Although many of the witnesses were initially under suspicion and a few of them were also soothsayers or healers, all of the attention suddenly began to focus on María Vásquez. Practically used as a magician scapegoat, the black healer was accused of acts as far back as six years and by people who had gone to her for help or had participated in similar activities.

An interesting series of cases involved several black and mulatto women who had immigrated to the northwest of Mexico, to San Miguel de Culiacán in Nueva Galicia. The Mexican northern frontier regions were mainly populated by indigenous peoples and in this particular community by about thirty Spanish families dedicated to farming, business, and mining. The first groups of blacks and mulattos to arrive in this zone did so as part of the entourage of Spanish captains and soldiers that had set out to explore and conquer this unknown part of the viceroyalty (Baena 2016, 40).

In the Mexican outer frontiers such as Nueva Galicia and Nueva Vizcaya, the presence of the Inquisition was null and the Church was aware that magical and superstitious beliefs and practices probably ran rampant with very little much done about it, as indicated by the scarcity in the number of files sent from there to the city of Mexico for legal execution. However, in the third decade of the seventeenth century, a general edict was pronounced of which one in particular was against astrologers, star-reading soothsayers, necromancers, and witch doctors (Baena 2016, 42–43). If there was an edict, it was normally generated by an outbreak of the type of activity described therein.

Many of the midwives were free mulatto women who sold vegetables and food on the side. The specific transgressions were committed by mu-

latto women, but Spanish and mestizo women are also mentioned in the
accusations. Since giving birth was a risky business and many mothers
and their newborns died in the process, there were certain practices commonly carried out by the midwives. Pregnant women traditionally wore
necklaces with relics, good-luck charms, and talismans to protect them.
While giving birth they invoked saints and lit candles. The trouble started
at the end of the birthing process when the midwives tried to deliver the
placenta. During this stage, they insisted that the mothers take off their
religious medals and at times, that they drink dirt mixed with water or
dirt from the hinges of three different doors (Baena 2016, 43–44, 48).
Removing the medals and drinking the dirty water were meant to help
expeditiously deliver the placenta. Drinking water with dirt seems to have
come from folk Jewish customs, indicating the great jumble of superstitious world customs inherited by the New World through European and
African settlers.

The mulatto midwives were generally widowed and thus free to move
about, but they were also in need of income. It appears from the testimonies that they did not believe they were involved in any wrongdoing. For
example, Isabel Arias, a thirty-year-old mulatto widow was admonished
by Juan de Cárdenas, an appointed minister of the Inquisition, for removing the religious relics at the birth of one of the babies she had delivered.
When she was scolded, she insisted that it was to ensure the birth of the
placenta. Even the Spanish women, who had learned this custom from
the mulattoes, insisted that they were following what they had seen and
learned. In several of the accusations, even when the women in labor
demanded that the relics not be removed, the midwives took them off
anyway to help in the expulsion of the placenta. After that, many times
they put a linen cloth on their abdomen.

Mulatto and Afro-Mexican, middle-aged, and elderly, widowed, and single women played a fundamental role in early modern Mexican wom-
en's medical caregiving. Age and widowhood status gave these women
freedom of movement, the need to be self-sufficient, and a certain social
standing. Economic and sundry goods exchange and interdependence

among Europeans, Indians, and castes allowed for permeable physical and imaginary social borders, thus permitting these midwife/medical women to gain the trust and respect of a broad range of clients. If pregnancy and childbirth involved both psychic and physical care and guidance, there were other members of the population that had similar psychological problems but unrelated to pregnancy.

New Spain medicine was a mishmash of various traditions. Pre-Columbian medical knowledge used a whole array of herbs and natural medicines that were still in apothecary shops well into the nineteenth century. Spanish settlers imported medieval religious practices of which, as Fernando Cervantes reminds us, "the Christian religion was itself intermingled with a great deal of magic. Necromancers, sorcerers, and conjurers of clouds often competed directly with parish priests in early modern Castile" (1994, 58). The wave of African slaves began an onslaught of medicinal folk practices that, when combined with other remedies, allowed for a wide variety of elixirs and beliefs.

It is not known if the number of mulatto and Afro-Mexican midwives was larger than any other group or whether that group was more frequently brought before the Inquisition. Whatever the case, they were perhaps the first example of economically upwardly mobile, aspirational females in the Americas. Their double macula was being female and mulatto, traits which still have not been forgiven in the scientific community.

NOTES

1. Jaffary reviewed a random sample of "fifty-three civil, criminal, and Inquisition documents involving Mexican midwives in the period between 1566 and 1888" (2016, 49).

2. The inquisitorial files that detail the trial carried out against Josepha de Zárate are: 1721, vol. 791, file 16, pp. 353–63, and 1723, vol. 61, file 8, pp. 124–252. The files are located in the Archivo General de la Nación México in Mexico City.

WORKS CITED

Aguirre, Gonzalo. 1973. *Medicina y magia: El proceso de aculturación en la estructura colonial.* Ciudad de México: Instituto Nacional Indigenista.

Baena, Fuensanta. 2016. "Negras y mulatas en el noroeste de Nueva España: La transgresión de la norma entre las parteras de San Miguel de Culiacán." *Revista Brasileira do Caribe* 17, no. 33: 37–51.

Behar, Ruth. 1987. "Sex and Sin, Witchcraft and the Devil in Late-Colonial Mexico." *American Ethnologist* 14, no. 1: 34–54.

Camba, Úrsula. 2008. "Altanería, hermosura y prosperidad: reflexiones en torno a conductas de negras y mulatas (siglos XVII–XVIII)." In *Mujeres en Veracruz: Fragmentos de una historia,* ed. Hernanda Núñez Becerra and Rosa María Spinoso Arcocha, 13–25. Ciudad de México: Gobierno del Estado de Veracruz de Ignacio de la Llave.

Cervantes, Fernando. 1994. *The Devil in the New World: The Impact of Diabolism in New Spain.* New Haven: Yale University Press.

Gonzalbo, Pilar. 2013. *Educación, familia y vida cotidiana en México virreinal.* Ciudad de México: El Colegio de México.

Gonzales, Rhonda. 2013. "No Friends in the Holy Office: Black and Mulatta Women Healing Communities and Answering to the Inquisition in Seventeenth-Century Mexico." *Journal of Pan African Studies* 6, no. 1: 1–19.

Jaffary, Nora. 2016. *Reproduction and Its Discontents in Mexico: Childbirth and Contraception from 1750 to 1905.* Chapel Hill: University of North Carolina Press.

Lagunas, Zaid. 2010. *Población, migración y mestizaje en México: Época prehispánica-época actual.* Ciudad de México: Instituto Nacional de Antropología e Historia.

Roselló, Estela. 2014. "La Madre Chepa: Una historia de fama femenina en el puerto de Veracruz." *Relaciones: Estudios de Historia y Sociedad* 35, no. 139: 69–91.

✢

Self-Denunciation before the Inquisition

The Case of Felipa Olaeta in Eighteenth-Century New Spain

YADIRA MUNGUÍA

In 1571, the Inquisition arrived in New Spain after Philip II ordered the establishment of the Holy Office in his American viceroyalties in 1569 (Campos Moreno 2001a, 19). The small number of cases in the sixteenth century multiplied and diversified within the next two centuries, and the prosecution of heretics, Judaizers, and sorcerers filled the pages of inquisitorial books that are preserved today in the archives. In this essay, I examine the unusual case of Felipa Olaeta (1796),[1] a young Spanish girl who voluntarily accused herself of heresy. Part of the evidence of her offense to the Catholic faith is based on the satirical verses the accused enjoyed singing at social gatherings. Olaeta apparently denounced herself on the advice of her confessor, aiming to obtain leniency during the proceedings carried out by the Holy Office. The characteristics and implications of these kinds of accusations allow us to see Olaeta's case as a guide to and example of the proceedings in cases of self-denunciation both from the part of the complainant and from that of the authorities.

Olaeta's case has been part of many studies in the last decades, but her case has not been analyzed in depth. María Águeda Méndez includes Olaeta in her *Catálogo de textos marginados novohispanos* (Catalog of Marginalized Texts from New Spain; 1992). In a later work, she expands on some of the outstanding issues and cases that are part of the *Catálogo* in her book *Secretos del oficio: avatares de la inquisición novohispana* (Trade Secrets: Avatars of New Spain's Inquisition; 2001). In the chapter devoted to *"Los 'Mandamientos de amor' en la inquisición novohispana"* ("The 'Commandments of Love' in New Spain's Inquisition" [2001, 102–3]), Méndez brings us closer to Felipa Olaeta, by mentioning that the defendant used to sing popular poems, collected several times by the Inquisition. However, she does not study this case in depth (102). Rather, Méndez focuses on Olaeta's scandalous poems, which were not of her own authorship, and were quite popular in celebrations. Olaeta performed some poems from *Mandamientos de amor,* satirical and blasphemous poems that metaphorically compare the unseemly inclination of a lover for her beloved to the Ten Commandments. According to Méndez, "Thanks to their popularity in Spain, *Mandamientos de amor* arrived in New Spain. In January 1799, Francisco Pérez Gallardo, a man born in Mexico and resident of that city, denounced a conversation among don José Cristóbal, Juan Salcedo, and the complainant [Olaeta] to the Holy Office" (2001, 100).

Olaeta's case was not the only one in which the satirical poems appeared; they were also part of another trial, in 1789, in which Pablo Lugo surfaces as the one who would sing them in social gatherings (Méndez 2001, 100). Thus, Felipa Olaeta's poetic interpretation is not of particular interest, as they were *coplas* (verses) of popular and extended use. The problem is that several people heard her at the wedding where she sang them. However, the poems recorded in Olaeta's case are fewer than the ones included in other trials, proving that she merely enjoyed singing them rather than composing them.

The poems Olaeta sang were just one of her main offenses against the Catholic faith, but were the most studied part of her case. For example, in Sara Poot Herrera's study of New Spain's marginalized literature, "El amor y los humores en el siglo XVIII mexicano" (Love and Moods in Eighteenth-Century Mexico), she alludes to the poems in Olaeta's case, but does not go into a specific study of her trial (2003, 1–23). Poot Herrera analyzes the blasphemous notes of that kind in satirical poetry.

In a more recent study of Olaeta's case, Rogelio Jiménez Marce sheds light on other aspects that do not have to do as much with the poems as they do with Olaeta's heretical propositions. He explains in detail the proceedings carried out against Olaeta and initiated by herself. Jiménez Marce refers to the errors of the dogma Olaeta incurs in, and to the statements related to matters of sexual nature (2014, 165). Although Felipa makes several statements on the latter aspect, here we will focus on the ones dealing with dogmatic issues. Apart from thereferences above, Olaeta's cases have not been thoroughly analyzed; nevertheless, her case illustrates how women were prosecuted for heresy in New Spain and shows us the vicissitudes that some of them went through in their inquisitorial trials.

Women before the Inquisition: Motivations and Procedures

Women had a leading role in New Spain, despite their conventional social and legal positions. Although to a much lesser extent than men, some women took part in the arts and sciences, and they had a major impact on society and even on politics.[2] From the sixteenth century onward in New Spain, we find outstanding women who were conquistadoras, such as Beatriz Hernández and María Estrada; founders of convents, such as Mariana de la Encarnación; and poets, such as Catalina de Eslava and Sor Juana Inés de la Cruz, as well as a significant number of religious women who served as role models in their convents and as spiritual leaders. Within this last group, some women narrated their religious experiences, and confessors wrote the biographies of some women's visions and extreme devotion (Muriel 2000, 496–505). However, discussions on matters of faith, exaltation of piety, and mystical visions were dangerous most of the time, as they could be mistaken for blasphemy and even heresy. As a result, nuns and mystics feared the harmful consequences of writing their experiences. For example, Sor Juana Inés de la Cruz's *Carta atenagórica* provoked a controversy within the Church precisely because of its theological content (1994, 412).[3] Many women were very close to falling into heretical opinions, comments, and statements, mostly due to either ignorance of the offense or the reduced scope of colloquial jargon. Olaeta's case will allow us to explore such propositions and their danger in this essay.

It is important to comment briefly on the Inquisition in New Spain and its relation to the women of this period to have a better understanding of what kinds of offenses the latter committed against the Catholic Church and the penances they received. This context will allow us to see the particularities of Olaeta's case. The establishment of the Inquisition in Spanish American territories had the same purpose as it had had in the metropolis, which was to eradicate heresy.[4] According to Inquisition manuals, heresy in its broader sense refers to an offense against the Catholic faith carried out by groups promoting deviant behaviors and beliefs, such as those of Judaizers, Muslims, and alumbrados, or Illumined, among others. Minor heresies—such as the ones in Olaeta's case—constitute religious errors, but not serious or disturbing in comparison to others. They relate more to blasphemy, outrageous words, and errors produced by ignorance (Dedieu 1992, 96). Heretics were defined as "those who are outside of the obedience and devotion of the Holy Roman Catholic Church, obstinate in errors and heresies, who always seek to pervert and turn the faithful and devout Christians away from our holy Catholic faith and, with their malice and passion, work with all intent to attract them to their contemptible beliefs, communicating their false opinions" (1992, 42).[5]

King Philip II considered that "the true remedy is to divert and exclude heretics and suspicious of heresy from all communication, punishing and removing errors" (Dedieu 1992, 42). The Inquisition's activity began after Pedro Moya de Contreras took the oath of faith in the Cathedral of Mexico in November 1571 (Medina 2010, 25, 50). Inquisitorial prosecution fluctuated depending on sociopolitical and economic circumstances, as Solange Alberro states.[6]

> In general terms, the establishment of the Holy Office in Mexico in 1571 was immediately followed by a significant increase in the volume of paperwork between 1610 and 1630, after a depression corresponding to the last years of the sixteenth century. The decade of 1630–1640 again shows a collapse in the volume of inquisitorial prosecutions, promptly corrected by the highest number of cases during the years 1640–1650, which was quite dramatic in comparison to previous years. (2015, 184)[7]

The Holy Office in New Spain prosecuted fewer women than men, with the exception of Judaizers, who were almost equally brought to court. According to Alberro, the Inquisition prosecuted crimes related to religious errors, with blasphemy, propositions, and heresy the most common (2015, 237). Additionally, there were offenses of a sexual nature, such as bigamy and solicitation, along with people prosecuted for Judaizing and for sorcery. The latter produced a great number of female cases and was seen almost benevolently by the inquisitors.[8] An overview of accusations and prosecutions during the seventeenth century shows that women were accused of crimes related to superstition and witchcraft; such practices were influenced by pre-Hispanic traditions and applied mainly to love magic. In the case of heresy and errors in religious matters, women's participation was less prominent than that of their male counterparts (Alberro 2015, 237–38). It is known that the Inquisition in New Spain was much more lax than the institution in Spain and was devoted mostly to cases of little social consequence, imposing sanctions comparable to the offenses. Alberro mentions a total of around 3,500 cases throughout the existence of the court, of which roughly fifty received significant sanctions. In addition, she states that "the number of victims, compared to any judicial instance then or now, does not justify in any way the sinister fame of the famous court, at least in America" (Alberro 2010, 29).[9] Consequently, recent historical approaches have demystified many aspects of the Holy Office's functioning.

Heresy and Inquisition

At the end of the eighteenth century in New Spain, the number of voluntary denunciations of women accusing themselves of heresy and error against the dogmas of the Catholic faith rose substantially; among them we find Felipa Olaeta's case. The allegations increased especially from 1770 to 1780 and kept doing so almost steadily until 1800. By the end of the century, the increase was in cases dealing, not with blasphemy and heretical propositions, but with crimes of bigamy and solicitation. There were eight autos de fe celebrated in the Plaza de Santo Domingo, Mexico City, in which the penitents marched exhibiting the banner of their offense (Medina 2010, 400–429).[10] However, none of the trials included instances of mixed heresy (*mixta de manifestación interna y externa*); since such instances were very rare, authorities prosecuted only men. Research conducted in the Archivo General de la Nación (Mexico) indicates that although the number of denunciations regarding cases of mixed heresy and self-denunciations in the second half of the eighteenth century increased, these cases were not necessarily prosecuted. On many occasions the lack of witnesses and the simplicity of the case led procedures to be either delayed or even discarded.

The reading of the edict written by the judicial vicar on February 11, 1769, prompted voluntary denunciations from women in the last decades of the eighteenth century (Medina 2010, 400–420). The edict denounces all those who fall into heretical propositions and issues outside the Catholic faith. This document states that charges would be prosecuted against anyone who "has blasphemed against God, our Lord, the Blessed Virgin Mary, or the saints, or disparaged their images, or held mass and heard confession without being priests or repeated the holy sacraments of Baptism or Confirmation, or abused them and that of Extreme Unction" (Medina 2010, 400–420).[11] This edict reveals the Inquisition's attempt to regain its power amid its decline in New Spain.

The edict invited priests and other religious people to inform and raise awareness among their parishioners on the severity of the issues and the importance of denunciation:

> Given that explaining the Christian doctrine to parishioners is considered the most effective means to uproot these and similar crimes, we strongly urge all parish priests to continue doing so, cautiously warning their parishioners, with the prudence required by this matter, against the vices that they must reject, and those they may note within their congregations, especially those against our holy faith. (Medina 2010, 407)[12]

The collaboration of witnesses against the defendants, whether or not it was voluntary, played a significant role in the functioning of the Inquisition as everyone became vigilant of everyone else's behavior and denounced any irregularities. After the edict, voluntary denunciations from women proliferated, especially in the decade of the 1770s, although not all of them led to prosecution. These denunciations were divided into two major groups. On the one hand were women who went to the Inquisition and denounced themselves, and those who allowed their confessor to present the case before the Holy Office. On the other hand were those confessors who asked permission of the Inquisition authorities to absolve any penitent that had fallen into religious errors, profanity, and heresies.[13]

In both groups, cases mostly referred to young maiden women: fewer than five were married, one was a widow, and none of them were nuns.[14] Their ethnic origins were varied: the young single women and some of the married women were Spaniards; there was a freed *parda* (mixed Black with indigenous) and two slaves: one of them was *mulata* (mixed Black with Spaniard) and the other one Black.[15] Additionally, these denunciations took place in the central territories of New Spain, particularly between Mexico, Puebla, and Oaxaca, which reveals the reach of the edict. These kinds of official documents influenced how both priests and parishioners denounced each other and served in turn as witnesses.

Voluntary Denunciations and Confessions

Although prosecution of heresy was at the core of the establishment of the Holy Office, specific cases of heresy were not numerous. For the inquisitors, accusations of this kind were complicated, as this crime was tedious and difficult to prove. They had to first encourage people to denounce themselves, and then find witnesses to corroborate heretic behaviors, producing a vigilantism that almost always complicated the cases (Dedieu 1992, 95). The first sentence in the manual of inquisitors by Nicolao Eymerico warns of the complications of this type of proceedings when he says: "Regarding heresy, one is to proceed quite simply, without the subtleties of lawyers, nor solemnities in the case" (2010, 1; Araya 2004). However, in practice, procedures normally took longer to conclude, even more so in New Spain, since due to bureaucratic instances, each trial had to be completed to be solved, including trans-Atlantic communications between Inquisition tribunals. According to the same manual, there were three ways to build a case: by accusation, by denunciation, or by inquiry. Once the case was opened, indictment was substantiated the moment authorities allowed informers to prove their accusations. However, they were subject to retaliation in case they failed to show enough evidence. Eymerico explains why inquisitors avoided such prosecutions:

> First, because [accusation] is a discontinued practice; second, because the informer puts him/herself in serious danger; and third, because it is long and litigious. [. . .] The second method of building a case, by virtue of

denunciation, is the most common. One person is reported by another as guilty of heresy, without the informer becoming part of it. [. . .] Inquiry is the third way of building a cause of heresy, and it is used when there is no informer or defendant. (2010, 4–5)[16]

Olaeta's case is included in a large number of self-denunciations, also called either voluntary denunciations or denunciations against oneself.[17] Many women opted for this option in order to avoid sentences greater than an economic sanction. The judges were generally more benevolent when it came to these kinds of complaints, as it allegedly was a recognition of the error and a sincere repentance. The confessors played an essential role in these cases since, most of the time, they were the ones identifying religious errors and heresies. Ordinarily, they advised the offenders to self-denounce, as they could not absolve them, due to the gravity of the sin. In general, women who reported themselves had the support of their confessors, who in turn served as commissioners of the Holy Office. That position allowed them to file a report, which normally did not carry severe penances. Such reports rarely exceeded ten pages, including both the confessor's petition to be granted the authority to absolve a penitent and the offender's voluntary denunciation. The briefness of these reports indicates the little attention Inquisition authorities paid to these denunciations. Only when other circumstances were also at play, specific cases were considered to deserve a longer trial, such as Olaeta's. In addition to the enunciation of errors, blasphemies, and heresies, Olaeta was accused of singing in public love songs known as "*Mandamientos de amor.*" Even if she was not the author of the lyrics, her public performance was reprehensible since the Inquisition had previously condemned the poems.

The Case of Felipa Olaeta

On May 11, 1796, Fray Francisco de Jesús María y José, priest and deacon of the Carmelite order in Mexico City, resorted to the Holy Office to denounce María Felipa Olaeta, a twenty-four-year-old Spanish maiden, of heresy on her behalf. Fray Francisco presented to the Inquisition authorities two documents: a letter in which he explained and justified Olaeta's case and another letter written by Olaeta. In his petition, Fray Francisco aimed to obtain the authority to absolve her and assign her a mild punishment by taking her repentance into account. Fray Francisco had been Olaeta's confessor for two years, and after hearing many of her sins, he considered that it was not within his competence to absolve her. In her account, she referred to deviant activities, blasphemy, obscene words, and above all, heterodox propositions. The main intention of Olaeta's confessor and the inquisitors was, without a doubt, to make Felipa see the errors she had incurred and assign a penance to absolve her. Even though the report is narrated in what seems to be serious dogmatic terms, repentance on Olaeta's part and her full willingness to confess resulted in a benevolent outcome. As will be discussed later, Olaeta's penance was less harsh than others as it did not include lashes. Instead, it involved repenting after understanding which errors she had committed, taking catechism classes for a year, periodically confessing, and avoiding public places and celebrations.

Olaeta excused her sins and mistakes by appealing to a lack of information on Catholic matters. She included information about her family and her education that explained her errors. As it reads in her self-denunciation, she identified her parents as Manuel Olaeta and María Manuela Herrera, and she mentioned that she was one of the middle children among several siblings. Although she did not elaborate, Olaeta stated that her relationship with her mother and one of her sisters, near in age to Felipa, was closer than with other members of her family. She also said they lived all together in the San Francisco neighborhood in Mexico City (AGNM 1796, 169). Apparently, her family was not overly attentive to churchgoing, resulting in a precarious religious education for Felipa. Although she argued that ignorance incited her to speak in such a wrong and scandalous manner, she did not blame her parents, but rather acknowledged her lack of interest in what she doubted about Catholic dogma. As time passed, she said, her doubts turned into serious misstatements leading to accusations of mixed heresy.

The proceedings carried out against Felipa Olaeta consist of several documents issued between May and June, 1796. The first is the request made by her confessor on May 11, in which he stated that without the Tribunal's authorization: "I am unable to absolve her from all the sins she has expressed to me during confession for a long time and to my satisfaction" (AGNM 1796, 163).[18] Consequently, Fray Francisco requested that he be granted the authority to judge her case. On May 21, 1796, the Holy Office accepted his petition and appointed him as commissioner responsible for Olaeta's case (AGNM 1796, 165).

In her file, the following document is written in Felipa Olaeta's own handwriting and highlights the errors and actions that she considers the most serious against the Catholic faith. Regarding her sins of word, she said: "I wish my heart would have broken into tiny pieces when pronouncing these infamous words that I uttered"[19] (AGNM 1796, 167). These expressions of willingness, acknowledgment of her errors, and repentance facilitated her absolution.

Felipa highlighted the following offenses she committed:

1. Lacking conviction about the virginity of Mary and the justification for fighting the Muslims.
2. Failing to comply with the sacraments of Eucharist and Penance, and wrongly complying with them due to her ignorance.
3. Singing and transcribing profane and heretical verses.
4. Ignorance and lack of understanding about hell.
5. Derision and mockery of holy images.
6. Judging God as cruel with regard to the imposition of corporal punishment.
   (AGNM 1796, 168)

Based on Olaeta's statements, Inquisition authorities asked Fray Francisco, in his role of commissioner, to interrogate her, asking a set of questions to which she should promptly respond. The questions mostly refer to Olaeta's dogmatic errors. On June 13, 1796, around 7:00 a.m., according to Fray Francisco, the interrogation began by his asking the accused to "kneel and make the sign of the Cross," and tell the truth under oath, to which she agreed. The commissioner asked Felipa the questions assigned by the Holy Office and wrote down in detail her responses.

In that interrogation, Olaeta provided information about her family and details about her mistakes. The examination was comprehensive and lengthy, and included a list of much more serious errors regarding the dogma than those mentioned earlier. This time, Olaeta expanded on what she had previously stated in the complaint and insisted on three issues: first, what she said she either did alone or only in her thought, and was heard only by her family; second, she acknowledged the magnitude of her errors; and third, she did so without knowing, as she was ignorant that what she said was wrong. She also mentioned that as a child she misbehaved by making gestures and insulting religious images. She then concluded by repenting and saying that she was ready to rectify her behavior.

However, she added new declarations that were more serious than the previous ones, such as not believing in indulgences nor in the graces of the Virgin Mary's apparition as the Virgin of Carmen (*la virgen del Carmen*), and thinking that they were inventions of the clergy and not a divine matter. By dismissing salvation, Olaeta exacerbated her heretical errors. She said that since the prize was only glory to God, she would like to go to hell. Furthermore, she stated that she did not believe in the Holy Trinity or in the Passion of Jesus. Also, she accused herself of going to the confessional to incite the priests with her beauty, instead of seeking forgiveness for her sins, which she said she was ignorant of at that time. However, after being accused of heresy, she acknowledged her mistakes and feared for her soul.

Throughout her interrogation, Felipa increased the number of her offenses, including childish trifles, misunderstood issues, and rhetorical games in family comments. Moreover, she expressed severe opposition to several dogmas, revealing not only a great ignorance of the essential elements of the Catholic faith, but she also made heterodox and heretical comments that cast doubt on truths of faith. Her comments show a restless mind that challenged orthodox principles. The description of her errors allows us to see her sins of word and her lack of faith both in religion and in the clergy, as she deemed as human inventions several dogmas and divine truths. Changes in her beliefs emerged from her readings, especially the *Spiritual Exercises* of St. Ignatius Loyola. Loyola's teachings opened her eyes and mind to Catholic dogma, and she then acknowl-

edged the errors she had committed. Once she finished her statement, it
was read back to her. Then, she agreed to everything said in it, and signed
the document, along with her confessor and prosecutor. That same day,
Fray Francisco delivered the documents pertaining to Olaeta's case to the
Holy Office (AGNM 1796, 186).

On June 15, Fray Francisco wrote a letter with his verdict on Olaeta.
He first thanked the Inquisition authorities for having trusted him and
appointed him as commissioner in this case. Then he declared that he
had interrogated the accused, trying to have her tell him the whole truth.
Additionally, he noted that in his role as mediator he considered Felipa's
health, sanity, and tranquility when asking the questions. Fray Francisco
apologetically summarized his work in this case as follows:

> And obeying this mandate of yours (as I should all), your Honor, I say
> that, according to the circumstances that are combined in María Felipa,
> such as: sex, age, character, knowledge of her own conscience, [. . .] I
> have pursued the purity of truth, with which she needed to explain to me
> in such serious matters, such as those belonging to our holy faith [. . .]
> at the same time that with every effort possible and despite the short-
> sightedness of my reason, I have tried to encourage and expand her heart,
> so that she candidly, purely and simply stated the truth, with full freedom
> and without any concerns that usually emerge in these predicaments.
> (AGNM 1796, n.p.)[20]

A few days after June 22, 1796, the inquisitorial commission pronounced its judgment in Felipa's case. Its determination advised her
amendment and reconciliation with the Church, as follows:

> Having seen the statement that in respect to our commission the Mas-
> ter Father, Fray Francisco de Jesús María y José has gathered against the
> [voluntary] penitent María Phelipa Olaeta for the crime of heresy, despite
> the horrendous and horrible crimes of which she has accused herself,
> wishing the remedy and spiritual healing of her soul, and responding to
> her candid confession and humble repentance, we have agreed to advise
> the Commissioner appointed to bring his penitent on her own volition [to
> our Court], to be reconciled with our Holy Mother Church.[21]

From this pronouncement, Felipa Olaeta should understand her "errors and horrors," and how far from the Church she was due to her sins, so that she would not commit any of them again.

After the abjuration, inquisitorial authorities allowed Fray Francisco to absolve her, and to impose the "spiritual penances and medicinal plants that are able to gently work the reform of this woman." They left to the Carmelite priest's competence the decision regarding her reinsertion in the Catholic life standards and its monitoring. On August 5, 1796, Fray Francisco absolved and reconciled Olaeta with the Church and sentenced her to:

1. One year of frequent participation in the sacraments.
2. Fasting for three years on bread and water every Friday, unless her health was compromised.
3. To pray part of the Rosary every day for three years.
4. To reflect on the Christian doctrine through Father Ripalda's Catechism.
5. To abstain for three years from public celebrations, holidays, games, and pastimes.
6. To regularly attend church and to meditate on Christ's Passion and death.
7. To keep good company and perform acts of faith, hope, and charity.
8. Finally, to make an act of contrition, with the following formulation: "I believe in God, I hope in God, I love God; I regret deeply having offended God."[22]
   (AGNM 1796, n.p.)

According to a later note in Olaeta's file, she was reconciled and acquitted, and she fulfilled the year of penance and confession with Fray Francisco de Jesús María y José. Felipa complied with the sacraments only after December 1796 since she had fallen ill the preceding months. It is possible that the other requirements of her penance were fulfilled in a similar manner, although there is no record of it.

Although inquisitorial cases were largely bureaucratic and normally took a great length of time to be resolved, in the case on Felipa Olaeta the proceedings went fast, were effective, and ended with a favorable outcome for all parties. As a result, her case reveals an unconventional side of the Inquisition.

The Inquisition in New Spain remains a controversial topic, as it has been since its establishment. As a branch dependent on its Spanish counterpart, it sought to regulate and control issues regarding religious dogma in a different space from that of the metropolis. The number of cases shows that the Inquisition in New Spain favored cases concerning Judaizers, alumbrados, and offenses involving unlawful interpersonal relations, such as bigamy. There were more men than women prosecuted for these offenses. Women were more often associated with cases of witchcraft, which were not so serious in this context, considering the multiplicity of ethnic groups. Dogmatic errors, heresies, blasphemies, and other offenses of word were also numerous, but in the case of women, their deeds had more to do with illiteracy and their lack of education than with any opposition to the Catholic religion, and errors occurred mainly from their misunderstanding of the dogmas.

Felipa Olaeta's arguments present a clear example of the lack of religious culture and the modern thinking that characterized the late eighteenth century. Her reasoning was based on common sense and tended toward enlightened ideas. Olaeta's case also shows us the bureaucratic side of some trials, and their efficiency, depending on the disposition and repentance of those who accused themselves. In her case, the correction of her mistakes led to a satisfactory outcome. These kinds of trials offer a different view of colonial society, and a different perspective of the Holy Office and its proceedings in the New World.

NOTES

1. In the documentation, her name varies between Felipa and Phelipa.

2. In *Cultura femenina novohispana* (2000), Josefina Muriel discusses women's different roles and positions in colonial society.

3. As is well known, Sor Juana Inés de la Cruz's *Carta atenagórica* caused a stir among

authors and theologians of its time and later. However, her name appears in a trial of the Holy Office, not for her work, but for the prohibition of the sermon *La Fineza mayor* by Francisco Xavier Palavicino, pronounced in San Jerónimo in her presence. See Elías Trabulse, Sara Poot Herrera, and Antonio Alatorre, among others.

4. In *Historia del Tribunal del Santo Oficio de la Inquisición en México,* José Toribio Medina studies the dynamics of the Inquisition in New Spain.

5. "Los que están fuera de la obediencia y devoción de la Santa Iglesia Católica y Romana, obstinados en errores y herejías, siempre procura pervertir y apartar de nuestra santa fe católica a los fieles y devotos cristianos, y con su malicia y pasión trabajan con todo estudio de atraerlos a sus dañadas creencias, comunicando sus falsas opiniones."

6. According to Solange Alberro, the Mexican Inquisition was responsible for monitoring a small percentage of the population in New Spain in the sixteenth and seventeenth centuries: 20 percent, or approximately 450,000 inhabitants, comprised of Spaniards Creoles, other Europeans, mestizos, African, mulattos, and Asian (2015: 29–30).

7. "En términos generales, se comprueba que la instauración del Santo Oficio en México en 1571 sigue de inmediato un aumento sensible del volumen de trámites, el que, luego de una depresión que corresponde a los últimos años del siglo XVI, no tarda en acentuarse vigorosamente entre 1610 y 1630; la década de 1630–1640 muestra de nuevo un derrumbe del volumen de trámites inquisitoriales, muy rápidamente corregido por el máximo, esta vez aparatoso, de los años 1640–1650."

8. In *Oraciones, ensalmos y conjuros mágicos del archivo inquisitorial de la Nueva España, 1600–1630* (2001), Araceli Campos Moreno analyzes how Inquisition authorities dealt with cases of sorcery, witchcraft, and magic in New Spain.

9. "la cifra de víctimas, comparada con cualquier instancia judicial de entonces o de ahora, no justifica de ninguna manera la siniestra fama del famoso tribunal, al menos en América."

10. As José Toribio Medina points out, the eighteenth-century autos de fe included blasphemous *indios*, bigamists, and perpetrators of other minor offenses, which were sentenced to exile, lashes, and public shame. Other prisoners considered more dangerous were separated from the rest. Those autos were celebrated on September 23, 1737, in Temamatla; March 18, 1770, in Santo Domingo; and in Mexico February 9, 1772; March 24, 1776; March 22, 1778; December 12, 1779; July 8, 1781; June 1, 1783; June 21, 1789. All of these latter were held at the famous Plaza de Santo Domingo in Mexico City.

11. "Que haya blasfemado de Dios, nuestro señor, la Santísima Virgen María, o sus santos, o menospreciado sus imágenes, o celebrado misa y confesado sin ser sacerdotes o reiterado los santos sacramentos del bautismo o confirmación, o abusado de ellos y del de la extremaunción."

12. "Por lo que considerando que el medio eficaz para desarraigar estos y semejantes delitos es la explicación de la doctrina cristiana, encargamos encarecidamente a todos los párrocos continúen en ella, advirtiéndoles a sus feligreses con la prudencia que el asunto

y la capacidad de estos demanda, los vicios de que deben apartarse, según la necesidad, que de igual expresión notaren en su partido, especialmente los que son contra nuestra santa fe."

13. The concept of heresy discussed here does not involve associations of beliefs outside the faith and refers to medieval and early Christianity heresies. Women and even men within this group usually committed heresy out of ignorance of the dogma, and not with the intention of going against it.

14. Nuns were not only prosecuted for heresy but also faced accusations of being credulous and false visionaries, and even demonic involvement was suspected in some cases. See Antonio Rubial, "¿Herejes en el claustro?" (2009, 19–34).

15. I have consulted the Inquisition section of the AGNM (Archivo General de la Nación in Mexico).

16. "Rara vez debe seguir un inquisidor este modo de proceder; lo primero, porque no está en practica; lo segundo, porque corre grave peligro el acusador; y lo tercero, porque es largo y litigoso. [. . .] El segundo método de formar sumaria en virtud de delación es el más usual. Uno es delatado por otro como reo de herejía, sin que el delator se haga parte. [. . .] La pesquisa es el tercer modo de formar causa por herejía, y se usa cuando no hay delator ni acusado."

17. In "Denunciar-denunciarse: la delación inquisitorial en Castilla la Nueva, Siglos XVI–XVII" (1992), Jean-Pierre Dedieu explains the workings of self-denunciation.

18. "hallo que todos pertenecen [. . .] Tribunal, sin cuya facultad, no puedo absolverla de ellos, ni [en todos] los demás pecados, que me ha manifestado con una confesión general que ha hecho conmigo, por largo tiempo, y a mi satisfacción."

19. "Quisiera que el corazón se me partiera en menudos pedazos al prorrumpir estas infames palabras que hablé."

20. "[. . .] y obedeciendo (como debo en todo) a este mandato de vuestra señoría Digo: que según todo el conjunto de circunstancias que concurren en dicha María Felipa, como son: sexo, edad, genio, conocimiento de su conciencia, [. . .] he hecho hacer de la pureza de la verdad, con que ha debido explicarme en materias tan graves, como las que pertenecen a Nuestra Santa fe, [. . .] al mismo tiempo que con todo el esfuerzo posible y en cuanto a la cortedad de mis luces han alcanzado, le he procurado animar y dilatar el corazón, para que con plena libertad y sin preocupación que las suele poseer en estos lances, dijese ingenua, lisa y llanamente la verdad. Me parece (salvo mejor juicio) que en efecto puede vuestra Señoría Ilustrísima darla [entero ejercicio] a toda su disposición."

21. "Habiendo visto la declaración que en virtud a nuestra comisión ha reunido el M.P. Fray Francisco de Jesús Maria y Joseph a su penitente Maria Phelipa Olaeta [espontanea] por crimen de herejía; sin embargo de los horrendos y horribles delitos de que se ha acusado, deseando el remedio y curación espiritual de su alma y atendiendo a su ingenua confesión y humilde arrepentimiento. Hemos acordado prevenir a dicho Comisario nombrado, que haga comparecer por sí y ante sí a la expresada su penitente, a la cual admitimos a la reconciliación con Ntra. Santa Madre Iglesia."

22. "Creo en Dios, espero en Dios, amo a Dios, me pesa entrañablemente de haber ofendido a Dios."

WORKS CITED

Alatorre, Antonio. 2007. *Sor Juana a través de los siglos (1668–1910)*. Ciudad de México: El Colegio de México/El Colegio Nacional/Universidad Nacional Autónoma de México.

Alberro, Solange. 2010. "Prólogo." In *Historia del Tribunal del Santo Oficio de la Inquisición en México*, 19–30. Ciudad de México: CONACULTA.

———. 2015. *Inquisición y Sociedad en México, 1571–1700*. Ciudad de México: Fondo de Cultura Económica.

Araya Espinoza, Alejandra. 2004. "De espirituales a histéricas: Las beatas del siglo XVIII en la Nueva España." *Historia (Santiago)* 37, no. 1: 5–32.

Archivo General de la Nación México (AGNM). Instituciones Coloniales, Inquisición, Vol. 1391, 1796. "Denuncia que hizo de sí misma Phelipa Olaeta, Doncella, de haber incurrido en el crimen de herejía mixta."

Campos Moreno, Araceli. 2001a. *Oraciones, ensalmos y conjuros mágicos del Archivo Inquisitorial de la Nueva España, 1600–1630*. Ciudad de México: El Colegio de México.

———. 2001b. "La voluntad cautiva: tres conjuros novohispanos parar atraer al amado." In *Lyra mínima oral: los géneros breves de la literatura tradicional*, 425–32. Madrid: Universidad de Alcalá

Dedieu, Jean-Pierre. 1992. "Denunciar-denunciarse: la delación inquisitorial en Castilla la Nueva, siglos XVI–XVII." *Revista de la Inquisición (Intolerancia y Derechos Humanos)*. https://dialnet.unirioja.es/servlet/articulo?codigo=157775.

Diccionario de Autoridades (1726–39). Accessed October 26, 2018. http://web.frl.es/DA.html.

Eymerico, Nicolao. 2010. *Manual de Inquisidores, para uso de las Inquisiciones de España y Portugal*. Ciudad de México: Maxtor.

Jiménez Marce, Rogelio. 2014. "Los imaginarios sexuales de una mujer Novohispana: El caso de María Felipa Olaeta." *Historia Agenda* 30:7–16.

Juana Inés de la Cruz, Sor. 1994. *Obras completas de Sor Juana Inés de La Cruz: Comedias sainetes y prosa*. Ciudad de México: Instituto Mexiquense de Cultura/Fondo de Cultura Económica.

López Forjas, Manuel. 2016. "Censura inquisitorial y prohibición de libros en La Nueva España: Una reflexión sobre la cultura escrita en México (Siglos XVI–XVIII)." In *Arte, cultura y poder en la Nueva España*, ed. Robin Ann Rice, 297. New York: Institute of Aurisecular Studies.

Medina, José Toribio. 2010. *Historia del Tribunal del Santo Oficio de la Inquisición en México*. Ciudad de México: CONACULTA.

Méndez, María Agueda, ed. 1992. *Catálogo de textos marginados novohispanos: In-*

quisición, siglo XVII: Archivo General de La Nación (México). Ciudad de México: El Colegio de México/Universidad Nacional Autónoma de México.

———. 2001. Secretos del oficio: Avatares de la Inquisición novohispana. Ciudad de México: Colegio de México.

Muriel, Josefina. 2000. Cultura femenina novohispana. Ciudad de México: Universidad Nacional Autónoma de México.

Poot Herrera, Sara. 2003. "El amor y los humores en el siglo XVIII mexicano." Hispanic Poetry Review 3, no. 2: 1–23.

Rubial, Antonio. 2009. "¿Herejes en el claustro? Monjas ante la Inquisición novohispana del Siglo XVIII." Estudios de Historia Novohispana 5: 19–38.

Trabulse, Elías. 1999. La muerte de Sor Juana. Ciudad de México: Condumex.

✝

The Personification of Erysipelas in Two Eighteenth-Century Spells from New Spain

CLAUDIA CARRANZA VERA &
JAIR ANTONIO ACEVEDO LÓPEZ

T hroughout the centuries, flower-bearing plants have received bo-
tanical and popular names given to them based on places, gods,
or sacred, legendary, and mythological characters. Consider the
stories of Hyacinth, Violet, and Narcissus, whose origins are found in
Greek mythology. Hyacinth is the name of a flower dyed by the blood of
a young man loved by Apollo, and representing prudence, spiritual peace,
and a craving for heaven in Christian symbolism, as well as joy. The violet
symbolizes humility and hidden love, as it represents Io, a girl courted by
Zeus, whom the god transformed into a heifer to save her from the fury
of his wife, Hera; violets sprouted to comfort the young woman from the
sorrows that her love had brought her. The last of these three flowers, the
narcissus, is a plant considered a harbinger of death due to its namesake's
tragic end; also because of its namesake, it is thought to symbolize self-
ishness and vanity (Morales 1997, 12–14).

Other plants take their name from Judeo-Christian saints, such as the
Damiana herb. It was named by the missionary Juan María de Salvatierra
(1648–1717) for Saint Damian, a Syrian martyr who, together with his
brother Saint Cosmas, is considered the patron of surgeons, pharmacists,
doctors, hairdressers, dentists, and spa workers; his protection covers all
those dedicated to health and well-being. Salvatierra learned of the properties, mainly aphrodisiac, attributed to the plant by the inhabitants of
southern Mexico; however, the name has transcended its place of origin.

Plants, as Cecilia López-Ridaura reminds us, also receive magical names, intended "to conceal the identification of the plant, on one hand, and on the other, to create the appropriate psychological environment to achieve the effects sought by [the] specialists in magic" (2015, 56).[1] In this sense, plants have been humanized or animalized in countless stories which mention their magical powers; a singular case is that of the famous mandrake, of which "it was said it had a soul with a human form that could kill its harvester with an agonizing scream if it was torn from the soil" (Rätsch 2011, 138).[2]

In America there are also many testimonies of a particular kind of humanization of the flora that took place thanks to the hallucinogenic effects caused by its ingestion; López Austin, for example, points out that to understand everything that escaped their knowledge, the ancient Nahuas consumed entheogenic plants such as the *ololiuhqui,* peyote, *tlitliltzin,* and tobacco: "Under the effect of these drugs one will find their personifications themselves: a small black man in the case of the *tlitliltzin,* venerable elders who are the peyote and the *ololiuhqui,* and sometimes even—after the conquest—Christ, and angels. They reveal to them the origin and the cause of their patients' illnesses, the location of stolen goods, and where a woman who has abandoned her husband can be found" (1967, 102).[3]

In some of the archives of the Holy Office in New Spain, we find several instances in which it seems that the herb called Santa María, which could well be peyote, acquires human characteristics. Its personification is mentioned repeatedly in a complaint made against a woman named Teresa Manzilla, who had told the declarant Nicolás López that

on one occasion, she had been ill, and she had called an *india* named Theresa—a neighbor of this jurisdiction, of the place they call *La Trinidad,* not knowing her last name or if she is married—, and that the abovementioned said to Teresa she would cure her, and that she should take the Santa María herb in a *temazcal,* or sweat house, in order to sweat with it. And from there she should take it out into a bedroom alone and stay there, and that no other person should be there, but that even if she saw several visions, she should stay calm and not be afraid, that she would sweat and heal. And to that effect, the aforementioned Teresa Manzilla took the herb in the temazcal, and from there she went into a bedroom. And being alone, she was overcome by great fear and began to scream and call people, and then Theresa entered and told her:

Now you see? You have frightened the herb by screaming and calling people.

She will not heal anymore. (Flores and Masera 2010, 216)[4]

In the same archive, Teresa Manzilla relates something even more interesting, as the Santa María herb takes the shape of a woman who informs a man, Cristóbal, of the whereabouts of a horse:

—Man, drink the rosemary and she will tell you where your horse is.

And the aforementioned Cristóbal drank it, to that effect, given to him by *El Pinto*. And that he rode a horse and arrived at a place they call Santillán. And that, there, the said Cristóbal told the declarant that he saw at his right side an *indita* (small indigenous woman), and that she told him:

—Dismount. Pick up that stone that is there.

And that he dismounted and picked it up. And that he pulled out a saddle blanket and a bit. And that he told the *indita*:

—¿Do you know this bit and this saddle blanket?

And that the aforementioned said yes, that they were his saddle blanket and his bit. And that then the aforementioned *indita* told him to turn around and see how big the world was, where he would go. That the shepherds had taken his saddle and horse, but not to worry, that next year it would come through his doors. And that, to that effect, after one year, when the shepherds came, one came to his doors, and he recognized his saddle and horse. And he claimed it.

And the declarant said that the same day he discovered the saddle blanket and the bit, the aforementioned *indita* told him:

—Know that this woman you are dealing with offends you with three or four individuals. (Flores and Masera 2010, 218)[5]

Plants also acquire healing, therapeutic, or aphrodisiac value from the resemblance of their leaves, stems, roots, or fruits to a particular organ of the human body, following the sympathetic principle that "like produces like"; for example, the *puyomate* was an indispensable element in the amorous magic practiced in New Spain, since its roots had a certain resemblance to the female and male genitalia; depending on their features, they were identified as male or female. The same patterns of nomenclature did not exist for ailments; few received names of persons and much less of saints, although they might be given a name that corresponded to their symptoms. Such a case is that of the disease called erysipelas, which has been known throughout the Hispanic world as "poisonous rose" or "evil rose," due to its similarities with that plant.

The name of the condition seems to derive from its main characteristics, since it is a cutaneous infection of bacterial origin that causes reddening and inflammation in the afflicted site—usually the limbs and the face—accompanied by fever and formation of sores. Additionally, as Ignacio María de Barriola explains, another reason for the analogy between the illness and the plant could be one of its more specific symptoms: "the exfoliation of the epidermis, or flaking, that perhaps was reminiscent of how roses lose their petals" (Barriola, 82, as quoted in Pedrosa 1993, 130).[6] This malaise was endemic in several regions of the Hispanic world, hence numerous documents have been preserved where it is discussed and possible methods for its cure are shown.

One of the most common means to combat the illness was the incantation "The Spell of the Rose," a poetic text of varying length that enjoyed great popularity in Spain and its territories in the early modern period. Several scholars have studied the incantation, whose use has been recorded in various American and Spanish regions as recently as the early twentieth century. However, there are not many studies in Mexico's Inquisition archives on its trajectory or on the personification of the illness. In this essay we focus on stories collected from the archives of the Holy Office in New Spain, where references to both the plant and the illness appear, as well as the link between them. These cases reveal the different reasons that they are assigned actions and even feelings, which humanize them; in addition, in several cases they are perceived as feminine entities or with traits specific to that gender.

The personification is evident in the prayer collected from Petrona de la Cruz in 1721, in the city of Oaxaca, Mexico. The woman claimed that a cousin had taught her how to cure or mitigate erysipelas reciting the following spell:

> I cure you, Rose,
> by the poison,
> by the sign of the Cross
> by the missal
> by the altar,
> go back whence you came,
> where no rooster crows
> or dogs bark.
> (AGNM, 1328)[7]

According to the literary scholar Francisco Rodríguez Marín, the oldest record of the formulaic poem comes from Castile and dates back to 1513. During the conquest and colonization of the New World, this resource against the illness did not take long to spread and take root among the population of New Spain. Therefore, it is not surprising that another version of this text exists, found in a letter signed by Friar Pedro de Alcántara Bazán in the town of Córdoba, Veracruz, in 1729. The letter is addressed to the inquisitors to whom he gives an account, in a respectful tone, of their work preaching and taking confession in the town of Alvarado. The friar relates that when encouraging the population to confess their sins, a certain "Don Francisco Bravo, a neighbor of Alvarado, introduced me to a black slave of his who was very old."[8] Alcántara Bazán calculated that he might be one hundred years old or very close, and recounts that the old man, named Pedro de San Antonio, recited the following poem:

> The one from the cursed hill
> Where five entered,
> Here I made my entry,
> With water and wind, I will take you,
> I will pull you by the root
> I will throw you into the water
> Where no rooster crows,

Or dogs bark,
Or child cries for its mother.
(AGNM, 1729, vol. 1328)[9]

Pedro de San Antonio assured him that the incantation was useful to cure erysipelas. The slave added that at the end of his recitation, he always requested that people should ask that "it be recited for the love of God and not for another purpose," for that gave a religious meaning to the dubious ritual (AGNM, 1729, vol. 1328).[10] This confirms the belief of Rodríguez Marín, who asserts that these healing methods were not exactly censored by the ecclesiastical authorities provided that in their execution accepted formulas were used, for example, words from Sacred Scriptures or prayers that appealed to the goodness of God, of the Virgin, or of the saints. However, given the ease with which reciters fell into excesses, some bishoprics, such as Toledo and Astorga, prohibited its practice from the mid-sixteenth century onward (2017, 19).

Both formulas recorded by the Holy Office of New Spain belong to the genre called "magic," that is, to words, phrases, or elaborate compositions, almost always in verse, that grammatically assume an imperative or desiderative mood. These are expressed in order to bring about a change in reality, either morally positive or negative, for which a pragmatic purpose was attributed to them. In these cases, as Araceli Campos points out, the word "is synonymous with power; not only are the needs externalized, but the intention is to achieve results by calling on occult or supernatural forces" (Campos 1999, 49).[11] Curses, prayers, spells, and enchantments form part of this genre, in which an invocation is made, usually addressed to a divine or supernatural entity, to achieve certain goals unattainable by natural means.

If we follow the guidelines established by Campos, the texts discussed here can be considered enchantments, since we can discern the intervention of supernatural forces in them to achieve a specific goal: to cure a disease. However, the examples do not comply with two essential characteristics of the definition she proposes for this genre: first, there is no request for saints or for Christ to help in carrying out the healing, since the formulas are addressed to the disease itself, which appears personified. Second, the tone used throughout the text is far from being supplicatory and submissive; instead it is imperative, since the illness is always reprimanded, pressuring it to leave the body (Campos 1999, 34). For these reasons, the texts better match the procedures of a different kind of spell, since a supernatural force is coerced and compelled to comply with the commands of those who pronounce them, which have as their intent to expel the illness or evil—in any of its possible manifestations—from a place or person where it causes havoc. It is reasonable, therefore, to call these spell exorcisms.

The formula recited by the slave Pedro de San Antonio is actually quite cryptic and its first lines incomprehensible. This can be due to several possibilities: that the sender had forgotten some part either before or after the third line, which is the only one that does not match the rhyme; that the receiver had not captured the entire text, because perhaps the slave recited the formula very quickly or its vocal articulation was not suitable; or that the informant knew only that fragment and had never noticed that the poem was incomplete. After all, it is a magical spell transmitted orally, so besides being susceptible to fragmentation, the content was less important than its effects.

The omissions can be observed at the beginning of the spell, since the first two lines seem hasty and incomplete. In the first, for example, the reference to the illness itself, of which we are only told that it is "the one from the cursed hill" (*la del monte maldito*), suggests a broader story; perhaps some lines preceded it in which it was specified toward which ailment the formula was directed. However, the number five in the second line (*que por cinco fue entrado*) recalls the biblical episode of the five wounds of Christ, so perhaps that passage occurs in other versions. This implies that, on occasion, the spell-exorcism incorporated religious references and a supplication addressed to the celestial court that fully transformed it into an enchantment.

The presence of Jesus Christ would not be unusual, since not only does the religious reference appear in numerous versions of this particular poem but also he is considered the main entity to whom formulas destined for healing are addressed, since Christ is perceived as an omnipotent physician, whose mention is sufficient to ensure health (Campos

2002, 157). This can be observed in the following case from the Inquisition archives in Spain; numerous versions are found in the different tribunals of the Iberian Peninsula in the sixteenth and seventeenth centuries. The following is from Murcia:

> My lord Jesus Christ
> Passing by the Mount of Olives,
> Met a knight
> Mounted on a horse.
> He exclaimed—Sir knight, How red is your outfit!
> And how red are your shoes!
> And what a red horse you ride!
> He responded:—I am the poisonous rose,
> Painful, malignant, evil.
> That entered the body of a man.
> I ate his flesh,
> I drank his blood,
> I broke his bones.
> —Since you are the poisonous rose,
> Painful, malignant, evil,
> That when you enter the body of the man,
> You eat the flesh, you drink the blood
> You gnaw at the bones.
> Go where no rooster or hen crows,
> Where no woman is with child or gives birth.
> Watch me throw you on the flames of the fire
> For them to burn and scorch you.
> —Do not cast me out, I shall go
> Where no rooster or hen crows
> Where no woman is with child or gives birth.
> (Pedrosa 1993, 128–29)[12]

This spell can be related in several ways to the previous one recited by Pedro de San Antonio, since in both cases there is mention of a hill and a similar description of the illness as *maldita* and *malvada*. The background would also explain the phrase "Here I made my entry" as part of the dialogue held in more extensive versions. In this way, the lines recited in the friar's letter can be considered a fragment of a composition of greater scale; in other words, the example in New Spain has many lacunae that we can only fill if we rely on other similar versions that give us clues about the missing lines of the text provided by the slave.

Unless a similar version is found, it is impossible to know whether the prayer that Petrona de la Cruz recited to the inquisitor in Oaxaca was due to the situation in which she was required to recite it or because of the position held by the recipients, since their assessment of the words was to affect her economic and physical condition. Indeed, it could be assumed that the speaker purposefully integrated sacred elements in the enchantment, likely from prayers and spells, to reduce the negative connotations of the verses and their curative powers. However, mentions of "making the sign of the Cross," "missal," and "altar" are often found in all kinds of magic formulas used in the New World, as they formed part of the constant admixture of the religious and the profane included in most magic practices.

It is important to note that the different texts have the dialectical aspects referenced by Campos; that is, the "you-I" game, where "in the dialogue between the invoking party and the invoked, the response to the requests is assumed to be a series of actions and not of words" (Campos 1999, 46–47).[13] Those who recited the spell knew that its utterance carried the necessary force to modify the undesired aspect of reality, and its use was guided by this conviction. In some cases, as in the Murcia example above, divine assistance was called on to overcome evil, as it was believed that the spell moved the will of Jesus Christ or the saints in favor of the speaker; in others, as is the case of the texts in New Spain, it was unnecessary to request divine intervention to eradicate the "illness of the rose": rather, the power of the enchanter was sufficient to compel the evil to leave the body it was tormenting. However, in either case, the treatment of the illness is always imperative and threatening: "I will pull you by the root" says the version of Pedro de San Antonio; "Watch me throw you on the flames of the fire" says the version recited in Murcia in the seventeenth century; "for you to go back to your place" says the Petrona version from the eighteenth century.

All of the versions also cast out the evil to where no rooster crows, dog barks, or child calls out for its mother. Rodríguez Marín comments that "sending evil far away, to places so remote it cannot return, is a frequent feature of the formulas of enchanters" (2017, 23).[14] The following, a twentieth-century version collected in Cuba, is a beautiful example that casts the illness to the bottom of the sea:

> Saint Bartholomew stood up,
> washed his feet and hands,
> took up his golden cane,
> went on his path,
> And met with an old woman
> Who was dressed in red,
> Red shoes on her feet,
> And immediately he asked her:
> —Where are you coming from?
> The old woman responded:
> —I am the poisonous rose
> Of pure purple red,
> I come from the bottom of the sea.
> —I shall send from heaven
> Lightning to burn you.
> May it burn you, may it scorch you!
> —No, no, I am leaving!
> No, no, I am going back to the sea!
> No, no, I am going back
> From where I launched!
>   Amen.
>
> (Pedrosa 1993, 137)[15]

Incantation-exorcisms and spells therefore have the power to ward off evil and to protect from misfortune and evil. Significantly, the disease erysipelas is always cast out to places where there is no connection whatever with humanity, or to places where children call out to their mother, and there are no domesticated animals like dogs, cats, or hens. In fact, it could be concluded that this feature is a typical closure for these kinds of formulas, as it also occurs in various compositions for dispersing damaging storms recorded by José Manuel Pedrosa, such as the one that is part of a Latin spell found on a slate rock in Carrio, an Asturian town, that disperses threatening storm clouds: "Let them go far from all your possessions, from the town, and from your buildings, let them go and fly to the hills, where no rooster crows or hen clucks, where neither the plowman nor the sower plants, where nothing exists that may be named. I conjure you, Paloraso, by the same lord as our brothers" (Pedrosa 2000, 67).[16]

Pedrosa explains the relationship between the spell against erysipelas and the Latin text as one that is based on the most evident fact of exorcising evil to a place where it can cause no harm, to the most remote and inhospitable confines of the world. However, he also points out that it can be part of a strategy, "in effect, it has always been believed that those are precisely the places that are the most comfortable, hospitable, and attractive to evil spirits: and, therefore, all our spells also extend an invitation—astute and suggestive—for them to retire to those places where they feel most at home" (Pedrosa 2000, 105).[17]

Up to this point it is evident that the formula was used as an exorcism, but it is also true that it could have been seen as a curse placed on the person affected by evil, where an unfortunate spirit could have been born. This is seemingly supported in a translation of the biblical Book of Job by the theologian friar Diego de la Vega, at the renowned convent of San Iuan de los Reyes in Toledo in 1604. Latin verses three and four say: "Pereat dies in qua natus sum, et nox in qua dictum est: Conceptus est homo. Dies ille vertatur in tenebras: non requirat eum Deus desuper, et non illustretur lumine" [Curse the day I was born / and the night it was said a manchild has been conceived! Let the day be darkness, / let God not regard it from above, / neither let light shine upon it]. Diego de la Vega translates it as: "Curse the day I was born and the night I was conceived. Beseech God that the night grow dark and cloudy, a solitary and sad night."[18] Up to this point he follows the Latin and Spanish versions; however, he adds the following: "so no rooster will crow, or dog bark, or bell, zither, or guitar be heard neither near nor far."[19] These last words were meant to impact the reader, since the hyperbole serves to intensify a fear of the site where no noise—the barking of dogs and the crowing of roosters—can ever be heard, and most importantly, the greater fear of being cursed and of never hearing any musical sound.

It is likely that the phrases used by the friar were reproduced constantly with the sense of a curse, as they express a complaint against birth itself, which is seen as the beginning of a wretched life that can only be compared to the inhospitable places that give birth and are home to all evils. This can be confirmed in the following song recorded by Margit Frenk in *Nuevo corpus de la antigua lírica popular hispánica de los siglos XIV al XVII* (New Corpus of Old Hispanic Popular Lyrics from the Fourteenth to the Seventeenth Centuries). The speaker complains using more or less the same topics:

> I was born at a miserable hour,
> No dog was heard, no rooster crowed.
> No rooster crowed, no dog was heard.
> Save for my fate, which cursed me.
> (Frenk 2003, 764)[20]

The typical formula used in spells is found in various lyrical compositions of the seventeenth century, and even in some early ballads, and thus extends beyond its own genre to other similar forms of literary expression, in this case popular poetry. A version of the spell of the rose from the twentieth century allows us to acknowledge the text's tradition, scope, and vitality, as well as its universality in the curing of erysipelas, a practice that can be found not only at other historical times, as we have seen here, but also in other cultures and languages, such as the following Serbian version cited by the scholar of medieval oral poetry John Miles Foley:

> Out from there comes the red horse,
> the red man, the red mouth,
> the red arms, the red legs,
> the red mane, the red hooves.
> As he comes, so he approaches,
> he lifts out the disease immediately;
> he carries it off and carries it away

across the sea without delay—
where the cat doesn't meow,
where the pig doesn't grunt,
where the sheep don't baa,
where the goats don't bleat,
where the priest doesn't come,
where the cross isn't borne,
so that ritual bread isn't broken,
so the candles aren't lit.
(Foley 2002, 192)

The editors of *Relatos populares* (Popular Stories), Enrique Flores and Mariana Masera, express their interest in this curative remedy; however, they do not stop at the similarities among the texts. As we can see, this time evil is metamorphosed into human and animal form: "Out of there comes the red horse, / The red man, the red mouth, / The red arms, the red legs, / The red mane, the red hooves. / As he comes, so he approaches, / He lifts out the disease immediately; / He carries it off and carries it away." What stands out in this version is the repetition of the word red (purple in other variants); the constant mention of the hills as a place of desolation where evil comes from and is expelled to (in one case, the bottom of the sea); and the characterization of the illness as an allegory that in some versions rides a horse and wears red shoes. Lastly, we find the dialogue between the conjurer or the healing entity—Jesus or Saint Bartholomew in the Iberian and Cuban versions, respectively—with a supernatural being that personifies the illness, which is either masculinized (Serbian version); feminized (New Spain and Cuban versions); or given masculine attributes but referred to as a woman (Spanish version). On occasion, the conversation ends with a plea for mercy by the erysipelas.

It is also interesting to note the two aspects that are most frequently feminized in the spell: the personification of the illness, and its main characteristic. This is not due to a simple generic correspondence between the gender of the noun and the adjective, but to an analogy between one and the other established through their association with the feminine: red and "poison" or "poisonous." Indeed, in the spell where the illness is represented as a horseman wearing red clothes, the entity identifies itself as feminine before Jesus Christ: "I am the poisonous rose." Although the name of the rose comes from the similarity between the disease's symptoms and the referred plant, why were the monikers of "poison" or "poisonous" used? This characteristic, the implications of which are entirely negative, has been frequently attributed to the feminine condition, as can be seen on phrases like "the scorpion has poison in the tail, and women in the mouth"[21] and "the snake and the women have the poison in the mouth";[22] Saint Bernard said that, like basilisks, females had poison in their gaze, that destroyed whoever was in front of them. Therefore, it can be thought that it is thanks to this feminine personification that the illness takes on its main quality, as it forms part of a series of epithets culturally assigned to women.

The other adjectives attributed to this personified illness are derivations from other negative characteristics, such as the inclination to do evil, that have been attributed to femininity since ancient times. Adjectives like "cursed," "malignant," and "evil" simply express the identification of the female condition that, through long tradition, is considered as an agent of evil. If we follow this same analogy, we are not surprised that the illness is considered a corrupting and painful, abominable entity deserving of complete eradication or at best, kept far away. It is also very interesting to note the compositions where the illness is given the physical representation of an old woman, since its description and ability to spread evil in horrendous ways have certain similarities to the figure of the witch. These similarities seem to be confirmed in the version recorded by the Holy Office of peninsular New Spain, since several of the activities attributed to the illness in its dialogue with Jesus Christ were also attributed to this personage: "—I am the poisonous rose, of pain, malice, evil / that entered the body of the man, / ate his flesh, / drank his blood, / scratched his bones."[23]

The Serbian text is the most ambiguous, as it is unclear whether the knight alluded to at the beginning of the spell represents the illness or the words that cure it, with the confusion originating in the verse "he lifts out the disease immediately," which may mean the person carrying the disease, or that which generates the disease in the person. However, the following section seems to confirm the identification of the gentleman with the cure, as it specifies that "he carries it off and carries it away / across the sea without delay." This specific case still varies from those found in the Hispanic world, where the man dressed in red assumes the role of the words that cure and thus, the action of exorcising the evil. The part of this example that does coincide with the Hispanic versions is the casting away of evil to an abandoned place, which in some versions is accompanied by a threat made by the healing agent to destroy the disease, resulting in the anguished pleas of the latter:

> —No, no, I am leaving!
> No, no, I am going back to the sea!
> No, no, I am going back
> From where I launched![24]

Because "illness" in Spanish is a feminine noun, it therefore assumes a feminine role in most versions that have lived on throughout the centuries, at least in the Hispanic tradition. This also occurs in other gendered languages, as we see in the following Serbian poem translated into Spanish in the twentieth century:

> I was walking along,
> When I met a woman
> and I asked her who she was:
> I am the rose, the poisonous one,
> Who is dressed in red,
> Wearing red shoes.
> —May God send you evil
> that tosses you into the sea
> so that you may not harm
> any little creature.
> (Portal de Nerpio Virtual website)[25]

With respect to the rites that tend to accompany the chanting of spells, the collector of the Serbian version comments that the person casting out the spell uses a knife or a piece of silver that is held to the injured part of the patient. According to Friar Pedro de Alcántara Bazán in 1729, the black slave Pedro de San Antonio "cured erysipelas with a lime cut in the shape of a cross and a few words."[26] In 1721, Petrona de la Cruz stated that while the prayer was being said, the sign of the cross was made with saliva on the affected part of the body "and a leaf of the herb called *lisa* was placed on top."[27] In 1668 at the Holy Office in Mexico City, a woman called María de la Concepción testified that, to cure erysipelas,

> She used nine leaves and then cut up another nine little pieces, saying the prayer or words, and responded that she did not use any more leaves because they corresponded to the nine months that our Lady held her precious son in her virginal womb, and that the leaves should be cut with scissors or a knife, and that this also cut off the erysipelas, and that burning the leaves burned the illness and they were cured. (Flores and Masera 2010, 134)[28]

These practices have similarities with others that have also been documented in different parts of Spain; for example, Francisco Seijo Alonso has recorded a ritual that was performed until not very long ago in the Valencian town of Canals, for which

> it was necessary to obtain several pots [. . .] of *alfalfa vera* [. . .] and have them on hand, along with some scissors, a glass with some water and salt. [. . .] Make three crosses over the part of the body affected by the evil while reciting the spell. [. . .] When proclaiming "Cursed one!" cut three pieces of alfalfa and place them in the glass, along with a teaspoon of salt. This is how the evil is cut off and dissolved, like "salt in water." Immediately pass the hand over the affected skin and repeat the spell and the other steps two more times (Seijo Alonso, 98–99, *as quoted in* Pedrosa 1993, 132),[29]

The following spell addressed to Saint Martha and the devil differs from the previous spells:

> Marta Martilla,
> May my child's godfather
> And my child's godmother
> Send me money
> And a man who is a good lover.
> And to see if this comes true,
> May the dogs bark
> And the rooster crow.
> And the Limping Devil
> Shall do this for me.
> (Flores and Masera 2010, 109)[30]

In this case, the devil and Martha are called on to attract the love of a man and are asked to offer tangible proof that they will obey the order through the barking of dogs and the crowing of a rooster, animals that, as we have seen, involve close association with humans. In another example, in her statement dated March 6, 1613, in Mexico City, María Álvarez indicated that after saying the magic words to attract a man, it was necessary to ensure that the entity addressed by the spell manifest itself, since "if as soon as the prayers were spoken, no doors were closed and the rooster crowed or the dogs barked, [. . .] it was a sign that good would happen, but if not, it would not" (AGNM, 1615, vol. 478, no file, 201).[31] What is requested, therefore, is proof that a contract between the conjurer and the preternatural forces being addressed will be carried out.

In summary, the prayer against erysipelas clearly had many versions in Europe that then circulated in America. The two cases cited are proof of its continued vitality in New Spain as they are not from the vice-regal period, but from the later colonial era. Unfortunately, the version from the seventeenth century needed to fill in the lacunae with terms that can be identified in later versions, which are not recorded in the archive, but only described. It is important to note that all of the variants show that the texts recited in Veracruz and Oaxaca must have their roots in different versions of the same prayer. Everything seems to indicate that the spell recited by the one-hundred-year-old slave omits the dialogue of the illness and the other entity, whether it be the conjurer or a biblical figure such as Christ. The Oaxaca spell is related to versions wherein the illness is rebuked directly; that is, there is not so much a dialogue as threats. It is likely that more versions of the spell exist in Mexico today.

The narrative element of these prayers, which reproduce a dialogue, easily may be seen as a battle between good and evil. The evil, in this case, is at times personified as an old woman, and at others as a young female defined solely by the color red and identified as malignant and evil. The brief formulaic style of spells which gives voice to the affliction has already been pointed out by Araceli Campos in her book on types of magic in New Spain.

The voice that heals the illness is also important as it is aligned with good; that is, the words that expel the evil. It is at this point that the Serbian text gains so much relevance, since in this version the cure is personified in a very similar way to the personification of the Hispanic versions cited here: a red horseman that, this time, drags the illness to the bottom of the sea. The closing formulas are nearly identical in most of the examples found, since they all make reference to sending the erysipelas to the end of the earth.

Lastly, we wish to point out the interesting nature of the texts gathered, since everything seems to point to the fact that the versions found in the inquisitorial archives in Mexico were previously unknown, and it is therefore necessary to incorporate them into the studies of the traditional cures for erysipelas. Most importantly, it would of great value to carry out a more thorough study of the humanization of illnesses and plants, as they appear as weak and vulnerable women who, through the slightest carelessness, become dangerous and merciless. They are unprotected old women who cause tremendous pain to the body; women who travel the roads spreading their evil, but in the end, beg forgiveness for their misdeeds. Such a study would enrich our understanding of how women were perceived in Hispanic society in the early modern and even contemporary periods.

* * *

NOTES

1. "a ocultar la identificación de la planta, por un lado, y por el otro, para crear el ambiente psicológico propicio para lograr los efectos buscados por [los] especialistas en la magia."
2. "se decía que tenía un alma con forma humana que podía matar con un grito agónico a su recolector si era arrancada de la tierra."
3. "bajo el efecto de estas drogas se va a encontrar con sus personificaciones mismas; un negrito en el caso del *tlitliltzin,* ancianos venerables que son el peyote y el *ololiuhqui,* y aun algunas veces—después de la conquista, claro está—con Cristo y los ángeles. Ellos le revelan el origen y la causa de las enfermedades de sus pacientes, el destino de las cosas hurtadas y el sitio en que se encuentra la mujer que ha abandonado a su marido."
4. "en una ocasión abía estado enferma ella i que abía llamado a una yndia llamada Theresa—vezina desta jurisdizión, en el paraxe que llaman La Trinidad, la qual no sabe si es casada ni su apellido—, y que la susodicha le dixo a la dicha Theresa que la curaría, y que abía de tomar la hierba de santamaría en un temascal, i sudar con ella. Y que de allí la abía de sacar a un aposento solo y recoxerse, y que no abía de aber persona ninguna, y que aunque biese barias visiones se estubiese quieta y no tubiese miedo, que sudaría i sanaría. Y que con efecto, la dicha Theresa thomó la hierba en el temascal, de donde salió a un aposento. Y biéndose sola, le causó mucho temor i empezó a gritar y llamar gente, y que entonzes entró la dicha Theresa i le dixo:
—¿Ia ves? Ia as espantado la hierba con gritar i llamar gente. No abía ia de sanar."
5. "—Hombre, vever la rosamaría y ella os dirá aónde está vuestro caballo.
Y que con efecto la vebió el dicho Christóval, abiéndosela dado El Pinto. Y que montó a caballo y que fue a dar asta el sitio que llaman Santillán. Y que, allí, le dixo el dicho Christóval a la que declara que vido a su lado derecho una yndiíta y que le dixo:
—Apéate. Lebanta aquella piedra que está allí.
Y que se apeó y la lebantó. Y que sacó un sudadero y un freno. Y que le dixo la yndita:
—¿Conozes ese freno y ese sudadero?
Y que respondió el susodicho que sí, que aquel era su sudadero y su freno. Y que entonzes la dicha yndiíta le dixo que volviese los ojos y viese quán largo era el mundo, que adónde abía de ir a dar. Que los pastores se abían llebado su silla y caballo, pero que no le diese cuidado, que a el año se le entraría por sus puertas. I que, con efecto, a el año, quando vienen las pastorías, llegó uno a sus puertas, y conozió su silla y caballo. Y lo cobró. Y dize la que declara que también le contó el susodicho que el mesmo día que descubrió el sudadero y freno, le dixo la dicha yndiíta:
—Sábete que esa muger con quien tratas te aze ofensa con tres o quatro sujectos."
6. "la exfoliación de la epidermis, o caída de escamitas, que quizá hayan hecho recordar el deshojarse de las rosas."

7. "Yo te curo, Rosa, / por la venenosa, / por el santiguar / por el misal / por el altar, / que te vuelvas a tu lugar, / donde gallo no canta / ni perro ladra."

8. "Don Francisco Bravo, vecino de Albarado, [que] me presentó un negro esclavo suio de edad muy crecida."

9. "La del monte maldito / Que por cinco fue entrado / Aquí hice mi entrada, / Con agua y con viento, cojeré, / De raíz te arrancaré / En el agua te lo echaré / Adonde gallo no cante, / Ni perro ladre, / Ni el niño llore por madre."

10. "con el interés de que le dixeran sea por amor de Dios y no con otro fin."

11. "es sinónimo de poder; no sólo se exteriorizan necesidades, sino que se pretende conseguir resultados suscitando fuerzas ocultas o sobrenaturales."

12. "Mi señor Jesu Christo / Por el monte Olivete andava, / Encontró un caballero / Que a caballo andaba. / Díxole:—Cavallero / Que de vermejo vistes / Y de vermejo calzas / Y de vermejo caballo cabalgas. / Díxole:—Yo soy la rrosa emoponzoñosa, / En dolorosa malina, malvada, / Que entró dentro del cuerpo del hombre, / Le comió la carne, / Le bevió la sangre, / Le rrasgó los huesos. / —Pues tú eres la rrosa emponzoñosa, / En venenosa, malina, malvada, / Que en más dentro del cuerpo del hombre / Le comes la carne, le beves la sangre / Le rroes los huesos. / Vete a donde no cante gallo ni gallina, / Ni mujer aya preñada ni parida. / Mira que te echaré en lenguas de fuego / Que te quemen y te abrasen. / —No me eches, que yo me iré / Donde no cante gallo ni gallina / Ni aya mujer preñada ni parida."

13. "el 'diálogo' entre invocante e invocado, el primero no recibe contestación del destinatario de la invocación; la respuesta a sus peticiones se supone que será de hechos y no de palabras."

14. "enviar lejos el mal, a parajes tan remotos de donde no le sea dado volver, es cosa frecuente en las fórmulas de los ensalmadores."

15. "San Bartolomé se levantó, / Sus pies y manos lavó, / Su bastón de oro cogió, / Por su camino tomó / Y una viejita encontró / Que de colorado viste / Y de colorado calza / Y en seguida preguntó: / —de dónde tú vienes? / La viejita respondió: / —¡Soy la rosa ponzoñosa / De puro rojo morado, / Y vengo del fondo del mar. / —Yo enviaré del cielo / Un rayo que te ha de quemar. / ¡Qué te queme, que te abrase! / —¡No, no, que ya yo me voy! / ¡No, no, que regreso al mar! / ¡No, no, que voy de regreso / A donde hube de zarpar! / Amén."

16. "Que se alejen de todas sus posesiones, de la villa y de aquellos edificios suyos, que *vayan y vuelvan por los montes, donde ni el gallo canta ni la gallina cacarea, donde ni el arador ni el sembrador siembran, donde no hay nada para darle nombre. Te conjuro a ti, Paloraso, por el mismo señor de nuestros hermanos.*"

17. "desde muy antiguo se ha creído, en efecto, que son justamente esos parajes los más cómodos, propicios y atractivos para los espíritus malignos: y, por tanto, todos nuestros conjuros contienen también una—astuta y sugerente—invitación a que se retiren a los lugares donde mejor pueden encontrarse."

18. "Mal aya el día en que nací y la noche en que fui concebido. Plega a Dios que sea noche escura y nublosa, noche solitaria y triste."

19. "que ni gallo cante, ni perro ladre, ni se oyga en ella voz de campana, ni de vihuela ni cithara."

20. "Quando yo nascí era hora menguada, / Ni perro se oÿa, ni gallo cantava. / Ni gallo cantava, ni perro se oÿa, / Sino mi ventura, que me maldecía."

21. "el alacrán tiene la ponzoña en la cola, y la mujer en la boca."

22. "la víbora y la mujer tienen la ponzoña en la boca."

23. "—Yo soy la rrosa emoponzoñosa, / en dolorosa malina, malvada, / que entró dentro del cuerpo del hombre, / le comió la carne, / le bevió la sangre, / le rrasgó los huesos."

24. "—¡No, no, que ya yo me voy! / ¡No, no, que regreso al mar! / ¡No, no, que voy de regreso / A donde hube de zarpar!"

25. "Iba camino adelante, / me encontró con una mujer / y le dije que quién era: / yo soy la rosa, la venenosa, / la que de colorado viste, / la que de colorado calza. / —Dios te dé un mal / que te arroje al mar / para que a ninguna 'creaturica'/ le hagas el mal."

26. "curaba la erisipela con vn limón partido en Cruz y unas palabra."

27. "le pone encima una oja de la yerba llamada lisa."

28. "se valía de nueve ojas y hacía después otros nueve pedaçitos diçiendo dicha oración o palabras, respondió que no se valía de más número de ojas porque los aplicaba a los nueve meses que nuestra Señora trajo en su vientre virginal a su hijo preçiosíssimo; y que dichas ojas se havían de partir con tixeras o cuchillo, que con eso se cortaba también la irisipela, y que, quemando las ojas, se quemaba y quedaban sanos de dicho mal."

29. "era necesario proveerse de algunos botes [. . .] de alfalfa vera [. . .] y tenerlos a mano, juntamente con unas tijeras, un vaso conteniendo un poco de agua y sal. [. . .] Se hacen tres cruces sobre la parte afectada por el mal y se dice el conjuro [. . .] al pronunciar '¡La maldita!' se cortan tres trozos de alfalfa y se depositan en el vaso, con una cucharada de sal. Así es como el mal se corta y se deshace, 'como la sal en el agua.' Acto, seguido se pasa la mano por la piel enferma y se repite el conjuro y todo lo demás otras dos veces."

30. "Marta, Martilla, / señor Compadre / y la Comadre / me ymbíe dineros, / y al hombre que quisiere bien. / Y para ver si es verdad, / que ladren los perros / y cante un gallo. / Y el diablo cojuelo / hará esto por mí."

31. "ssi acabando de decir las dichas oraciones no cerrar puertas o cantar gallo o ladrar perro [. . .] era señal de que había de suceder bien y si no, no."

WORKS CITED

AGNM (Archivo General de la Nación México). Inquisition, 1613, vol. 478, no file.
———. Inquisition, 1729, vol. 1328, no file.
———. Inquisition, 1668, vol. 1328, no file.

Campos Moreno, Araceli. 1999. *Oraciones, ensalmos y conjuros magicos del archivo inquisitorial de la Nueva España, 1600–1630.* Ciudad de México: El Colegio de México.

———. 2002. "Ensalmos novohispanos, palabras magicas para curar." In *La otra Nueva España: La palabra marginada en la Colonia,* ed. Mariana Masera, 155–65. Barcelona: Universidad Nacional Autónoma de México/Azul.

Flores, Enrique, and Mariana Masera, eds. 2010. *Relatos populares de la Inquisición Novohispana: Rito, magia y otras "supersticiones," siglos XVII–XVIII.* Madrid: Consejo Superior de Investigaciones Científicas/Universidad Nacional Autónoma de México.

Foley, John Miles. 2002. *How to Read an Oral Poem.* Champaign: University of Illinois Press.

Frenk, Margit. 2003. *Nuevo corpus de antigua lírica popular hispánica de los siglos XIV al XVII.* Ciudad de México: Fondo de Cultura Económica/Universidad Nacional Autónoma de México/El Colegio de México.

López Austin, Alfredo. 1967. "Cuarenta clases de magos en el mundo náhuatl." *Estudios deultura áhuatl* 7: 87–117.

López-Ridaura, Cecilia. 2015. "De la mandrágora al peyote: Plantas brujeriles en España y América." In *Las minorías: Ciencia y religión, magia y superstición en España y América (siglos XV al XVII),* ed. Antonio Cortijo Ocaña and Ángel Gómez Moreno, 52–62. Santa Barbara: eHumanista.

Méndez, María Águeda. 1992. *Catálogo de textos marginados novohispanos: Inquisición: Siglos XVIII–XIX.* Ciudad de México: Archivo General de la Nación/El Colegio de México/Universidad Nacional Autónoma de México.

Morales, Ramón. 1997. "Plantas y cultura popular: la etnobotánica en España." *Quercus* 139: 12–14.

Nerpio Virtual website. "Oraciones y rezos para curación: erisipelas (disipelas)." *Nerpio Virtual,* http://www.nerpio.org/cultura/rezos/disipela.htm. (Accessed October 12, 2018.)

Pedrosa, José Manuel. 1993. "El *conjuro de la rosa* y la curación de la erisipela: Poesía, magia y medicina popular en España y América." *Asclepio: Revista de Historia de la Medicina y la Ciencia* 45: 127–42.

———. 2000. "Un conjuro latino (siglo VIII) contra la tormenta y la cuestión de orígenes de la poesía tradicional románica y europea." In *Entre la magia y la religión: Oraciones, conjuros, ensalmos,* 63–111. Gipuzkoa: Sendoa.

Rätsch, Christian. 2011. *Las plantas del amor: Los afrodisíacos en los mitos, la historia y el presente.* Ciudad de México: Fondo de Cultura Económica.

Rodríguez Marín, Francisco. 2017. *Ensalmos y conjuros en España y América.* Querétaro: Universidad Autónoma de Querétaro.

✝

The Cultural Construct of the Witch

Inquisitorial Discourses

GRACIELA RODRÍGUEZ CASTAÑÓN

From the European Middle Ages through the nineteenth century, countless treatises were written to catalog, explain, disseminate, or repress the practices of witchcraft, sorcery, and superstition. One such treatise, the *Malleus Maleficarum,* dates back to 1486; its first part deals with the Catholic faith and the different types of witches, while its second part explains the methods used in witchcraft and how to combat them. It incorporates a subsequent addition to the main text on the judicial trial and how to deal with it; the treatise served an explicitly instructive purpose and as a resource for many later treatises (Kramer and Sprenger 2006).

In 1613, the infamous Pierre de Lancre, after serving as inquisitor in the Basque country, published his *Tableau de l'inconstance des mauvais anges et démons, où il est amplement traicté des sorciers et de la sorcelerie.* This disturbing book added a central column to what could be called the edifice of witchcraft. Its author, a merciless persecutor of witches, graphically recounted the transgressions that characterized the women of Euskal Herria: all were, according to him, images of Eve, all willing to break the commandments, all regular attendants at the coven, all worshipers of the devil, all witches. His opinion follows the stereotype of the influential *Malleus Maleficarum* and is consistent with those of other scholars who helped outline the demonological characteristics attributed to women as the greatest transgressors in western culture (Ortiz 2018).

In the extensive list of texts communicating similar concepts during the early modern period, the works that stand out are those by Jean Bodin, *De magorum daemonomania, Libri IV,* 1581; Martín Delrío, *Disqui-*

sitionum magicarum, libri sex, 1600; Francisco Torreblanca, *Epitomes de-
lictorum in quibus aperta, vel occulta invocatio daemonis intervenit,* 1618;
Gaspar Navarro, *Tribunal de superstición ladina, explorador del saber, astucia y poder del demonio,* 1631; and Johann Wier, *De praestigiis daemonum et incantationibus ac veneficiis,* 1660 (Zamora Calvo 2016, 187–250).
The moral obligation to evangelize, coupled with the political anxiety to
preserve the hegemony in the known world produced a specific type of
discourse delivered by specialists who spoke against preternatural evil,
superstitions, heresy, magical practices, and other transgressions in order
to safeguard orthodoxy by persecuting and punishing those considered to
be representatives of the devil and thus ensuring the achievement of the
divine plan of salvation (Alberro 1993).

The demonologists' discourse, therefore, contained a high degree
of apostolic conviction in carrying out their uncompromising struggle
against evil. Since the texts composed for this purpose were supported
by the scholastic tradition and other authoritative voices, demonologists
recognized other theologians with similar views and followed verdicts
qualified as undeniable, chiefly the Bible, with emphasis on the New Tes-
tament and the texts of the patristics. It is worth pointing out that scholars developed a discursive tradition against magic, and their corpus de-
noted a special character with analogous arguments, although not entirely
similar in the details. Their theses and explanations were not consigned to
merely accusatory theories with misogynist overtones, but covered everyday reality through the persecution of propitious victims, or scapegoats,
on which fell both the symbolic violence of the sign of malignancy and
the physical violence of the inquisitorial proceedings, which included torture and often recommended secular execution.

The stage of the European witch mania, which had critical episodes at
various times between the sixteenth and eighteenth centuries, illustrates
the links between the demonologic texts and judicial practice. In this historical sense the theoretical side of demonology was as important as the
side that carried out the inquisitorial resolutions. The infamous *Malleus
Maleficarum,* the work of witch persecutors Heinrich Kramer and Jacob
Sprenger, is considered by some the prototypical text of ecclesiastic co-
ercion against witchcraft. Although, in the Catholic world, other texts,

such those by Nicholas Remy and Martín del Río, had supplanted the authority of the *Malleus,* according to William Burns, "its ubiquity, however, must have made it an important contributor to the ideas that many educated people held of witches and the proper way to deal with them" (160).[1] Later, in the Baroque period, the constant reissuance of demonological texts initiated an era in which myths about witchcraft and the powers of demons extended and intensified as truths, achieving scholarly specialization and the further elaboration of their characteristics.

Therefore, the witchcraft myth and its classification as a crime of heresy follow a path that explains their hold, which, from the Middle Ages to the Baroque, never ceased to spread, thanks to the oral and written dissemination of the ideas proposed in the treatises and manuals. The concepts' significance must have been perceived from the first censorial review of each extraordinary phenomenon considered as an actual disturbance. Inquisitors and eminent theologians suspected the disturbance, but they were precluded from recognizing it. Despite the deserved ill fame of Kramer and Sprenger's text, we should not deem those who criticize magic and witchcraft as solely sadistic and religious fanatics, although these did exist. Most of the critics, however, were in reality humanists who strove to understand the presence of evil in the world. Paradoxically, that concern directed their writings toward the construction of a myth, one fostered by the legal trial through the model of trials of heretics (Eymeric 1983).

Through the sustained pace of public interest, the topics of demonologic discussions—witchcraft, divination, diabolical pact, covens, demons, succubi and incubi, heretical manifestations, demonic possession, etc.—constituted a serious matter that was studied and debated by ecclesiastical and secular experts. The witch exemplifies a polysemic concept that has been shaped from the outside and comes from this discursive tradition, its intrinsic definition, its connotations and denotations, its referents and contexts. In brief, almost all the semantic framework that substantiates, characterizes, and identifies the figure results from its syntagmatic denominational construction, rather than from the subject's ontological identity. Its qualification as transgressive, therefore, ensues precisely from the descriptive discourses that constructed it.[2]

In other words, we have been given the definition of a witch by a censoring power in an era of dogmatism and we have been told what, who, and how a witch is; her iconological profile, a result of this fiction, is embedded in the collective imaginary to such a degree that it overrides logic, despite the fact that, *sensu stricto,* the fiction does not exist. The systematic violation of a rule or precept in this case does not operate as an eventual error caused by a congenital liability of the subject, nor for any eventual mistake in the exercise of passion or understanding, but constitutes its very essence. The witch is a transgressor by the very fact of being, and the transgression is implicit; it sustains and define her identity; it resides in her flesh, her bones, her sentiments and ideas, always acting as an essential emanation, from the commonplace to the extraordinary.

From passive personal identity, she turns to active militancy; the witch is an enemy of society, of religion, of procreation, of the divine plan, so she goes through the world as an active and harmful agent, killing children, causing impotence in husbands, destroying crops, making women ill, poisoning waterholes, becoming the tool of evil on earth in order to cause as much damage as possible and to comply with the mandates of her master, the devil, whom she has sworn to serve and love. To arrive at this motley scheme, the witch has had to go through a series of ideological transformations. Hers is a refined cultural archetype that fluctuates between improvisation and artifice, justification and speculation, censorship and inertia. The formation of this peculiar transgressor required several elements that today can be listed and exposed thanks to their sociological permanence.[3] Although it is not possible to determine an accurate chronology of the integration of each intervening factor in the witch's design, any analysis could start by targeting the negative bias against women that developed within the core monotheistic religions of the Middle East and the West (Pérez 2010).

The witch was primarily female owing to obvious reasons of community patronage, theological patriarchy, and dominant misogyny, formulations of social realities that were expressed colloquially, such as the man speaks, the woman listens; the father commands, the daughter obeys; the male thinks, the female feels.[4] At the base of this prejudice against women, however, was an ignorance of female physiology and psychology.[5] If medieval poetry, the courtly love tradition, and the chivalric romance had described her as a mystery, a beloved tyrant who was able to enchant with her gaze, the songs of minstrels and common perception described her in terms close to madness, ingratitude, inconstancy, charlatanism, and falsehood. Ignorance of others provokes fear; fear, in turn, leads to violence. In the collective imaginary that invented the witch, there is a double urge to exercise violence; men's lack of knowledge of female physiology, which was perceived as unclean and inferior to the male body, made women highly suspect, since the other is always the one guilty of evil, of the lie, of disaster. And it turns out that the target of this double prejudice, the closest strange, different unknown is the woman next door. The history of witchcraft has two ideal victims: foreigners and our close neighbors.

The individual fear of being bewitched, of losing one's property, or dying by poison combined with the self-imposed suggestions of simple minds who appropriated the frightening tales recounted from the pulpit by those who reiterated the myth. The conspiracies by ecclesiastics that would occasionally cause anti-witch crusades, along with the comforting recourse of blaming someone else for our own evils and errors, such as in the case of erotic spells, resulted in immediate accusations and denunciations of women next door as witches. Collective fear, in turn, arises when the community goes through a time of crisis. Official responses and traditional recourses of faith seem to run out. Cries for miracles and remedies, via prayers, penance, pilgrimages, and sacrifices, among other acts, take place with no result. Concern is rampant, ignorance points to likely culprits, a single woman is chosen, suspected for rarely being seen at church, despised by her neighbors, or noted because one day she muttered a profane prayer, someone saw her operate a mysterious ritual, or perhaps she attended a woman in labor (Fernández 2017).

In sum, the discursive tradition that decried all kinds of unorthodox beliefs and practices invented the "woman witch" as the scapegoat, using a system of religious judiciary control that defended male identity, and continued to feed a generational contempt for women. The result was the characterization of the witch brought on by duality, prejudice, and superstitious beliefs about the feminine. There is, indeed, inoculated in this belief system of magic, a factor of authoritarian perception of gender, obviously inequitable, obviously biased by sexual dimorphism and a disproportionate valuation of the ancient historical-societal role of the warrior father, provider and advocate, as superior to the domestic mother, who generates and sustains life.

This inequitable but close relationship is still authorized by numerous founding myths and their interpretations, conveniently and hastily conceived from the control of faith. Placed in the space of evil, the woman loses her humanity, eradicating her soul and ceasing to be part of the flock; she repeats the myth of the rebellion against the father and suffers the fall. She is no longer a child of God; she is the witch. It is easy to redirect the biblical exegesis and accept it as a doctrine of required learning. The prejudice against intrinsically malignant femininity depends on its continuity through the strategy of its antithesis: in reality, it is the malignancy that has been feminized, partially excluding, in passing, the man from the sphere of evil, increasing his power to exercise free will, while the woman's is undermined because it is subject to lust. As an example, consider an inquisitorial trial included in Flores and Masera's *Relatos populares de la Inquisición Novohispana* (Folktales of the Inquisition in the New Spain; 2010) on a witchcraft case dating from 1748, in which the baker Francisco Javier presents himself to the Holy Office to denounce his lover, Juana la Castañona, as a witch. One night, waking to find his throat and legs covered in welts and Juana transformed into a ball of fire, he decides to leave her, thinking she had put a spell on him.

Not by chance do most of the demonological treatises devote a special essay or section to explain their version of gender difference, presuming it as truth. The terms serving as arguments that contrast with masculinity abound; women are weak, occupy an imprecise space between beast and man, show a tendency toward sin, are easily corrupted, are given to pleasure, have a perverse nature, and so on; hence the many contemporary accusations of misogyny against the notions of earlier theologians. However, it is not enough to assert that women are imperfect and prone to error due to their weak will, excessive sensuality, and scarce intelligence; instead, in order to corroborate these hypothetical assertions, it is necessary to exemplify, develop theories, authorize verdicts, and compel the acceptance of indisputable treatises in order to censure, prosecute, and punish such an affiliate of evil: the witch. Thus, demonologists, evangelists, and inquisitors worked in tacit agreement with essential and authorized notions against illicit magical practices and necromancy, assembling a complex network of censorship and control that applied to all genres and social strata, but whose transgressive subject was always prefigured as female (Ciruelo 2005).

The discourse against witchcraft, a forceful cultural product of Renaissance and Baroque scholasticism, is not only a necessary ingredient of the deeply rooted figuration of the witch, but it also works to give voice to perceptions about her. Once a discourse against witchcraft is drafted, it is possible to describe its transgressive activities. There is activated a demonization of the domestic sphere, in particular activities dealing with food and caregiving, and which constitute the traditionally female semiotic system, such as kitchen utensils, food preparation, care of farm animals, attention to religious matters, preservation of the family traditions, and care of infants and children, all tasks pertaining to women and forming part of their obligations. These activities can be easily linked to the threat of witchcraft, whose fantastical narrative occupies the same spaces as the household: goblins are small demons at the service of the sorceress, the animals around her are familiar demons—that is to say, helpers of hell assigned by Satan himself on her initiation into the coven—poisoning potions and ointments for flying are boiled in the cauldrons, young children are offered to the devil, and female children inherit the mother's malevolent vocation.

Just as the fat of an unbaptized newborn was rendered into ointment in order to lard the witch's naked body so she could attend the nightly meetings mounted on a common object, animal, or familiar, so the social assimilation of the fantastical narrative that shapes witchcraft is needed in order to understand how it influences society. It is a discourse that qualifies, censures, anathematizes, and punishes on the basis of institutional power and theological knowledge: in other words, one imposed from the top, which functions on the individual and collective consciousness as an external force in search of control and unification. This scholarly discourse must also be considered as transitioning and transforming in the collective and popular imaginary (Castrillo 2011).

In the majority of inquisitorial trials that contain some aspect of the witchcraft myth, the doctrinal and dogmatic explanations result from the deceptive and deceived voice on the statement of the accused, since, in general, the defendant does not know the doctrinal twists and turns given the offenses for which she is under interrogation. She has only a version of the accusation and glimpses the danger and seriousness of her future judgment thanks to the tone and insistence of the judges and prosecutors. The trial itself works as a lesson by which the accused will learn the offenses she is charged with; if nothing is learned, the result is the same: it is the system that usurps the voice, putting in the mouth of the accused what it wants to hear and writing it down on paper. The woman accused of making a pact with the devil, of blasphemy and apostasy—after denying in a first instance such accusations and demonstrating through her prayers her complete adherence to the Christian flock—finally admits her guilt and declares herself a witch and enemy of religion, thus appropriating the discourse that subjugates her, until she firmly believes that, perhaps unknowingly and after torture, she was a witch, after all.

The woman, guilty in her own mind, comes before the inquisitors convinced of being a witch: she has already assimilated the deviant precepts of the phenomenon, thanks to constant doctrinal propaganda, her own needs, and lack of judgment. In these cases, the indicted woman does not await torture to confess her alleged crimes since she has internalized the demonological discourse so entirely that all that is left is to criminalize, redirect, and multiply her offenses against the divinity in order to strengthen the coercive vigilance of faith, which calls again on torture as support. What should be noted is that the discourse is socially accepted and assimilated, becoming a personal pattern and a common belief equivalent to faith in God, while constituting the idea of witchcraft and driving its persecution.

This discourse, at first specialized and then commonplace, combined with local and popular beliefs to form strong patterns of collective thought, thanks in part to yet another source, that of the fantastic, that promoted the witch as a transgressive figure. The mythical stories of witchcraft were communally adopted in part due to their far-fetched nature, and the social compulsion for fiction led to the formation of improbable narratives. Thus, the concept of the witch is sustained by mythological fabulation, particularly by fictions originating from the same discourse that identifies and fears it, by the communal (mythical-historical) religious narrative, and by the literary creation that deploys and recycles it culturally. The interaction of these sources resulted in a stereotypical image of the witch, to such a degree that the character itself absorbed opposing characteristics, and various feminine traits and attitudes ended up arbitrarily subsumed within the fiction (Scott 1996).

The figure of the witch, therefore, assumed various aspects, as the character was constantly reconstrued, gaining or losing prominence and attributes according to the versions and concerns of the time and place. Nonetheless, the stereotype endures because it is part of a tradition useful for the explanation of the social imaginary. Its oral, written, and now electronic transmission ensures the constant presence of the basic myth, which supports its functional syncretism within contemporary culture. Amid the primacy of logical rationalism in a time of disbelief, confusion, and doubt, the most vilified female image of the past remains bound still to the quality of unredeemed transgressor. The witch is not dead.

NOTES

1. María Jesús Torquemada claims that Spanish inquisitors paid little attention to the *Malleus,* perhaps due to its exaggerations (2000, 34).

2. One of those who laid the theoretical foundations for diabolical sects and witches was St. Augustine in his writings of *De civitate Dei* and *Divinatione daemonum.*

3. The witches in New Spain, as well as the witches in Europe, used to fly, suck the life from children, employ hallucinogenic substances, and transform themselves into animals. They were usually mestizo or mulatto, unmarried, and old (Flores and Masera 2010).

4. According to Nachman Ben-Yehuda, between 200,000 and 500,000 witches were executed in Europe from the fourteenth to the mid-seventeenth centuries, 85 percent or more of whom were women (1980, 1).

5. It should not come as a surprise that male physicians' incursion into obstetrics and the printing of numerous gynecological treatises developed mainly from the sixteenth century on.

WORKS CITED

Alberro, Solange. 1993. *Inquisición y sociedad en México.* Ciudad de México: Fondo de Cultura Económica.

Ben-Yehuda, Nachman. 1980. "The European Witch Craze of the Fourteenth to Seventeenth Centuries: A Sociologist's Perspective." *American Journal of Sociology* 86, no. 1 (July): 1–31.

Burns, William. 2003. *Witch Hunts in Europe and America: An Encyclopedia.* Westport, CT: Greenwood.

Castrillo, Hernando, 2011. *Historia y magia natural, o ciencia de filosofía oculta.* Madrid: Maxtor.

Ciruelo, Pedro. 2005. *Reprobación de las supersticiones y hechicerías.* Madrid: Maxtor.

Eymeric, Nicolai. 1983. *Manual de Inquisidores: Para uso de las inquisiciones de España y Portugal.* Barcelona: Fontamara.

Fernández Juárez, Gerardo. 2017. *Brujería y aquelarres en el mundo hispánico: Una antropología de contrastes.* Quito, Ecuador: Abya-Yala.

Flores, Enrique, and Mariana Masera, eds. 2010. *Relatos populares de la Inquisición Novohispana: Rito, magia y otras "supersticiones," siglos XVII–XVIII.* Madrid: Consejo Superior de Investigaciones Científicas/Universidad Nacional Autónoma de México.

Kramer, Heinrich, and Jacob Sprenger. 2006. *Malleus Maleficarum.* Barcelona: Reditar Libros.

Ortiz, Alberto. 2018. *Ficciones del mal. Teoría básica de la demonología literaria para el estudio del personaje maligno.* Barcelona: Calambur Editorial.

Pérez, Joseph. 2010. *Historia de la brujería en España.* Madrid: Espasa Libros.

Scott, Walter. 1996. *La verdad sobre los Demonios y las Brujas.* Barcelona: Humanitas.

Torquemada, María Jesús. 2000. *La Inquisición y el diablo: Supersticiones en el siglo XVIII.* Seville: Universidad de Sevilla.

Zamora Calvo, María Jesús. 2016. *Artes maleficorum: Brujas, magos y demonios en el Siglo de Oro.* Barcelona: Calambur.

✝

Marital Pains, Heterodox Cures

Alternative Economies of Sorcery and Witchcraft during the Cartagena de Indias Inquisition

ANA MARÍA DÍAZ BURGOS

In January 28, 1613, almost three years after the establishment of the Inquisition Tribunal in Cartagena de Indias (modern-day Colombia), Doña Lorenzana de Acereto, a twenty-seven-year-old Creole (*criolla*), wife of the royal scribe of the port city, was imprisoned for sorcery and superstition. Among the accusations made against her, Acereto was charged with casting spells, practicing love magic, and occasionally attempting to murder her husband. One of the most dangerous practices denounced by witnesses was her supposed attempt to knowingly give her husband deadly powders made from the seeds of a fruit commonly referred to as *pini piniche,* or beach eggplant (*berenjena de playa*). She emphatically denied these accusations and, in her defense and to show her pious intentions, went on to offer a brief account of the origin of the fruit and how she used it. The witnesses, however, told a different story. They not only revealed the household's marital tensions but also took pains to show how Acereto had processed the seeds and to detail the effects they supposedly caused. On October 1, 1613, about ten months after being jailed in the Inquisition prison, she was sentenced to a spiritual penance, an onerous fine, and banishment from the city for two years. Nonetheless, her husband appealed her sentence and, as a result, by the end of 1614, Acereto was absolved and reimbursed for the fine.[1]

Twenty years later, on January 28, 1633, Doña Elena de la Cruz, a forty-year-old Spaniard living in Tolú, a neighboring town southwest of Cartagena, and wife of a prominent captain, was arrested on charges of witchcraft, heresy, and apostasy. In her third inquisitorial hearing, Doña

Elena confessed that approximately six years prior, rumors of her husband's infidelities had triggered her jealousy. Driven by anger, de la Cruz
consulted a priest, looking for possible solutions to palliate her marital
woes. The priest, however, advised her to contact two women known as
witches in her town. After meeting these women, she participated in various Sabbaths, or *juntas,* renounced her Catholic faith, and, finally, became
a witch herself. In her confession, all these steps were presented as part
of the proceedings. Through these actions, she not only secured access
to the means of confirming the rumors about her husband and carrying
out her revenge, but also acquired a small horse, named Cambalache,
that was gifted with special qualities. On February 6, 1634, de la Cruz's
sentence involved the confiscation of her property, the wearing of a peni-
tential habit during an auto de fe celebrated at Cartagena's cathedral, and
banishment from Tolú for four years.[2] A few months after the auto de fe,
de la Cruz's husband appealed her sentence. In the meantime, the inquisitors learned that de la Cruz had been spreading the word that she had
agreed to accept the charges to avoid torture, statements which clearly vi-
olated inquisitorial secrecy. Thus, three months after her initial sentence,
the inquisitors opened another trial against her. Unfortunately, before this
latter case was resolved, de la Cruz died in 1636.[3]

For the inquisitors, the ways in which Acereto and de la Cruz deployed
regulated and regulating discourses—whether scientific or religious—
for heterodox purposes explicitly manifested the women's spiritual devi-
ance. As Pedro Ciruelo had stated in his 1530 demonology manual, *Reprobación de las supersticiones y hechicerías,* illnesses "had to be treated
in two different ways: naturally, with medicines; or spiritually, through
prayers, but refrain from any attempt to cure through sorcery as if from
fire" (Ciruelo 1952, 90).[4] Any other approach suggested nothing short of
a pact with the devil and thus threatened Catholic orthodoxy.[5] From a
theological perspective, the devil interfered with people's physical and
spiritual health and caused illnesses that affected their souls. In contrast, early modern physicians considered lovesickness "a genuine illness,
with its own specific symptoms and remedies," usually associated with
melancholia. The safest recommendation was "to partake in sexual relations with the man in question . . . as long as one abided by restric-

tions imposed by Christian mores." However, when this was not possible, the physicians suggested different kinds of "distractions and therapeutic activities . . . to restore harmony to both body and mind that had no place in the world of female magic" (Tausiet 2014, 70). In the midst of the perceived insufficiencies of medical and spiritual approaches to everyday female suffering, women like Acereto and de la Cruz often engaged in solutions that escaped and contravened orthodox practices.[6]

In this essay, I focus on the materiality of Acereto and de la Cruz's practices as well as on the discourse with which they tried to justify it. It is useful, therefore, to consider materiality following anthropologist Victor Buchli, "not so much as physics, but as a cultural process" (Buchli 2002, 18–19). This approach allows us to shift our emphasis from an object itself to its production, circulation, and use, and, in turn, to analyze how subjects participate in these trials. The cases in question prove themselves to be fertile ground for this inquiry because, among the details offered by witnesses and defendants, those that provided material evidence of deviant practices were of particular interest to inquisitors, and they returned to them in hearing after hearing. The material lives of the objects used in such practices functioned as the material manifestations of the purposes, beliefs, and meanings of the practitioners.[7] Moreover, inquisitorial interest in the economies of witchcraft and sorcery makes sense in the context of early seventeenth-century Cartagena de Indias. At the time, that city was considered to be one of the most significant ports in South America due to its commercial, naval, and slaveholding importance to the Spanish Monarchy.[8] As such, inquisitors became aware that the influx of peoples, goods, and knowledge in the port city and its neighboring regions allowed for the formation of extra-official networks and exchanges among locals and foreigners intended to fulfill needs that exceeded and challenged the social, religious, and economic colonial order.

In the context of the heterodox practices recorded in Acereto and de la Cruz's cases, an emphasis on materiality provides not only an inventory of the existing remedies to treat women's afflictions, but also an account of the role of those involved in procuring them. The multiple descriptions of these objects, their uses, and their effects given to the Inquisition authorities reveal different instances of the relationship that the defendants and their witnesses established with the objects and their meanings. Moreover, the accounts related to these objects shed light on the tensions between the expectations and needs of women like Acereto and de la Cruz. By insisting on this kind of materiality, the records involving objects such as the pini piniche powders and the horse Cambalache open up a dialogue—even if fragmentary—among those inscribed in and affected by the practices, as well as unveil the alternative economies and heretical beliefs that the Inquisition was seeking to disband.[9]

In their search for solutions, Acereto and de la Cruz participated in alternative economies through which people from across the social spectrum traded words, objects, and rituals intended to solve marital and extramarital conflicts that did not find remedies within the limits of orthodoxy. These networks helped women like Acereto and de la Cruz to supplement the deficiencies of a system that excluded afflictions that could not be explained or addressed under its premises. These networks benefited from the local, peripheral, and foreign resources that coincided in Cartagena and the surrounding towns, which played a prominent role in the circulation of the goods and different kinds of knowledge necessary for many unorthodox practices. Oftentimes, in Cartagena's inquisitorial cases, African and Afro-descendant inhabitants of those areas occupied significant positions in these alternative economies insofar as they served as brokers, having access to particular local products and knowledge of the area's flora and fauna. The village of Tolú, where de la Cruz dwelled, was one of these peripheral areas. Tolú was a small coastal town southwest of Cartagena, officially known for its agricultural production and, unofficially, for its central role in Caribbean contraband.[10] While Tolú was mentioned in Acereto's case as a town where there existed an herb for the preparation of an effective love potion, it was not until the 1630s that the village emerged as the epicenter of witchcraft (AHN, Acereto, 47r).

Between 1610 and 1613, a round of witnesses contributed details that revealed how Acereto procured the necessary materials for her practices, what kinds of intermediaries she had, the procedures by which she prepared, used, and distributed the ingredients, and, in some cases, even the specific results or side effects of the practices. One of these practices was the use of powders—crushed substances—made of different kinds of materials to appease spouses and lovers. Powders were effective precisely because they were subtle and camouflaged easily when mixed with food or beverages and were considered a means for women to take control of their relationships (Few 2005, 679; Sánchez Ortega 1991, 67; Ceballos Gómez 2002, 180–81). Depending on the purpose or the dosage, the powders could be intended either to reconcile with or reject the person who consumed them.[11] In this way, the pini piniche powders functioned as a *pharmakon* (medicine, philter) with the potency of either healing or killing.[12] As José Enrique Sánchez Bohórquez states, women like Acereto tried to take revenge on their husbands by drawing on such herbs, powders, and concoctions to impair their senses (Sánchez Bohórquez, I, 212).

According to witnesses, after trying different kinds of powders, Acereto decided to use the ones made from the pini piniche plant. In her defense, she explained that five years earlier, a certain Don Alonso had given her a small fruit of pini piniche. He did not live in Cartagena, but instead was visiting the city, and when they met, he told her about the plant's properties. The powders of that fruit, she was told, were very effective to improve or tame men's condition. She said she took the little seeds because she was interested in "improving her husband's condition," or taming his temperament. The Inquisition authorities took this as an attempt to kill her husband and judged her accordingly. They were not mistaken: the pini piniche (as *Solanum persicifolium*) was also known to belong to the poisonous *solanaceae* family.[13] In addition, the Inquisition cataloged the usage of the plant's fruits as diabolical due to their hallucinatory effects and the subsequent effects of visual disruption and physical weakness (Rey Bueno, 120). As Don Alonso told Acereto, when its thorns were ground and altered through sorcery, they could be used to tame whoever ingested them.

Although Acereto denied having given her husband the pini piniche powders to get rid of him, and there is not record of the exchange between Acereto and Don Alonso, other testimonies presented different accounts of what occurred with those powders. Inquisition authorities questioned five witnesses about the pini piniche. Even if some of the testimonies did not offer details of the practice, they provided contextual information to understand its impact within and outside Acereto's house. In mentioning the preparations for the use of the pini piniche powders and their effects, witnesses disclosed how people, products, and information flowed to and from Acereto's house. As a result, rumors about the marital tensions between Acereto and Del Campo spread to the streets and public squares, making them common knowledge among Cartagena's society.[14]

Two witnesses offered differing narratives of the pini piniche episode: Lorenzana de San Marcello, a twelve-year-old niece of Acereto and a novice at the convent of the Discalced Carmelites at the time of her confession, and Sebastián Pacheco, a public functionary who worked for Del Campo. In her account, San Marcello offered the perspective of an eyewitness to the preparation, usage, and effects of the powders. San Marcello had seen Acereto test the powders on one of her slaves and mix them in her husband's food. San Marcello declared that after receiving the pini piniche from the shadowy Don Alonso, who had in turn collected the plant at the beach, Acereto gave it to Joana, one of her most obedient slaves. According to San Marcello, Acereto asked Joana to grind the tips of the pini piniche thorns, mix the powders into an amaranth stew, and serve the dish to Sebastián, the slave who had agreed to test the powders' strength. After eating the stew, Sebastián "went crazy, and then [Acereto and her slave Joana] gave him a small bowl of oil that made him vomit everything he had eaten, which made him healthy again" (Acereto, 13v–14r).[15] San Marcello added that after seeing powders' effect on her slave, Acereto used them to poison her husband and a lunch guest, whose name she did not remember, but who is later identified as Sebastián Pacheco. San Marcello concluded her testimony by mentioning that both men fell gravely ill, but that the physician Julio de Alvarado cured them. As in the case of the slave, Alvarado gave Pacheco and Del Campo oil, and as a result, they vomited and were cured. The known side effects of the pini piniche powders not only on her husband, but also on Pacheco, triggered a public scandal about Acereto's marital problems and her attempted murder.

As a regular visitor to Acereto and Del Campo's household, especially during lunchtime and in the evenings, Pacheco gained knowledge of their domestic daily lives and drew close to one of their servants, with whom he had a child. Pacheco declared that he saw and heard about the flow of people coming and going from Acereto's house, such as slaves, lay religious (*beatas*), women reputed to be herbalists and sorceresses, and others of ill fame. He believed that they all came by to participate in spells, pagan prayers, and potions against Del Campo (Acereto, 24r). According to Pacheco, who morally condemned Acereto, the movement of people and products that resulted in the substances mixed in Del Campo's food and beverages was aimed to allow her the opportunity to see her lover, the sergeant Francisco de Santander, as it was publicly known (Acereto, 24v).

The use of pini piniche powders represented the most extreme attack not only to Del Campo, but also to Pacheco himself. As a consequence, he narrated his account as a victim of the side effects of the powders. Catalina Tolosa, one of the slaves of Acereto and her lover, told him that her mistress asked her slave Joana to mix the pini piniche in with Del Campo's food, so he would be poisoned. Pacheco stated that once Joana camouflaged the powders in the main dish,

> [Another servant] brought to the table a plate of eggplants covered with eggs, and both Del Campo and he [Pacheco] ate everything. As this witness [Pacheco] left Del Campo's house, on the streets everybody told him that it seemed he was dying and asphyxiating, and some people recommended that he go for bloodletting, so he asked the barber to do it. [Pacheco also said] that Del Campo and he ran a high fever until midnight, as someone from Del Campo's house told him, and that Del Campo was talking nonsense, and he [Pacheco] said he complained to Doña Lorenzana because she did not warn him whenever she put something bad in the food for her husband, as she had done in the past. (Acereto, 24v)[16]

This account differs from San Marcello's in the way that Pacheco was healed. Although the physician and the barber did not leave any record of the treatment they provided to Del Campo and Pacheco, the fact the latter asked for additional assistance outside Acereto's house emphasizes the poisonous properties of the powders. Even if San Marcello mentioned that both men consumed the oil and vomited, for Pacheco it was apparently not enough, since he had to stop for a bloodletting on his way back home.[17] Pacheco's illness became public and triggered more rumors of Acereto's intentions against Del Campo. Additionally, by mentioning that

Acereto had prevented him from consuming food intended only for Del Campo, Pacheco underscored how often Acereto deployed these kinds of practices to harm her husband.

In her defense, Acereto denied the accusations, saying that after receiving the fruit from Don Alonso, she made the powders, and with the excuse of taming Del Campo's condition, she later threw them into the pot to serve to all at her table. However, contrary to her expectations, everyone fell sick after the meal (Acereto, 57r). In her account, Acereto did not mention either the test run with the slaves, or the details of who fell ill after eating the eggplants with fried eggs. Moreover, she distanced herself from the side effects of the powders, emphasized her good intentions, and mentioned once again the enmity between her and Pacheco. After Acereto's response to the accusations, the inquisitors summoned three more witnesses to confirm her statements regarding her quarrels with Pacheco. Although, in the end, the authorities disregarded some of his statements given his fame as a gossiper and a drunkard, his account on the effects of pini piniche confirmed San Marcello's testimony to a certain extent.

All at once, San Marcello and Pacheco's testimonies gave a complete range of the material elements involved in the procurement, preparation, and consumption of the pini piniche powders. The trials that made possible the use of the powders and their side effects provided the newly established Inquisitorial Tribunal not only with sufficient proof to further its case against Acereto, but most importantly, they gave the authorities access to the heterodox practices that preexisted their arrival, and that they were committed to sever. The inquisitorial record also reveals how Acereto inserted herself into these practices by seeking affiliations from across the social spectrum to skirt the social restrictions on mobility placed on women and thus obtain what she needed to resolve her marital issues.

Inquisitorial control mechanisms intensified in the years after Acereto's case, as can be gleaned from the second auto de fe in 1622 where the concept of witchcraft was linked specifically with relation to African or Afro-descendant women.[18] From this moment on, the alliances and networks seen in the previous case were punished with more zeal as inquisitors prosecuted a specific group under the premises of witchcraft.

The growing fear of an outbreak of witchcraft and its relation to the African and Afro-descendant population in the jurisdiction of the Cartagena Tribunal marked the last years of Juan de Mañozca's tenure as inquisitor. This intensification of inquisitorial scrutiny continued throughout the next two decades with his successors, Domingo Vélez de Asas y Argos and Martín de Cortázar y Ascárato.[19] Whereas in the first auto de fe there were six women prosecuted for sorcery and none for witchcraft, by 1634, witchcraft cases abounded and targeted mostly African and Afro-descendant women, with the exception of Doña Elena de la Cruz, a white Spanish woman (Splendiani 1997, II, 297–326). Such an increase in prosecuting witchcraft reveals the fears and beliefs of the inquisitors Vélez and Cortázar regarding the influence of the Afro-descendant population in the area of Tolú. As Luz Adriana Maya Restrepo explains, in urban and rural areas Afro-descendant women prosecuted for witchcraft during the 1630s participated in gatherings aimed at figuring out different ways to achieve their freedom, opposed slavery, and subverted the colonial order (Maya Restrepo 2005, 593–94). Consequently, the inquisitors increased their control mechanisms, resulting in a witch hunt in Cartagena and its surrounding areas.

De la Cruz's case is not particularly different from other cases of the period in regard to its description of the initiation into witchcraft, its pact with the devil, and the participation in the Sabbaths, or juntas.[20] The juntas celebrated in Tolú and neighboring areas were similar to the ones recorded in Cartagena, in which the participants practiced blasphemy, dances, sexual intercourse, and flight. Some of de la Cruz's witnesses offered meticulous reports of the places she attended and how she behaved. Those who confirmed her active participation in the juntas were in the Inquisition prison facing similar charges. Since providing information about others seemed to be an effective strategy for the defendants to fulfill confessional requirements in front of the inquisitors, defendants entered into a cycle of denouncing and accusing as many people as possible to show their willingness to cooperate with the authorities during the hearings (White 2005, 12). As a result, hearsay and rumor played an essential role in the prosecution of witchcraft as it increased the number of possible participants in deviant practices.

Although in de la Cruz's argumentation, the statements related to those gatherings serve as a preamble to explain the resources she used to resolve her sufferings, much as in Acereto's case, the testimonies related to the small horse Cambalache provide an account of the circulation of goods and unorthodox knowledges inscribed in witchcraft practices. As previously mentioned, de la Cruz's first stop in her quest to treat her marital woes was a visit to a priest, Miguel Camino, who was also a commissary of the Holy Office. It was Camino who recommended that she visit two women from Tolú that were widely known as witches: Ana de Ávila, a black woman, and Ana María, a mestizo woman (AHN, de la Cruz, 54r). Ávila, in turn, put her in contact with Luisa de León, an Afro-descendant woman also from Tolú, who would help her find out whether or not her husband was cohabiting with Magdalena de Arellano, a mestizo woman, as she had heard. De la Cruz added that León confirmed her suspicions and persuaded her to become a witch to carry out her vengeance (AHN, de la Cruz, 54v). León promised that after participating in the juntas and meeting the Great He-Goat (*cabrón*), "she would enjoy pleasure and amusement aplenty, and would be able to take revenge on whomever she liked, and in particular her husband" (AHN, de la Cruz, 55r).[21] The jealous doña confessed that she could not resist this promise.

In her declaration, de la Cruz skillfully admitted that, driven by her passion and her thirst for revenge, she went and talked to these women and that she knew that her participation in the juntas was against the Catholic faith. Yet she claimed her motivations were legitimate: not only because her husband was cohabiting with someone else, but more importantly because she followed a priest's suggestion to find a way to cure her marital pains through alternative means. However, some of her witnesses provided a different account of the relationship between de la Cruz and Ávila. For instance, Lieutenant Julio de Arce and his daughter María de Arce insisted that de la Cruz had had a close relationship with Ávila for several years and, in fact, visited her frequently. Instead of accusing Ávila as a witch, he said that de la Cruz openly shared her unorthodox practices and dispositions with the woman, and his daughter confirmed this (AHN, de la Cruz, 13r).

On the fourth hearing, on June 17, 1633, de la Cruz mentioned the Limping Devil, her companion during the juntas, and three other elite women from Tolú who also participated in the juntas happening in the public square and on the beach (AHN, de la Cruz, 56v). In this instance, de la Cruz narrated in great detail the way in which attendees at the gatherings shared dances, blasphemies, sexual encounters, and food. These gatherings, she noted, had consistently taken place since she had become a witch seven years prior. Additionally, de la Cruz said that, after one of those juntas, Ávila came to her house and informed her that there was a special small horse named Cambalache and a young male rider charged with taking de la Cruz to the farm where her husband was living with his lover, Arellano. De la Cruz took it all in stride and decided to go along with the rider and the special horse. That said, Ávila warned her against mentioning the name of God, the Virgin Mary, or any saints while riding Cambalache. That evening, de la Cruz went to the farm and came back to her house before the rooster sang. The small horse had been so fast that they had covered fourteen leagues in less than six hours, a journey which typically would have taken a day to complete (AHN, de la Cruz, 58r).

Compared to Acereto's, de la Cruz's alternative economy was more performative and, because of this, more dangerous, in that she had to participate physically in the trial by being part of the ceremonial juntas and by traveling to the site of her husband's infidelities. These differences speak to the Inquisition's classification of these women's deviant practices as sorcery, as in Acereto's case, and witchcraft, as in de la Cruz's. In this sense, the differences between both become relevant. Although inquisitors in Cartagena followed European treatises that discussed the differences between sorcery and witchcraft, the classification of practices and the specificities of sentences varied according to local cultural meanings as well as the socioeconomic and racial circumstances of the defendants.[22] As scholars have shown, whereas charges for sorcery fell on individuals, accusations of witchcraft involved groups or collectives.[23] Of the two, sorcery was seen as the lesser evil. Technically, sorcery practices did not require an explicit pact with the devil, but witchcraft did. That said, both kinds of practices defied social and religious hierarchies and presented challenges to the authorities due to their supernatural nature (Maya Restrepo 2005, 530). Sorcery included spells, pagan prayers, and love magic practices, while witchcraft made use of supernatural and psychic powers to cause major physical, emotional, economic, or social damage, and involved participation in nocturnal gatherings to practice diabolical idolatry. In the cases of Acereto and de la Cruz, as we have seen, these differences are also inscribed in the alternative economies in which they participated.

One similarity between the cases is that the stated goal of de la Cruz's trial, like Acereto's, revolved around the attainment of an object that would have otherwise been out of her reach: Cambalache, the gifted horse capable of unreal speeds. If, with Kathryn Joy McKnight, we understand inquisitorial scenarios "as structured interactions that expressed cultural paradigms, worked with recognized plots and produced anticipated, 'though adaptable,' outcomes," we can approach de la Cruz's willing confession as a nuanced account that did not limit itself to describing her as a witch, but that brought to bear her marital woes, registered her husband's unlawful behavior, and, thus, inscribed her within the paradigm of a troubled wife (McKnight 2016, 155–56).

Unfortunately for de la Cruz, different witnesses testified that they saw her riding the small horse in different roads at midnight. The small horse's appearances allowed inquisitors to associate her precisely with the deviant practices of witchcraft. Although de la Cruz declared that she visited her husband's farm just once, many witnesses said they either saw, or heard that other people had seen her, on separate occasions. For instance, Doña Ana Jacinta de Benavides, wife of the lieutenant Bernardo Saenz, provided one of the first accounts on de la Cruz to the Inquisition authorities in Tolú.[24] She said that Miguel, the foreman in charge of Barrasa's farm, told her he had seen de la Cruz on a small horse wandering around the farm several nights (AHN, de la Cruz, 34r). Then, Hernando, Saenz's slave, mentioned that while he was making the evening rounds one night, he saw "a black bulk that seemed like a cow by the side of the road. It was standing on two legs, and showed him its horns and cow's head as it was stepping backwards. He stopped and tried to see what was happening, but only saw half a body" (AHN, de la Cruz, 37r–37v).[25] After this episode Hernando came down with a fever that lasted for almost a week, and he believed that his encounter with that bulk caused his illness. He also affirmed that Joan Bran, a slave of Francisco Barros, told him and other people that one night in the summer of 1632, while he was on his way to the farm where he lived, he ran into de la Cruz. According to Hernando, Bran mentioned that she was riding her small horse and did not respond to his presence, but kept quiet and continued on her way (AHN, de la Cruz, 36v). De la Cruz denied riding Cambalache save for the one time she had already confessed to. She insisted that she normally rode a white-colored male mule that she had at her farm, which Juan de Acosta gave to her in exchange of another mule (AHN, de la Cruz, 79r).

In his account, however, Bran denied Hernando's testimony involving him. Instead, he declared that once, when Captain Barrasa was living on his farm, while on his way to buy cacao for her owner, he had seen de la Cruz riding her small horse and entering a hut located on a hill in her husband's farm. Bran said that de la Cruz was waiting for news about her husband.[26] In his testimony, Bran also mentioned another encounter with de la Cruz: one evening when he was returning home, he saw a bulk apparently formed of termites crossing the road. As he approached it, he made the sign of the Cross several times, uttering the name of Jesus aloud. Then he saw at one side the same small horse that de la Cruz would ride, and moments later, the bulk transformed into Doña Elena herself. After the transformation, de la Cruz rode off on Cambalache to her farm. Bran followed her and upon arriving at her farm he did not see her anymore. When he asked about her, someone told him she was in Tolú. Despite his confusion and fear, he ran to his place and there he fell ill (AHN, de la Cruz, 45r; 70v). In her defense, de la Cruz said that she never ran into Bran at night. Instead what he could have seen was the devil, which sometimes took her shape to harm others in her stead (AHN, de la Cruz, 79v). Even though de la Cruz argued she had not caused Bran's illness, the inquisitors held her responsible not only for the devil's deceptive personification, but also for Bran's ill health (Moreno Rodríguez and Valenzuela Candelario 2010, 32). However, when the inquisitors interrogated another witness, Joan de Tordesillas, a priest from Tolú, he said that he had not witnessed any activities related to de la Cruz. Instead, he emphasized that he did not believe those rumors, as they were all lies Black people would tell (*embustes de negros*) (AHN, de la Cruz, 41r).

After the episode with Cambalache, the Inquisition authorities sought for more information about all the time she had engaged in a "bad life" (*mala vida*), not only for the period she mentioned in her confessions, but for the thirteen years that people from Tolú had known her as such (AHN, de la Cruz, 64v and 68v). According to the accusations, de la Cruz omitted key information regarding her deviant practices, such as having initiated several people into witchcraft as a *madrina* (godmother) to other witches, celebrating juntas in the main church of Tolú and the patio of her own house, and exhuming bodies from the local cemetery. In the remaining hearings and with the hope of reducing her penance, de la Cruz provided more details about the juntas and denounced more people. Unfortunately, the inquisitors ruled against her, giving her a condemnatory sentence.

To conclude, even if the results and the women's ways of accessing these alternative economies varied in each case, in their confessions both women framed their heterodox means as having an orthodox purpose: the restoration of the well-being of their marriage and household in the face of circumstances without any approved spiritual, medical, or lawful solution. Despite their rhetorical efforts to legitimize their actions, and because the Inquisition was an institution interested mostly in regulating means and proceedings, Doña Lorenzana and Doña Elena's trials resulted in sentences involving public penance, banishment from their towns, and a monetary fine. Although their husbands later appealed the sentences for the sake of the family's honor and to recuperate the hefty fines paid to the Inquisition, they could not erase from their inquisitorial records the traces of the circulation of knowledge and material goods engaged in by these women.[27]

NOTES

1. The complete case of Doña Lorenza de Acereto is located in the Archivo Histórico Nacional in Madrid (hereafter AHN), Inquisición, 1620, file 1.

2. The complete case of Doña Elena de la Cruz is located in AHN, Inquisición, 1620, file 8.

3. For a discussion of the causes that provoked the second trial of de la Cruz, see Tejado Fernández (1954, 115–16), and Ceballos Gómez (2011, 135–36).

4. "las dos diligencias que deben hacer en todas sus enfermedades: una natural de

medicinas y otra espiritual de devociones. Y guardese como del fuego de querer sanar por vanas hechicerías."

5. For a discussion on the impact of Ciruelo's work, see Zamora Calvo (2005, 77–80), and Kamen (2014, 293–94).

6. For a discussion on medical practices that included treatment of female physical illnesses in Cartagena during the first half of the seventeenth century, see Lux Martelo (2006, 39–95), and Sotomayor Tribín (2008, 60).

7. Ceri Houlbrook and Natalie Armitage discuss the materiality of magic from an archaeological perspective (2015, 12–13). For an anthropological viewpoint, see Appadurai (2013, 3–63). For a historical review of the concept of material culture and the area of material culture studies, see Hicks (2010, 25–98) and Findlen (2013, 3–27).

8. For an overview of Cartagena's economic relevance during the sixteenth- and seventeenth-century Atlantic trade, see Maya Restrepo (2000); Vidal Ortega (2002); Meisel Roca (2006); Newson and Minchin (2014); and Gómez (2017), among others.

9. Pablo Gómez explores the ways in which material culture in seventeenth-century Caribbean therapeutics sheds light in social, spiritual, political, and cultural dynamics (2017, 144).

10. Tolú is located in the Morrosquillo Gulf, an area known during colonial times for its agricultural production and proximity to swamps and streams. During the eighteenth century, pirates and corsairs constantly attacked Tolú (Ruíz Rivera 2005, 168–77).

11. Powders similar to the pini piniche ones would be mentioned in inquisitorial trials again. For example, a similar fruit was mentioned in the case summary of Doña Rufina de Rojas in 1644. Rojas, a seventeen-year-old woman from Seville, was accused of giving her husband: "an herb called wild eggplant (*berenjena de monte*), which was used to cause sensory deprivation." Although she did not indicate who was her provider, the effects were like those of the pini piniche powders on Acereto's husband about thirty years earlier (Splendiani, II, 121).

12. According to Jacques Derrida, *pharmakon* refers to both cure and poison and is the substance that "makes one stray from one's general, natural, habitual paths and laws" (429).

13. According to Alain H. Liogier, the *Solanum persicifolium* comes from a shrub natural to the Caribbean coastal zone. This shrub protects the soil through its thorns, keeping cattle from grazing near it, and produces small red, blue and white flowers, and small red fruits (470).

14. For analyses of rumor and gossip regarding heterodox practices and their social and inquisitorial effects, see Silva Prada (2016, 172), Stewart and Strathern (2003, 38–39), and Ceballos Gómez (2002, 355–65).

15. Sebastián "se volvió loco y después le dieron a beber una escudilla de aceite volvió todo lo que había comido y con ello estuvo bueno."

16. "trajeron a la mesa un plato de berenjenas cubiertas con huevos y este testigo y el dicho Andrés del Campo comieron de ellas y acabando de comer salió este testigo de

la casa y fue por la calle y todos le decían que se iba muriendo y ahogando que se fuese a sangrar y este testigo llamó al barbero y se sangró. Y este testigo y el dicho Andrés del Campo tuvieron una calentura cada uno que les duró hasta más de media noche y la gente de su casa le dijo que a este testigo que el dicho Andrés del Campo decía mil disparates y después este testigo se quejó a la dicha doña Lorenzana porque no le avisaba cuando enviaba alguna cosa mala a la mesa para su marido como le había dicho antes."

17. According to humoral medicine, illness was perceived as a repository flow of humors and putrefied matter. Treatments to cure body obstructions involved bloodletting, purges, and ointments, among other things (Moreno Rodríguez and Valenzuela Candelario 2010, 32).

18. The prosecution for witchcraft decreased in Europe from the 1620s, as Jeffrey Watt indicates (687). The Cartagena Tribunal prosecuted forty-five cases in 1632 and 1634, according to Maya Restrepo (2005, 512–14).

19. Inquisitors considered Tolú the epicenter of witchcraft during the first half of the seventeenth century. They designated the outbreak of the 1630s as the conjuration (*complicidad)* of the witches from Tolú.

20. For analyses of juntas in Nueva Granada, see Sánchez Mojica (2016, 153–67); White (2005, 6–9); McKnight (2016, 168–70); Maya Restrepo (2005, 501–15); Borja Gómez (1998, 288–95); and Ceballos Gómez (1994, 93–95).

21. "con lo cual tendría muchos gustos y pasatiempos y tomaría venganza de quien quisiera y en particular del dicho su marido."

22. For a discussion on the main early modern treatises of penology and demonology see Zamora Calvo (2005, 21–136), and Herzig (2010, 51–80).

23. For the distinction between sorcery and witchcraft in Nueva Granada, see Ceballos Gómez (1994, 86–90), and Borja Gómez (1998, 275).

24. Witnesses in de la Cruz's case presented their declarations in front of Diego Morán de Chávez, a commissary of the Inquisition in Tolú, instead of Cartagena.

25. "vio al lado del camino un bulto negro y que le pareció baca y estabaparado en los dos pies y hizo de ver la cornamenta y la cabeza de baca y yba rerculando asia atrás y se paro para ver lo que hera y no pudo ver mas del medio cuerpo."

26. Since folio 44v is illegible, the information Bran declared must be examined in the Inquisition attorney's summary located later in the case (AHN, de la Cruz, 70v).

27. An expanded version of the discussion related to the case of Doña Lorenzana de Acereto appears in Díaz Burgos 2020. ·

WORKS CITED

AHN (Archivo Histórico Nacional). Inquisition, docket 1620, file 1. "Doña Lorenza de Acereto muger de Andres del Campo vecino de esta ciudad de Cartagena, Cartagena año de 1612."

———. Inquisition, docket 1620, file 8. "Doña Elena de la Cruz vecina de la villa de Tolú desta governacion muger de Francisco Barraza, Cartagena año de 1631."

Appadurai, Arjun. 2013. "Introduction: Commodities and the Politics of Value." In *The Social Life of Things: Commodities in Cultural Perspective*, 3–63. Cambridge: Cambridge University Press.

Borja Gómez, Jaime Humberto. 1998. *Rostros y rastros del demonio en la Nueva Granada: Indios, negros, judíos, mujeres y otras huestes de Satanás*. Santafé de Bogotá: Editorial Ariel.

Buchli, Victor. 2002. "Introduction." In *The Material Culture Reader*, ed. Victor Buchli, 1–22. Oxford: Berg.

Ceballos Gómez, Diana Luz. 1994. *Hechicería, brujería, e Inquisición en el Nuevo Reino de Granada: Un duelo de imaginarios*. Medellín: Editorial Universidad Nacional.

———. 2002. *"Quyen tal haze que tal pague": Sociedad y prácticas mágicas en el Nuevo Reino de Granada*. Bogotá: Ministerio de Cultura.

———. 2011. "Ante las llamas de la inquisición." In *Historia de la vida privada en Colombia*, ed. Jaime Borja and Juan Pablo Rodríguez, Vol. I, 111–40. Bogotá: Taurus.

Ciruelo, Pedro. 1952. *Reprobación de las supersticiones y hechicerías*. Madrid: Joyas Bibliográficas.

Covarrubias, Sebastián de. 1611. *Tesoro de la lengua castellana o española*. http://fondos digitales.us.es/fondos/libros/765/500/tesoro-de-la-lengua-castellana-o-espanola/

Derrida, Jacques. 1998. "Plato's Pharmacy." In *Literary Theory: An Anthology*, ed. Julie Rivkin and Michael Ryan. Malden, MA: Blackwell.

Díaz Burgos, Ana María. 2020. *Tráfico de saberes: Agencia femenina, hechicería e Inquisición en Cartagena de Indias (1610–1614)*. Madrid/Frankfurt am Main: Iberoamericana/Vervuert.

Few, Martha. 2005. "Chocolate, Sex, and Disorderly Women in Late-Seventeenth and Early-Eighteenth-Century Guatemala." *Ethnohistory* 52, no. 4: 673–87.

Findlen, Paula. 2013. "Introduction. Early Modern Things: Objects in Motion, 1500–1800." In *Early Modern Things: Objects and Their Histories, 1500–1800*, ed. Paula Findlen, 3–27. Abingdon, Oxon/New York: Routledge.

Gómez, Pablo F. 2017. *The Experimental Caribbean: Creating Knowledge and Healing in the Early Modern Atlantic*. Chapel Hill: University of North Carolina Press.

Herzig, Tamar. 2010. "Flies, Heretics, and the Gendering of Witchcraft." *Magic, Ritual, and Witchcraft* 5, no. 1: 51–80.

Hicks, Dan. 2010. "The Material-Cultural Turn: Event and Effect." In *The Oxford Handbook of Material Culture Studies*, ed. Dan Hicks and Mary C. Beaudry, 25–98. Oxford: Oxford University Press.

Houlbrook, Ceri, and Natalie Armitage. 2015. "Introduction: The Materiality of the Materiality of Magic." In *The Materiality of Magic: An Artefactual Investigation into Ritual Practices and Popular Beliefs*, ed. Ceri Houlbrook and Natalie Armitage, 1–14. Oxford and Philadelphia: Oxbow Books.

Kamen, Henry. 2014. *The Spanish Inquisition: A Historical Revision*. New Haven: Yale University Press.

Liogier, Alain H. 1995. *Descriptive Flora of Puerto Rico and Adjacent Islands*. San Juan: Editorial de la Universidad de Puerto Rico.

Lux Martelo, Marta. 2006. *Las mujeres de Cartagena de Indias en el siglo XVII*. Bogotá: Uniandes.

Maya Restrepo, Luz Adriana. 2000. "Los afrocolombianos." In *Geografía humana de Colombia: Los afrocolombianos*, Vol. VI, 11–52. Bogotá: Instituto Colombiano de Cultura Hispánica.

———. 2005. *Brujería y reconstrucción de identidades*. Bogotá: Ministerio de Cultura.

McKnight, Kathryn Joy. 2016. "Performing Double-Edged Stories: The Three Trials of Paula de Eguiluz." *Colonial Latin American Review* 25, no. 2: 155–56.

Meisel Roca, Adolfo. 2006. *Geografía física y poblamiento en la Costa Caribe colombiana*. Cartagena: Banco de la República.

Moreno Rodríguez, Rosa M., and José Valenzuela Candelario. 2010. "Lenguajes de enfermedad en el siglo XVIII: La experiencia de enfermar ante el Tribunal Inquisitorial." *Historia Social* 66: 23–39.

Newson, Linda A., and Susie Minchin. 2014. *From Capture to Sale: The Portuguese Slave Trade to Spanish South America in the Early Seventeenth Century*. Leiden: Brill.

Rey Bueno, Mar. 2008. *Historia de las hierbas mágicas medicinales*. Madrid: Nowtilus.

Ruíz Rivera, Julián Bautista. 2005. *Cartagena de Indias y su provincia: Una mirada a los siglos XVII y XVIII*. Bogotá: El Áncora Editores.

Sánchez Bohórquez, José Enrique. 1997. "La hechicería, la brujería y el reniego de la fe, delitos comunes entre blancos y negros esclavos." In *Cincuenta años de inquisición en el Tribunal de Cartagena de Indias, 1610–1660*, ed. Anna María Splendiani, 209–31. Bogotá: Centro Editorial Javeriano.

Sánchez Mojica, Darío. 2016. "La bruja negra como alteridad abismal del poder esclavista: Cartagena de Indias, 1618–1622." *Nómadas* 45:153–67.

Sánchez Ortega, María Helena. 1991. "Sorcery and Erotism in Love Magic." In *Cultural Encounters: The Impact of the Inquisition in Spain and the New World*, ed. Mary Elizabeth Perry and Anne J. Cruz, 58–92. Los Angeles: University of California Press.

Silva Prada, Natalia. 2016. "El Tribunal de la fe censurado: Prácticas rituales, pasquines y rumores contra la Inquisición novohispana (1602–1734)." *Fronteras de la Historia* 21, no. 1: 148–82.

Sotomayor Tribín, Hugo A. 2008. "Cirujano licenciado Pedro López de León y su libro *Práctica y teoría de las apostemas* (Siglo XVII)." *Historia de la medicina* 18, no. 1: 53–64.

Splendiani, Anna María, ed. 1997. *Cincuenta años de inquisición en el Tribunal de Cartagena de Indias, 1610–1660*. Bogotá: Centro Editorial Javeriano.

Stewart, Pamela J., and Andrew Strathern. 2003. "Rumor and Gossip, an Overview." In *Witchcraft, Sorcery, Rumors and Gossip*. Cambridge: Cambridge University Press.

Tausiet, María. 2014. *Urban Magic in Early Modern Spain: Abracadabra Omnipotens,* trans. Susannah Howe. Basingstoke: Palgrave Macmillan.

Tejado Fernández, Manuel. 1954. *Aspectos de la vida social en Cartagena de Indias durante el seiscientos.* Sevilla: Escuela de Estudios Hispano-Americanos.

Vidal Ortega, Antonio. 2002. *Cartagena de Indias y la región histórica del Caribe, 1580–1640.* Sevilla: Consejo Superior de Investigaciones Científicas.

Watt, Jeffrey R. 2010. "Love Magic and the Inquisition: A Case from Seventeenth-Century Italy." *Sixteenth-Century Journal* 41, no. 3: 675–89.

White, Heather Rachelle. 2005. "Between the Devil and the Inquisition: African Slaves and the Witchcraft Trials in Cartagena de Indies." *North Star: A Journal of African American Religious History* 8, no. 2: 1–15.

Zamora Calvo, María Jesús. 2005. *Ensueños de razón: El cuento inserto en tratados de magia (siglos XVI y XVII).* Madrid/Frankfurt am Main: Iberoamericana/Vervuert.

✛ CONTRIBUTORS ✛

JAIR ANTONIO ACEVEDO LÓPEZ received his BA from the Universidad Autónoma de Zacatecas, Mexico, and his MA from El Colegio de San Luis, Mexico. His most recent articles focus on love spells used during the sixteenth and seventeenth centuries in New Spain. He has participated in several national and international symposiums on literature and history. He was research assistant to Fernando Lara at El Colegio de México, and he currently does research under the direction of Claudia Carranza Vera, at El Colegio de San Luis, Mexico.

CLAUDIA CARRANZA VERA is a researcher and professor at El Colegio de San Luis, Mexico. She received her PhD from the Universidad de Alcalá de Henares, Spain, and is the author of *De la realidad a la maravilla: Motivos y recursos de lo sobrenatural en Relaciones de sucesos hispánicas (s. XVII)* (2014). She has coedited several books, including *Del inframundo al reino celestial: Entidades sobrenaturales en la tradición oral* (2018). Her main research topics focus on popular literary prints, the oral tradition from the Golden Age to the present, and fantastic and wonderful elements in oral tradition. In addition, she created the project "Supernatural and Fantastic Characters and Places in Oral Tradition from Mexico and Latin America."

ANA MARÍA DÍAZ BURGOS is assistant professor of Hispanic studies at Oberlin College. She received her MA and PhD from Emory University and specializes in transatlantic early modern literature, visual culture, and gender studies. Her research on female agency and the Spanish Inquisition includes her book *Tráfico de saberes: Agencia femenina, hechicería e inquisición en Cartagena de Indias* (2020), as well as journal articles in

Colonial Latin American Historical Review (2013) and *Edad de Oro* (2019), among others.

CECILIA LÓPEZ-RIDAURA received her PhD from the Universidad Nacional Autónoma de México (UNAM), and she is a professor in the bachelor's degree program for Intercultural Literature in the Escuela Nacional de Estudios Superiores (ENES) in Morelia, UNAM, Mexico, where she also is in charge of the editorial department. Her research work is focused on popular literatures and witchcraft in New Spain.

BEATRIZ MONCÓ REBOLLO is professor of social and cultural anthropology at the Universidad Complutense, Madrid, Spain, where she received her PhD. She is the author of numerous articles and book chapters. Her work on religiosity and beliefs of women includes *Antropología de género* (2011) and *Mujer y demonio: Una pareja barroca* (1989). In 2013, she directed the master's program in feminist studies at the Universidad Complutense, Madrid.

YADIRA MUNGUÍA received her PhD in Latin American literature from the Benemérita Universidad Autónoma de Puebla, Mexico. She is an associate professor in the humanities at the Universidad Panamericana, Guadalajara, Mexico. Her publications on conventual literature include *Respuesta a los Enigmas de Sor Juana* (1999), *Enigmas ofrecidos a la soberana asamblea de la Casa del Placer* (2019), and journal articles in *Edad de Oro, Hipogrifo: Revista de Literatura y Cultura del Siglo de Oro,* and others.

ALBERTO ORTIZ is professor of literature at the Universidad Autónoma de Zacatecas, Mexico. A member of the Mexican National System of Researchers (SNI), he includes among his research interests theoretical approaches to the figure of evil in literary works. Among his publications are *Tratado de la superstición occidental* (2009); *Diablo novohispano: Discursos contra la superstición y la idolatría en el Nuevo Mundo* (2012); *El aquelarre: Mito, literatura y maravilla* (2015); and *Ficciones del mal: Teoría básica de la demonología literaria para el estudio del personaje maligno* (2018). He has also coedited several books related to New Spain studies.

He is currently preparing an edition focusing on the battle against diabolical evil in western culture.

SONIA PÉREZ-VILLANUEVA, a scholar from the Basque Country,
Spain, holds a PhD in Spanish Literature and Cultures from the Univer-
sity of Birmingham in England. She is currently an associate professor of
Spanish studies at Lesley University in Cambridge, Massachusetts. Pérez-
Villanueva has published *Vida y sucesos de la Monja Alférez, Catalina de
Erauso: An Early-Modern Autobiography* (2014), and she has authored
numerous book chapters, as well as articles in scholarly journals such as
Bulletin of Hispanic Studies, Edad de Oro, and *Hispanic Review.* In 2018,
Pérez-Villanueva coedited the special issue "Violence against Women:
Representations, Interpretations, and Education" for the Sage journal se-
ries *Violence against Women.*

ROBIN ANN RICE is professor and researcher at the Universidad Popular Autónoma del Estado de Puebla, Mexico. She received her PhD from
the Universidad de Navarra, Spain. She is coauthor of the study, notes,
and edition of Sor Juana Inés de la Cruz's *El cetro de José* (2020) and
El mártir del Sacramento (2019). She has published books, articles, and
book chapters on subjects such as Sor Juana Inés de la Cruz, Calderón
de la Barca, and New Spain female hagiographies, as well as Inquisition
archives on women.

GRACIELA RODRÍGUEZ CASTAÑÓN is professor and researcher of
history at the Universidad Autónoma de Zacatecas, where she received
her PhD. She is the author of numerous studies that focus on the culture
of New Spain and on inquisitorial cases, including *Transgresión mágica e
inquisición novohispana en Zacatecas* (2014) and *Magia, hechicería e inquisición en Zacatecas* (2015). Her work on Mexican colonialism includes
her contribution to *Magia y Siglo de Oro: La relación de la tradición dis-
cursiva antisupersticiosa y la literatura en español de los siglos XVI y XVII*
(2007) and her participation in a series of investigative articles titled *El
discurso Inquisitorial alrededor de la hechicería y brujería en el Zacatecas
colonial* (2008, 2009, 2010).

MARÍA JESÚS ZAMORA CALVO, PhD, Universidad de Valladolid, Spain, is an associate professor of Hispanic studies at the Universidad Autónoma de Madrid, Spain. She has authored *Ensueños de razón: El cuento inserto en tratados de magia* (*siglos XVI y XVII*) (2005) and *Artes maleficarum: Brujas, magos y demonios en el Siglo de Oro* (2016); and she has edited seven books, the most recent of which is *Cruces y áncoras: La influencia de Japón y España en un Siglo de Oro global* (2020). Other publications have included book chapters, as well as articles in *Bulletin Hispanique, Archivium, Cauces: Revue d'études hispaniques, Rassegna Iberistica,* and *Artifara,* among other journals. Currently she leads the research group "Mentalidades mágicas y discursos antisupersticiosos (siglos XVI, XVII y XVIII)" at the Universidad Autónoma de Madrid. Since 2018, she has served as editor of the journal *Edad de Oro.*

✤ INDEX ✤